PROGRESSIVE PREJUDICE

PROGRESSIVE PREJUDICE

Exposing the Devouring Mother

LESLIE CORBLY

BOMBARDIER
BOOKS

Published by Bombardier Books
An Imprint of Post Hill Press
ISBN: 979-8-89565-170-4
ISBN (eBook): 979-8-89565-171-1

Cover Design by Jim Villaflores

All people, locations, events, and situations are portrayed to the best of the author's memory. While all of the events described are true, many names and identifying details have been changed to protect the privacy of the people involved.

BOMBARDIER BOOKS

Post Hill Press
New York • Nashville
posthillpress.com

Published in the United States of America
1 2 3 4 5 6 7 8 9 10

TABLE OF CONTENTS

PREFACE

For years I doubted the wisdom of translating my experiences into writing. During this time, I grappled with whether my desire stemmed from fear or prudence. An innate fear resided behind my desire to tear the veil separating society from the experiences of those hiding on the periphery of progressive privilege. Yet, upon further examination, the jagged pieces of my life fit into a mosaic displaying the embodiment of the type of personhood progressive culture detests and fights tirelessly to eradicate, via perverse methods of mental colonization actualized through emotional manipulation and psychological abuse.

Because progressive views are culturally privileged, victims of this worldview are culturally marginalized. This leaves their lives unknown, undefined, and unexamined, causing them to languish, in various forms of disenfranchised grief.[1] The disenfranchisement of those who do not fit within a progressive ideological framework is at the core of current cultural conflict over

---

1 A phrase coined by Dr. Kenneth J. Doka in 1989. "Publications – Kenneth J. Doka, Ph.D." Accessed January 31, 2025. https://drkendoka.com/media/.

human rights and dignity. Because the narratives of this conflict are framed in progressive terms, the conversation builds on the premises supporting progressive beliefs.

The results of the 2024 general election show the American public is growing weary of progressive dogma, but why?

Understanding the election results requires analyzing issues that, at first blush, are far afield from the initial line of inquiry. This is because it requires abandoning the assumption that history is a long march toward justice and equality and instead recognizing that human history is the story of human beings with a predisposition toward seeking god-like authority to bend the world to fit their desires.

America was the first nation in the world to explicitly ground its political system, and therefore moral credibility as a nation, on the premise of human equality. Since then, the nation—and increasingly the global community—continue to dispute what equality is and how to ensure its legal protection. The American experiment in self-governance assumed an innate connection between equality and responsibility because our founders knew freedom without accountability is chaos.

The progressive vision redefines equality to equity. This is a linguistically subtle change, but practically destroys political equality. Rather than focusing on legal equality, progressives seek to control outcomes. Of course, to determine what an ideal outcome is, those on the left need a benchmark representative of an ideal outcome. The benchmark chosen is the measure of material, worldly success. Because America was founded by white, Christian, heterosexual men descended from Europe, this group has traditionally wielded the most political power. In search of equality, those on the left want to redistribute that power to groups they describe as "historically marginalized."

CULTURAL UPHEAVAL

The twentieth century saw a rise in the strength of progressive ideas that pushed against the ideals of the founding. Although historically expansive, the American founders' concept of equality disenfranchised large swathes of the American public, most notably African Americans and women. Over the course of the past one hundred years, the United States has drastically changed its political power structure in a progressive direction, both in terms of the size of government and the scope of increasingly niche demographic interests that determine the nation's cultural and political trajectory.

Although it would be nice if expanding political enfranchisement came with no negative trade-offs, reality proves this is a false, naive belief. Instead, the natural, ingrained human desire to lust after power and control means that when new voting blocs enter the game of politics, they bring with them positive *and* negative changes. This by no means undermines equality; it is undoubtedly best to ensure all people have the right to participate in the political process. However, pretending the historically marginalized will vote in everyone's best interest, rather than working to protect themselves, even if this harms others, is naive.

In the wake of the advancements of the twentieth century, the citizenry of the twenty-first century faces new challenges to equality that stem from twentieth century—not nineteenth—historical events. Progressives remain locked in the past, incapable of gazing past the navel of the nation's founding flaws. This means the left excels at critiquing traditional religious worldviews dominant during the first phase of US history. However, leftists are allergic to self-reflection and struggle to analyze how their own worldview causes harm.

Simply put, when a society enfranchises historically marginalized groups, it risks allowing resentment to fuel political and cultural change. The classic progressive phrase stating that "equality feels like oppression" to groups with systemic cultural advantage is correct. The problem is that oppressed groups change over time, and leftists' worldviews are now the epitome of privilege. Thus, when their sacred ideas are challenged, for example through the overturn of *Roe v. Wade*, this intellectual friction feels like an attack.

Nowhere is this easier to observe than in social norms surrounding issues impacting the relation between the sexes and the relationship between children and adults. The largest group of disenfranchised Americans, and therefore those who remained locked in legal inequality, are children. This inequality is unique because it is innate. Children cannot be equal to adults because they lack the capacity for consent, thus their best interest is protected primarily through parental relationships supported by the state. Mothers and fathers are presumed to operate in a child's best interest. Even in circumstances where children are endangered by their parents leading to their placement in foster care, the goal, if at all feasible, is to reunite children and their biological parents.

However, the bond between mother and child has been destroyed. In a quest to become like men, women have demanded to be treated as gods, thus transforming children from people worthy of protection to either a curse to avoid or an accessory to wear. Mothers are no longer expected to protect their children, unless they *want to*. Generations born after *Roe v. Wade* lived in a world where their existence was a matter of maternal opinion. Children have no right to exist. They are the only group people feel comfortable routinely disparaging, and the only group whose value is subjectively defined. Children are discussed as if they were the worst outcome of consensual sex. They are told their annoying, inconvenient presence destroys their mothers' body, dreams, and ability to compete with men for social status and power. Children are increasingly described as burdens, and childcare is a tedious duty passed to those forced to trade the glory of a career for the mundane horror of raising the next generation.

Unwanted children, those born into poverty, and the disabled are routinely used as justifications for abortion. Women, envious of the power of men, have become like their oppressors, guaranteeing independence by passing their pain to the one group of people that can never fight back, for the enfranchisement of children is a political impossibility. This foundational shift of power is often explored in the abortion context, but its broader impact is rarely discussed.

This is a mistake because the implications of the belief that women have a human right to kill human beings they created is immensely profound. Like all forms of human oppression, once one group of people (women) are granted rights superior to others (children), the impact affects every facet of society, culture, and law, either directly or indirectly.

MORAL PURITY AS POLITICAL POWER

This cultural upheaval the nation is experiencing requires contextualization, and to understand the present, it is essential to face the social taboo of critiquing women. In writing *Progressive Prejudice*, I elucidate how progressive beliefs and practices that assume the moral superiority of women marginalize and socially destroy the lives of individuals whose value is insufficiently tied to the desired outcomes of female interests.

Progressive beliefs, like all worldviews, are broad and complex, but this book tackles only those progressive views related to women's rights in society. And, although there are notable outliers, the vast majority of progressive culture accepts women as the just arbiters of human worth. Leftists generally accept the idea that women have the *right* to create and kill human beings in utero for any reason or none at all. Democrats capable of articulating any regulations on abortion are a dying breed. This is because, while claiming to fight for equality, women successfully enshrined moral superiority into law. Access to birth control levels the reproductive playing field. Abortion, however, does not stop conception; it kills human beings.

The Democratic Party protects this procedure with religious zeal—and for good reason. Women are one of the largest and most consistent of its voting blocs, and since approximately one-fourth of women have killed at least one of their children by the age of forty-five, there is an enormous political incentive for women to cherish this "right" as well as a high social cost placed on opponents who question the morality of abortion and its downstream social consequences.[2]

---

2 "Abortion Is a Common Experience for US Women, Despite Dramatic Declines in Rates." Guttmacher Institute, October 19, 2017. https://www.guttmacher.org/news-release/2017/abortion-common-experience-us-women-despite-dramatic-declines-rates.

There has long been a sizable gender gap between men and women, with the former favoring Republicans and the latter voting primarily for Democrats.[3] As women gained more political influence over the course of the twentieth century, the Republican Party was increasingly incentivized to avoid the appearance of offending half of the electorate. This led to a political discourse that, at least emotionally, favored female interests. Criticizing men was perceived as punching up; the reverse was true of critiquing women.

However, women *are equal* to men, both in their capacity for good, and their propensity toward corruption. And, as Lord Acton famously stated, people love "to get as much power as circumstances allow, and nobody will vote for a self-denying ordinance." Since men and women both crave power, they are equally prone to corruption, and that corruption can be expressed either through broken masculine or feminine traits.

Unhealthy masculinity is widely discussed, often referred to as "toxic masculinity," but perversions of femininity remain a social taboo. This must change. The archetype of female predation is the devouring mother, a woman who perverts her role of caretaking by devouring her children through emotional manipulation and covert psychological destruction. Because this perversion of femininity relies on the child's belief that the mother operates in her best interest, it is the ultimate betrayal and most oppressive form of tyranny. In *God in the Dock*, C. S.

3 "Gender Differences in 2024 Vote Choice Are Similar to Most Recent Presidential Elections." Center for American Women and Politics, December 28, 2024. https://cawp.rutgers.edu/blog/gender-differences-2024-presidential-vote.

Lewis described how this type of dominion is more wretched than overt oppression:

> The robber baron's cruelty may sometimes sleep, his cupidity may at some point be satiated; but those who torment us for our own good will torment us without end for they do so with the approval of their own conscience.[4]

My unique life circumstances are inextricably linked to this book because my life has always existed under the weight of female oppression, and pain tends to reveal social problems hidden to those who live under relational luxury.

The harsh realities of life propelled me to engage in both belief formation and cultural critique from my earliest years. Because of this, the combination of cultural analysis and autobiographical description serves as a powerful medium for conveying the silent suffering imposed on those whose experiences have been delegitimized by progressive prejudice. This unique format offers readers a lens to observe the ways in which progressive values degrade the worth of individuals whose existence and beliefs do not align with narratives promoting and/or strengthening the progressive grip on cultural power.

---

[4] Lewis, Clive Staples, and Walter Hooper. *God in the dock: Essays on theology and ethics*. Cambridge: William B. Eerdmans, 1970.

CULTURAL COMMENTARY WITHOUT CONDESCENSION

Among the many problems facing progressives in the Trump era is their tendency to scorn those whose viewpoints diverge from their own. The "uneducated" are looked upon with pity and condescension. While the Republican Party and Donald Trump may benefit from progressive hubris, the American public loses when one of the most powerful political parties openly views the public with contempt.

This book approaches issues of philosophic, ethical, cultural, and political importance as they actually occur. It blends the autobiographical and cultural because people always exist at the intersection of the theoretical and practical. No one forms their beliefs in a relational or historical vacuum. Reason and rationality are inherently tied to the culture and social conditions of each individual's life. Cultural commentary is the self-consciousness of people's collective experience. Thus, when commentary is narrowed to viewpoints comfortable to those with social power, the collective mind constricts. When it is broad, the mind expands.

This book offers a perspective missing from mainstream conversations because it articulates the philosophical, cultural, and political implications of subjugating children beneath the boot of maternal oppression.

Some people believe the exploration of issues of philosophy and ethics is best suited for the ivory tower of intellectual elites, but in truth, this practice is remarkably practicable and utilized by all human beings throughout all cultures and historical eras. Philosophy is not beyond the ordinary. Whether conscious or not, everyone from the fast-food cashier to the CEO of a Fortune 500 company engages in philosophic and ethical analyses.

The structural relationship between a person's philosophy—or value system—and their behavior, holds true across any given system of belief. The Amish do not utilize modern technology because the use of such technology violates the principles of their philosophy A committed feminist would never take a vow to submit to her husband because such a vow violates a fundamental principle of her moral code.

Thus, to understand the world of the present moment, it is essential to understand the philosophical assumptions that undergird the worldviews of the predominant culture.

PROGRESSIVE PRIVILEGE AND FEMALE SUPERIORITY

Even the most outwardly "open" worldview contains taboos, the discussion of which is risky for individuals who live within its mental walls. Indeed, it is with these mental walls that all people—and therefore all cultures—contend. "For we do not wrestle against flesh and blood," wrote the Apostle Paul, "but against the rulers, against the authorities, against the cosmic powers over this present darkness, against the spiritual forces of evil in the heavenly places.[5]" Whether one is a Christian is largely irrelevant to the truth of what Paul said. There is an undeniable, and perpetual, battle between ideas within all human cultures.

---

[5] Ephesians 6:12 (ESV) *The Holy Bible: English Standard Version.* Wheaton, IL: Crossway, 2016.

Progressivism arose in the twentieth century. Like all philosophies, it has variations and factions. Just as Catholics bicker with Protestants and Protestants endlessly fight among themselves, so too do those who adhere to the various types of progressive philosophies. The branches of Christianity have common denominators uniting the faith, such as the belief in Jesus's divinity, and leftist systems of belief are similar. Progressive viewpoints are, broadly speaking, characterized by a commitment to atheism and women's rights.

Note that the use of the term "progressive" in this book intentionally draws from the ways these ideas are used in practice, not through academic inquiry. This is because progressive beliefs derive significant power from their indefinability. Unlike religions, leftist beliefs have no canon. Thus, adherents to leftist beliefs often goad their opposition into endless definitional disputes that subvert the intellect. Without a canon of thought, progressive ideas sit in an endless sea of information, making it nearly impossible to create consensus about what the ideology *is*. However, while progressive ideals are by nature difficult to define, progressive culture is fairly easy to identify. Nearly every college campus in the United States is saturated in progressive beliefs. This allows an analysis of progressive ideas to emerge through a different method. Rather than consulting a nonexistent authoritative scriptural text, progressive culture is better understood in the realm of relational experience.

Presently, the West is approximately three generations deep in postmodern cultural development. All sectors of institutionalized cultural power, from literature and cinema to technology, education, law, and journalism, are driven by a population that is overwhelmingly leftist and progressive in belief orientation. Thus, the gatekeepers of the cultural conversation control the terms of the moral debate, and those who question the central doctrines of progressive thought do so at their own peril.

Because progressive moral assumptions, such as a "woman's right to choose" and "truth is relative," serve as the default moral settings in cultural communication, progressive ideas come with an unearned power and corresponding privilege. Subcultures that would otherwise gather to question progressive dogma are stifled before they can flourish. In her pamphlet, *Checking Progressive Privilege*, Carrie Lukas summarizes the cultural privilege that is baked into the air every person in modern American culture breathes. Among the list of privileges—all of which are accurate and worthy of contemplation—several, in particular, serve as the backbone of understanding the progressive water in which we swim. They are paraphrased below:[6]

- Voices highlighted by women's magazines are progressive. When alternative female perspectives are discussed, it is with the intent to disparage or belittle their personhood and/or politics.
- Popular media is created almost exclusively on a progressive philosophic foundation, depicting conservative beliefs as "bigoted," "hypocritical," or "out of touch," with no corresponding scrutiny applied to progressive cultural beliefs.

---

[6] Lukas, Carrie L. 2019. *Checking Progressive Privilege*. Encounter Books.

- When attending social events, progressives need not hide their beliefs because they are *presumed* to rest on a morally just foundation. On the contrary, those with views in opposition to progressive causes speak with an unknown cost, fully aware their views may result in disparaging insults and slurs from the notoriously "tolerant" left.
- The education system, from K–12 through all levels of collegiate and post-collegiate studies, are taught almost exclusively by those with a commitment to progressive thought, and who view beliefs contrary to progressive axioms with open hostility and revulsion.

Given the cultural power propping up progressive thought, it is an exercise in mental gymnastics to pretend as though progressive values maintain cultural dominance through merit alone.

PAINTING A PICTURE OF PROGRESSIVE PREJUDICE

Progressive appeals to emotion drive its cause forward. From civil rights to the LGBTQ campaign run on the trite tautology "Love is love," progressive politics is full of emotions and human experience. Emotional appeals are among the most powerful tactics of the progressive cause because postmodern philosophy—practically embedded in widespread progressive cultural messaging—rejects the existence of absolute truth, thus allowing for a type of relativism conducive to emotional influence. Because this philosophy is impossible to act out—people cannot live without acting as if some moral predicates are *absolutely* true—the search for truth becomes absurd. This leaves little other than emotions to serve as the foundation for the practical absolutes humanity requires to function.

In response to the emotionalism of the left, the center-right has a strong tendency to abandon the realm of experience. This is famously expressed in conservative commentator Ben Shapiro's catchphrase, "Facts don't care about your feelings." Although there is value in pointing out the limitations of feelings, such a sentiment can be taken too far. On one level, Shapiro's catchphrase is undoubtedly true, but when overutilized, it reduces human beliefs to a type of rationalism that denies the holistic nature of human thought, a process that is an infinitely complex interplay between emotion and logical reasoning.

The power of progressive emotional appeals comes from the lack of scrutiny applied to their human interest stories. Because progressives define the terms of cultural debate, they can control what subjects are allowed to be viewed with sympathy versus scorn. Rather than abandoning emotion entirely, conservatives would do well to follow the advice of *Mad Men*'s Don Draper, "If you don't like what is being said, change the conversation."[7] This can only be done by unapologetically beginning cultural analysis from predicates contrary to progressive dogma and, while building on mutually exclusive foundational beliefs, clearly showing the harms a culture perpetuates when it mindlessly accepts progressive philosophy as if it were fact, rather than the convenient fiction it has always been.

---

[7] "Trailer: Change the Conversation: *Mad Men*: Season 7 Premiere." YouTube, March 20, 2014. https://www.youtube.com/watch?v=aSDTNFFvtVQ.

This is a difficult task because, given the moral relativism incentivized by postmodern philosophy, the landmines of progressive dogmas are opaque and constantly evolving. But, like pornography, you know a progressive first principle when you see it, if only because of the vitriol that necessarily accompanies questioning the foundational beliefs of the unseen, and unnamed secular goddess, for surely no modern god would rule in male form.

Through a series of unfortunate (or divine) events, my life exists at the intersection (pun intended) of the dogmas and corresponding consequences that come with progressivism's most impactful claims in relation to humanity, specifically the belief that women possess an inalienable "human right" to abortion without legal limitation.

Unfortunately, the progressive stranglehold on all levels of the US educational system ensures that most children—including those born in the hands of abusive mothers—are never allowed to question the basis of progressive predicates. Instead, questioning moral presuppositions is reserved for religious beliefs, not philosophies rooted in the respectable theologies built out by philosophy and gender studies departments. This leaves millions of children who languish in horrific conditions unable to process the natural line of inquiry that accustoms abuse, namely: "Am I *innately* valuable?" "Am I *innately* loveable?" "Is my worth subject to the value my mother assigns or is it *inherent*?"

Progressive abortion dogma cuts off the inquisitive child's ability to ask such questions because it states, as a matter of fact, that children are choices. And there is one thing everyone knows about choices—*sometimes they are wrong*. Unfortunately for the curious child, to question how a child can be a mistake is to commit secular blasphemy. "My body, my choice" means "Accept my assessment of human value, *no questions asked*." The cultural messaging, discussed at length in this work, details the enormous barriers of entry abused children must overcome when questioning whether abortion or other progressive dogmas, in practice or rhetoric, has caused them emotional harm.

The progressive weaponization of empathy and love impacts the unwanted child more than any other category of person, but it by no means is limited to this demographic. Like all internal predispositions, a habit of weaponizing empathy in one sphere of life quickly spreads to other dimensions of politics and society. Thankfully, unlike millions of children, I existed outside of progressive culture, notably public education, during my formative years. This gave me the space to observe and critique progressive cultural values without the emotional pressure that comes with personal entanglement with progressive relationships.

My earliest memories involve the abortion question, because "half-aborted" is one of the first words I learned. The first full sentence I recall learning was a simple statement "Leslie is half-aborted." Of course, as a child, a natural follow-up question emerges in the mind, "What is half-aborted?" To answer this question, I had to ask another, more specific question, namely, "What is abortion?"

Soon, I learned the secret name bequeathed to me as a child placed an asterisk next to my personal identity. Television interviews galore featured "empathetic," "loving," and "tolerant" feminists all too eager to remind me that a child unwanted and abused by her mother was, quite literally, better off dead. Thus, from an early age, it was clear to me that a progressive knowing my life story was directly proportional to the likelihood they would pity my existence. "At what point will this person think, consciously or not, '*Her mother should have aborted her, the pain is too great*'?" Emotional involvement with progressives is poison to my soul.

To relate to a progressive has always required either the refusal to share personal experience or the acceptance that my life, in their eyes, may have unequal worth. Such is the inequality on which progressive philosophy rests, and such is the quality of the invisible barrier between maternally abused/unwanted children and the progressive world.

This is a collection of essays specifically examining the oppressive nature of progressive culture through a combination of cultural critique and autobiographical account of the belief formation process.

Ultimately, this work was created to assist younger generations increasingly skeptical of progressive power structures, out of a commitment to nurturing the next generation's understanding of equality, human dignity, the transformative effects of cultivating virtue despite insurmountable suffering, and the need for analysis of cultural dogmas that cause incalculable, albeit silent, anguish.

CHAPTER 1
Abortion

HALF-ABORTED

"Leslie is half-aborted," was the first sentence I recall learning. This singular fact meant personal consciousness was tied to an inherent tension between life and death, making philosophic exploration the most practical pursuit of my life.

Yet, from the earliest of ages I struggled to answer the most basic question of my predicament: "What is half-aborted?"

Many days, the elusive meaning behind the phrase "half-aborted" lingered in the air as my mom angrily retold my birth story. The story was told in numerous forms, but most often she circled the living room in a state of distress that, to a detached observer, resembled a mixture of anger, honesty, and vindictive rage.

"Vengeance!" she cried, shaking her fists high and arching her back toward the floor. "Vengeance against those who have stolen the hearts of my children!" Degradation, she said, was a bottomless pit, and—one by one—her children had become more susceptible to corruption. The first was corrupted in grade school. Then, each child in the seven-sibling lineup was corrupted at an earlier age, until she gave birth to an almost lifeless child. This child was so stained by the touch of evil that to describe her as fully human would be a classification error. Instead, my poor, loving mother was left with a child who lived between heaven and hell. She was neither fully dead nor alive. Neither fully human nor demon. Although no physical attempt to end her life in utero had been made, half-aborted was the most appropriate descriptor of Leslie's state of being.

My siblings and I watched Mom's familiar performance, awaiting our father's arrival home from work that guaranteed an end to the verbal torment.

But the temporary muting of verbal abuse did little to alleviate the internal questions haunting my mind. In search of answers, I asked Mom endless questions about half-aborted, why the descriptor had fallen upon me, and how I could remove its affixation to my name. Hours of conversation brought me no nearer to answers, instead entrenching me into a harsh reality from which I could not escape. This name, once known, gave others a manipulative power over me from which there was no liberation.

Mathematics—Mom's area of expertise—presented me with one of my first glimpses of what half-aborted meant in practice. Missing one too many questions, failing to neatly "show my work," or any other range of errors could lead her to use the phrase, patronizingly reminding me of my inferior status.

"I must remember you are half-aborted," she said, shaking her head in disappointment. "It's a miracle you can even add at all. You will never be normal. Everything will always be harder for you. Tasks that take others minutes will take you hours."

Over time, I learned to hide the emotional disturbance accompanying her words. I taught my hands not to shake, and crushed emerging tears before they could well in my eyes. For the pain of the words paled in comparison to the torment of enduring Mom's attempts to comfort me after thoroughly destroying my self-worth. Compassion brought no relief when intermingled with contempt.

And contempt was communicated daily. When my birth story was not spoken, math problems were missed. On days when I was lucky enough to avoid hearing of my half-aborted status through these typical means, Mom found creative ways to bring attention to my position, often in the form of numerous reminders of how others in society would view my humanity should they be made aware of the descriptor she chose to associate with my name.

The degree to which she believed her own web of lies regarding the corruption of her children is impossible to assess, but the intentional nature of her actions showed she was fully aware of the burden her words placed on my back.

"No one will accept you," she said. "The closer you become to people, the more likely they are to reject you because you will remind them of what they wish did not exist. You are defective, broken...abnormal, and those are the people no one wants to love. The more they learn of your life, the more they will view you with a mixture of pity and scorn. It will not matter whether they pity or scorn you more; either way they will never see you as an equal."

Behind these words was a subtext any child could intuitively understand. Should society learn of my predicament, they would wish I had been fully—rather than half—aborted.

The strain between my mom and I grew stronger with time as my will to assert dignity clashed with her quest for absolute relational control. At times, I questioned the wisdom of her words; was she speaking from a place of truth or a desire for dominance? An answer to this question approached me through the medium of television, specifically the words spoken by commentators during the contentious national season accompanying presidential elections.

By the 2000 presidential election, I was eight years old, with an unlimited curiosity for questions of morality and justice. Naturally, I took a keen interest in the ideas and debates discussed on TV, filtered through the nonsensical lens of America's binary Republican and Democratic political system.

Politics was not an uncommon topic of familial conversation. Most such discussions were raised by my mother during homeschool hours or through sibling banter brought on by the machinations of my older brother's insatiable desire to annoy one of my sisters using various Socratic methods designed to test her ability to defend her naturally compassionate inclinations.

Through these discussions, I was aware of the general political stances held by the adults around me. The home was "Christian," pro-life, and hated government intervention into economic activity. Taxes were viewed with scorn and the government—indeed bureaucrats of all stripes—were seen as power hungry, corrupt actors interested in exerting control over matters they had no just authority to regulate.

As George Bush and Al Gore faced off in a deeply divisive election, I sat curled up on my parents' couch, pretending to have no interest in the debates while internally fixing my mind exclusively on the words of the candidates and the commentators who debriefed their performances post-debate.

I waited with bated breath, eager to hear the candidates speak on the topic of abortion. Their answers fell within the range of normal opinions on the matter, with Democrats favoring strong protections for the procedure while Republicans argued for barring abortion.

Both argued on humanitarian grounds for positions that were mutually exclusive, making it instantly clear that one of these two beliefs, although intended to convey compassion, was in fact a commitment to cruelty. Later, as commentators discussed the viewpoints presented, one justification for abortion crystallized the hatred of life inherent to the procedure's defense.

"Abortion is a form of mercy," the commentator argued. She continued, laying out the reasons unwanted children who "are abused and maltreated" by resentful parents are better off aborted than born.

My mind returned to Mom's words: "The more they learn of your life, the more they will view you with a mixture of pity and scorn. It will not matter whether they pity or scorn you more. Either way they will never see you as an equal." The hatred between Mom and myself could not negate the truth she spoke. Mom's statements were punishingly brutal, but they were not lies.

Internally, I connected the dots between support for abortion and scorn for those who suffer seemingly senseless earthly pain. "*If pro-choice people learn I am half-aborted, they will likely wish I had been aborted rather than living the life of pain handed to me*," I thought.

With this realization came the undeniable effects of dehumanization: "*Within this worldview, children are not their mother's equal. They believe it is moral and just to subjugate children under the domination of mothers. Mom has the sole right to assign my worth and value at birth.*"

With this knowledge, I sensed a threat to my existence and rejected a core tenet of the moral system of the current historical era. "*Supporting abortion is not justice. It is not compassion. It is inequality. It is prejudice.*"

DEFINITIONS

The nexus between the justification of abortion as a woman's "human right" and maternal abuse of power was an obvious reality for me from a young age. However, the circumstances surrounding my unorthodox childhood nickname represent an aspect of the abortion debate routinely denied, and therefore undiscussed. Thus, the most socially, politically, and culturally relevant issue of the twenty-first century has been pushed to the back of the public's mind, allowing the grave consequences of abortion to be dismissed and denied.

Abortion is almost universally framed as a women's issue, related entirely to a woman's bodily autonomy and rights. Occasionally, the implications of abortion are discussed in terms of a father's interest in his child's growing life, in relation to the pain a child can or cannot experience in utero, or whether there is a meaningful distinction between a human being and a person.[8] But how abortion impacts children as a social class is almost never addressed.

This is because it is generally assumed that, to the extent children are victims of abortion, most of this victim class is dead.[9] It is also because the sidelining of children's voices, perspectives, and pain aligns with progressive political priorities by keeping the focus of sympathy solely on women.

In reality, beneath the surface of seemingly compassionate progressive arguments in support of abortion is an age-old prejudice against individuals conceived and born in adverse circumstances. Never does the ever-watchful eye of progressive empathy meet the plight of children harmed by abortion rhetoric, which often suggests children born into persistent suffering are better off dead. Such children are relegated to the rhetorical equivalent of "medical waste," where their pain and experiences are cast aside by a progressive culture that celebrates cruelty under the guise of compassion.

Although it is possible to deny reality, truth has a nasty habit of never dying. Despite the pro-choice movement's best efforts, it is impossible to disconnect the link between mothers and children in utero versus mothers and children outside the womb. Whether one uses the term "fetus" or "child" to describe the developing life in utero, it is indisputably a human being in the earliest stages

---

8 *Dobbs, State Health Officer of the Mississippi Department of Health, et al. v. Jackson Women's Health Organization, et al.* (United States Supreme Court, June 24, 2024).

9 "Why We Exist." The Abortion Survivors Network, accessed January 29, 2025. https://abortionsurvivors.org/about/.

of the human life cycle.[10] Thus, once a woman is aware of her pregnancy, she is in relation with the growing life inside her, and how she treats that life is a profound statement of her viewpoints surrounding the equality—or lack thereof—between mothers and their children.

Derogatory terms such as "clump of cells" may obscure reality to the willfully ignorant, but in practice, the phrase underscores the inequality created by a culture hellbent on supporting the dogma of abortion as a "human right." Endearing terms are used to describe unborn children at baby showers, while unborn children of the same gestational development are described using nakedly inhumane language. Popular pro-abortion rhetoric refers to the unwanted unborn as "parasites," "clumps of cells," or "fetal tissue" to hide the humanity of this human demographic. These efforts can border on the absurd, such as an attempt by *The Guardian* to persuade the public that reprinted pictures from MYAbortion Network showing the gestational sac, without an embryo, are accurate representations of a normal, healthy, ten-week unborn child.[11,12]

---

10 Jacobs, Steven Andrew. "Biologists' Consensus on 'When Life Begins.'" SSRN, August 6, 2018. https://papers.ssrn.com/sol3/papers.cfm?abstract_id=3211703.

11 Noor, Poppy. "What a Pregnancy Actually Looks like before 10 Weeks – in Pictures." The Guardian, October 19, 2022. https://www.theguardian.com/world/2022/oct/18/pregnancy-weeks-abortion-tissue.

12 Waters, Emma. "UK Newspaper Takes Pro-Abortion Deception to Next Level." The Heritage Foundation, October 25, 2022. https://www.heritage.org/life/commentary/uk-newspaper-takes-pro-abortion-deception-next-level.

Although this article was debunked by pro-life[13] and pro-choice critics,[14] millions of online users have been exposed to the images as a literal representation of fetal development. The images' reach includes the 527,000 TikTok followers of Bronte Remsik, a medical resident who debated conservative *The Daily Wire* host Michael Knowles on the topic of abortion.[15] Ironically, in an attempt to combat Knowles' "misinformation" regarding the nature of fetal development, Remsik held the photos up to the camera during a debate.[16] Additionally, Jessica Valenti, a pro-choice activist with over 292,000 followers on X (formerly Twitter),[17] posted the same image with the caption "Just a reminder that this is what an 8 week pregnancy/abortion looks like."[18]

Such attempts to whitewash the reality of abortion are understandable. For the pro-abortion progressive, the stakes are high. If the pro-life position—that abortion is the innocent killing of valuable human life—is correct, then support for abortion as a "human right" is nothing more than the use of violence as the just predicate for women's rights.

---

13 Waters, "UK Newspaper Takes Pro-Abortion Deception to Next Level."

14 Donley, Greer, and Jill Wieber Lens. "Those Pregnancy Tissue Photos Were Destined to Backfire on Abortion Rights Supporters." Slate, October 27, 2022. https://slate.com/news-and-politics/2022/10/guardian-pregnancy-tissue-photos-abortion-rights-misfire.html.

15 Remsik, Bronte. "Dr. Bronte TikTok." TikTok, accessed January 29, 2025. https://www.tiktok.com/@bronteremsik.

16 Knowles, Michael. "Michael Knowles DEBATES Viral Pro-Choice Activist | Bronte Remsik." YouTube, December 3, 2022. https://www.youtube.com/watch?v=yiNW84kJy_k.

17 "@JessicaValenti." X, accessed January 29, 2025. https://twitter.com/JessicaValenti.

18 @JessicaValenti, January 10, 2024, 8:22 PM.

Progressives, believing themselves empathetic and compassionate, are understandably psychologically uneasy with the idea that their support of a "human right" results in incalculable cruelty perpetrated against children. And although the humanity of the unborn alone should stir people to prevent their legal killing, we should also consider that the cost of abortion "rights" is carried by all children—half-aborted, aborted, and unaborted alike.[19]

THE PROGRESSIVE CULTURAL RESPONSE TO *DOBBS*

In June 2022, the US Supreme Court issued a ruling in *Dobbs v. Jackson Women's Health Organization*, overturning *Roe v. Wade*, the 1970s case establishing abortion as a right guaranteed by the Constitution. By overturning *Roe*, decisions regarding the legality of abortion remained in the authority of states and, in some states, trigger laws banning abortion at early stages of pregnancy took effect.[20] Thus, depending on geographic location, some women were unable to access abortion. This created a new social class: Dobbs babies, or children born due to the closure of abortion facilities in states banning the practice. Such babies are a glaring, living example of abortion's cost. These children owe their lives to the closure of an abortion clinic and will grow up in a society that views these closures, and by extension their births, as evidence of

[19] "Latest Survivor Stories." The Abortion Survivors Network, accessed January 29, 2025. https://abortionsurvivors.org/services/.

[20] "State Laws Restricting or Prohibiting Abortion—CRS Reports." Congress.gov, December 10, 2024. https://crsreports.congress.gov/product/pdf/LSB/LSB10779.

injustice. In short, they will grow up with a scarlet letter placed next to their name, courtesy of progressive culture.

Never has it been clearer that the justification of abortion as a "human right" requires a commitment to legal and cultural inequality that places the worth of children under the power and control of subjective maternal judgment regarding human value. Indeed, a Slate article, pushing back on The Guardian's disingenuous representation of preborn life, boldly makes this claim, stating it is reductive to reduce fetal life to a meaningless "clump of cells."[21] This, the authors argue, risks alienating women who have a profound sense of loss following miscarriage. Instead, the value of preborn life should be determined solely by the pregnant mother because it is just to "[a]llow the pregnant person to define the pregnancy's meaning."[22]

Asserting preborn life only has value to the extent it is assigned by the child's mother fundamentally alters the mother-child relationship from a bond predicated on unconditional love to a twisted power dynamic in which children exist only at the pleasure of maternal overlords.

This makes it all the more ironic that many progressives seek to live by a creed that states there are "no moral absolutes." Despite their attempts to banish absolute truth, the ultimate and unconditional power they grant the mother in the mother-child relationship reveals that progressives do utilize a hierarchy of values. They may have rejected traditional Judeo-Christian conceptions

---

21 Donley and Lens, "Those Pregnancy Tissue Photos Were Destined to Backfire on Abortion Rights Supporters."

22 Donley and Lens, "Those Pregnancy Tissue Photos Were Destined to Backfire on Abortion Rights Supporters."

of the divine for a secular vision, but their beliefs hardly reside outside the structure of hierarchical thinking.

These cultural gatekeepers, in true postmodern fashion, take the identity of God and fracture it, selling the scattered attributes for parts. Professors and the "expert" class divvy up His all-knowing trait, serving as God-like figures over their fiefdoms of knowledge. Google and the government corner the market on His omnipresence. But it is women who seek to retain an iron grip on His mercy, love, and judgment.

Women are progressive culture's judges of the value of human life.

Kamala Harris's attempt to win a presidential campaign almost solely on supporting abortion perfectly encapsulates the absolute nature of the power women seek to wield, without question or qualification. This is echoed in the popular progressive idea that there is no such thing as a "good" or "bad" abortion.[23]

In this structure, modern mothers are analogous to gods within a polytheistic belief system, each serving as the final arbiter of the moral value of human life within the jurisdiction of their individual homes. Progressive culture asserts mothers alone have the just authority to determine whether a human being should live or die. Without the "right" to make such a unilateral decision, women are deemed to be "oppressed," treated as subhuman while living in a "tyrannical patriarchy" as described in dystopian literature, like *The Handmaid's Tale*.

---

[23] Donley and Lens, "Those Pregnancy Tissue Photos Were Destined to Backfire on Abortion Rights Supporters."

This is ironic, because the God-like authority wielded by American women does not come with the corresponding scrutiny brought to bear in religious settings. The God of the Bible is routinely derided as "cruel" by non-theist critics for His allegedly inhumane treatment of human life, yet women who decide to abort their children rarely receive such criticism. If women believe they have the just authority to determine the value of human life, then this exercise of raw power should come with corresponding scrutiny. Otherwise, society must be prepared to treat mothers as if their decisions regarding their children's value is assumed correct, by granting their opinions the weight of what has traditionally been associated with God-given authority.

Imagine a world in which a woman's decision to voluntarily conceive and then abort her child, thereby causing the child to exist only to feel pain and death, were scrutinized as often and with as much zeal as divine judgment?

Developments following the death of *Roe v. Wade*, the Supreme Court decision that ruled abortion was a right protected by the US Constitution, provide us with a unique cultural opportunity to critique our once all-powerful, maternal goddesses.

Kamala Harris built her entire 2024 presidential campaign around the phrase "Trust Women."[24] Her message was simple: her opposition, in this case Donald Trump, neither trusts women to make decisions for themselves nor respects the "freedom of women or the intelligence of women to know what's in their own

---

[24] @KamalaHarris. X, August 6, 2022, 9:46 AM; @KamalaHarris, July 15, 2023, 2:51 PM.

best interest."[25] In contrast, she holds herself as someone different, stating that she and her party "trust women."[26]

Harris's message was compelling, but only because confronting the morality of women is a cultural taboo. Her loss may have shown this taboo is on thin ice, but the way abortion was handled at the presidential and vice-presidential debates solidifies the reality that questioning women is still political suicide.

In the presidential debate, Trump faced harsh lines of questioning about abortion, with moderators asking why women should trust him on the issue given inconsistent statements about his support or opposition to Florida's six-week ban on the procedure. Yet, in deference to Harris and contrary to the facts, moderators stated, "There is no state in this country where it is legal to kill a baby after it's born."[27]

This statement ignored the reality that there have been several babies left to die after failed abortion procedures, including in Minnesota, the home state of Harris's running mate, Tim Walz.[28] However, more importantly, this served as a layup for Harris, who was given a golden opportunity to retain control over the framing

---

[25] Lucey, Catherine. "Harris in Arizona: 'We Trust Women.'" *The Wall Street Journal*, accessed January 29, 2025. https://www.wsj.com/live-coverage/harris-trump-election-10-31-24/card/harris-we-trust-women--zSSZu1jLCOYT76C2XTpN.

[26] Lucey, "Harris in Arizona: 'We Trust Women.'"

[27] Hoffman, Riley. "READ: Harris-Trump Presidential Debate Transcript." ABC News, September 11, 2024. https://abcnews.go.com/Politics/harris-trump-presidential-debate-transcript/story?id=113560542.

[28] "Here's Exactly How Born-Alive Infants Were Denied Protection Under Minnesota Law." MCCL, October 10, 2024. https://www.mccl.org/post/here-s-exactly-how-born-alive-infants-were-denied-protection-under-minnesota-law.

of the debate. Still, the most compelling appeal to the morality of women is embedded in Harris's response to a question asking if she supported any restrictions on abortion. Confidently, yet incorrectly, she stated firmly that "nowhere in America is a woman carrying a pregnancy to term and asking for an abortion."[29,30] According to Harris, not only was this not happening, but to question whether it would be, was "insulting" to women.[31]

Now, imagine if moderators of the presidential debate were neutral on the issue of abortion, rather than pro-choice. A fair line of questioning for Harris would look something like this:

> Ms. Vice President, you have stated women should be "trusted" to determine whether abortion is appropriate, how do you answer a skeptic who believes it is sexist to grant only women the right to create and destroy human life?
>
> Furthermore, in the wake of the *Dobbs* decision, a ruling you vehemently oppose, researchers determined there were a minimum additional

29 "The Mom Who Had an Abortion at 8 Months, Then a Surprise Pregnancy." *The Cut*, June 6, 2018. https://www.thecut.com/2018/06/she-had-an-abortion-at-8-months-then-a-surprise-pregnancy.html.

30 Godfrey, Elaine. "The Abortion Absolutist." *The Atlantic*, May 12, 2023. https://www.theatlantic.com/politics/archive/2023/05/dr-warren-hern-abortion-post-roe/674000/.

31 Hoffman, "READ: Harris-Trump Presidential Debate Transcript."

> 30,000 births within a year of the decision.[32] This means some children are born because of the *Dobbs* decision, how do you answer those who view your stance on abortion as dehumanizing to the children born as a result of the Supreme Court's decision? Additionally, does your belief that children born because of the *Dobbs* decision should not exist undercut your emphasis on social belonging and inclusion?

Of course, these questions are not asked because the moderators of presidential debates agree with the underlying premises of pro-choice rhetoric, and since abortive women are a major voting bloc, even those who are pro-life know it is in their best interest to speak carefully on the issue.

Discourse highlighting children impacted by abortion cannot occur in mainstream outlets because it complicates support for the procedure, which is highest when women's interests are magnified, while the fetus is treated as mere maternal property. The strength of pro-abortion propaganda is highlighted in a discourse between billionaire Republican ally, Elon Musk, and an abortion survivor. During the audience question and answer portion, a woman described how her mother tried, but failed, to have

[32] Levitt, Michael, Tinbete Ermyas, and Ari Shapiro. "After the Dobbs Decision, Birth Rates Are Up in States with Abortion Ban States." NPR, November 24, 2023. https://www.npr.org/2023/11/24/1215152734/after-the-dobbs-decision-birth-rates-are-up-in-states-with-abortion-ban-states.

her aborted, before asking whether Musk would consider being pro-life.[33]

In response, Musk did what no Democrat would ever do. First, he showed compassion to the woman, stating he was glad she had not died. He then stated he views abortion after viability as "murder," before getting to the root of the issue: the destruction of the mother-child relationship. The modern left has instilled in young women a "terror" of pregnancy, making it out to be the worst possible thing a woman can experience. "This is the issue we face," Musk said, "the relentless push in education to terrify girls and women that if they get pregnant their life is over."[34]

IMPACT OF *DOBBS*

Millions of children face questions surrounding their value and worth, and this is particularly true of children who face the horrors of maternal abuse.[35] However, the direct link between maternal abuse and the issue of abortion, a problem I was forced to face at an early age, only directly affects a small, but growing, number of children.

---

[33] Secular Pro-life. "Abortion Survivor Asks Elon Musk His Stance on Abortion." YouTube, November 5, 2024. https://www.youtube.com/watch?v=p1Uu64Wl9Z4.

[34] Secular Pro-life, "Abortion Survivor Asks Elon Musk His Stance on Abortion."

[35] Khoury, Jennifer E., Lina Dimitrov, Michelle Bosquet Enlow, J. D. Haltigan, Elisa Bronfman, and Karlen Lyons-Ruth. "Patterns of Maternal Childhood Maltreatment and Disrupted Interaction Between Mothers and Their 4-Month-Old Infants." *Child Maltreatment* 27, no. 3 (2022): 366–377. https://doi.org/10.1177/10775595211007567.

Despite the profound impact culture will have on the lives of these children, they are rarely discussed, or when mentioned, they are spoken of with disdain. After all, they are the result of a "human rights" violation. In the words of Alison Gemmill, assistant professor at the Johns Hopkins Bloomberg School of Public Health, they are indicative of "an assault on reproductive autonomy."[36]

Imagine the experience of a Dobbs baby who looks out into the medical community only to find contempt at her existence. After gazing into the darkness of the medical community's hatred of her life, she may quickly glance at online comment sections, exposing herself to more of the casual hatred common progressive cultural messaging communicates. In the *New York Post*, a commenter writes, "All this says to me, is a whopping 32,000 people who needed an abortion [emphasis added] were denied one and forced to birth a child they do not want. Yay for those unwanted children. I have no doubt a 'large percentage' of them will proceed to have excellent unwanted childhoods, followed by top-notch unscathed lives."[37,38]

When observing popular media, these children will watch powerful movie stars, such as Anne Hathaway, describe abortion

---

[36] *Dobbs v. Jackson Women's Health Organization.*

[37] Tietz, Kendall. "Overturning of Roe v. Wade Led to 32,000 Additional Births, Study Finds." *New York Post*, November 25, 2023. https://nypost.com/2023/11/25/news/overturning-of-roe-v-wade-led-to-32000-additional-births-study-finds/.

[38] *Dobbs v. Jackson Women's Health Organization.*

as "another word for mercy."[39] As they face the onslaught of shame, they may confuse Hathaway's hatred for truth, leading to an internalization of self-hatred and a belief in their own worthlessness. In the midst of their emotional perplexity, they will see actresses like Michelle Williams receive resounding applause at star-studded events for declaring her self-made career was only made possible by "employing a [woman's] right to choose."[40] Women, they are told, must vote for "self-interest."[41] In justification of this position, the same pro-choice activists cite the actions of men who have—through the voting booth—created a world that "looks so much like them."[42] Women, as the "largest voting body," she argues, should create a country that "looks more like us."[43] Dobbs babies will observe how *TIME* magazine described Williams's advocacy as "impassioned,"[44] while CBS lauded her for "shining the spotlight on abortion rights."[45]

---

39 Johnson, Julia. "Watch: Anne Hathaway Tells the View 'Abortion Can Be Another Word for Mercy.'" *Washington Examiner*, November 1, 2022. https://www.washingtonexaminer.com/news/1149018/watch-anne-hathaway-tells-the-view-abortion-can-be-another-word-for-mercy/.

40 Greenspan, Rachel E. "Michelle Williams Makes a Passionate Plea for Abortion Rights in Golden Globes Acceptance Speech." *TIME*, January 6, 2020. https://time.com/5759356/golden-globes-2020-michelle-williams/.

41 Waters, "UK Newspaper Takes Pro-Abortion Deception to Next Level."

42 Waters, "UK Newspaper Takes Pro-Abortion Deception to Next Level."

43 Waters, "UK Newspaper Takes Pro-Abortion Deception to Next Level."

44 Waters, "UK Newspaper Takes Pro-Abortion Deception to Next Level."

45 Cohen, Li. "Michelle Williams Advocates for Abortion Rights in Golden Globes Acceptance Speech." CBS News, January 6, 2020. https://www.cbsnews.com/news/golden-globes-michelle-williams-advocates-for-womens-rights-in-golden-globes-speech/.

What will be noticeably absent were the voices of those willing to question how the unwanted children spoken of may process death's praise. The profound contempt these children will face from society is difficult to fathom, yet impossible to deny. In Williams's ideal world, created by women, Dobbs babies do not exist; they would have been erased before they could be born. Their lives are a women's rights tragedy.

THE MENTAL SUBJUGATION OF CHILDREN

Of course, neither unwanted children nor Dobbs babies are monolithic groups. Inevitably many will be pro-choice or prolife for a range of reasons. Some will hold nuanced and complex views on the topic of abortion, others will pick up their beliefs through cultural osmosis.

Regardless, these views will be informed and shaped by a culture steeped in progressive values, the belief abortion is the foundation of female equality, and the culturally normative idea that the arbitrary assignment of worth to human lives is not only justice, but opposition to such a system is oppression. Within this belief system, the dehumanization of children serves as the predicate for the self-sufficiency and self-actualization of mothers whose God-like decisions are beyond the scrutiny of mere mortals. Children will learn they must sacrifice themselves at the altar of mother god because this form of dehumanization is just, good, and beautiful.

Indeed, under the Biden-Harris administration, a federal law of questionable constitutionality was weaponized to target prolife protesters demonstrating at abortion clinics. Calls—which were ultimately successful—for President Trump to pardon these pro-life Americans have increased,[46] but their prosecution stands in stark contrast to pro-choice protests. Over ninety pro-life pregnancy centers were targeted by pro-choice protests after *Dobbs*, but the federal government only prosecuted three individuals.[47] On the left, protesters have always been selectively lauded.

The naturally curious unwanted child who seeks to understand why his life has less value than his mother's will intuitively understand the danger associated with targeting the abortion rights status quo. This inquisitive child seeks to understand, but knows knowledge is a double-edged sword that can lead to profound social consequences. Thus, the unwanted child faces the tension between curiosity and conformity to authority that has existed within all cultures throughout time regardless of the prevailing viewpoint. He will see the demonization of those who attempt to present reasonable pro-life viewpoints as they are universally met with fierce resistance from the gatekeepers of social knowledge. This will clarify for him the age-old truth that "knowledge is power," and, accordingly, those in possession of power are loath to share in its spoils.

Although unwanted children, particularly Dobbs babies, have a stronger incentive to explore questions regarding abortion, all

---

46 "Thomas More Society Petitions President Trump to Pardon 21 Pro-Lifers Targeted by Biden DOJ." Thomas More Society, January 15, 2025. https://web.archive.org/web/20250117222348/https://www.thomasmoresociety.org/news/thomas-more-society-petitions-president-trump-to-pardon-21-pro-lifers-targeted-by-biden-doj.

47 Richardson, Valerie. "Trump Urged to Pardon 21 Pro-Life Activists Convicted in Biden Administration's Crackdown." *The Washington Times*, January 15, 2025. https://www.washingtontimes.com/news/2025/jan/15/trump-urged-pardon-21-activists-convicted-biden-ad/.

children are surrounded by pro-choice rhetoric. They are implicitly aware that questioning the morality of a woman who aborts her child is tantamount to heresy against progressive norms. The pro-abortion activist community is now generations old, and the feminists who have championed the "right to choose" have passed their broken understanding of human life into the bloodstream of their children.

I have observed glimpses of this reality when engaging in honest, deeply personal discussions of abortion with several friends. Below is a narration representative of the cumulative nature of those conversations. Although singular pronouns are used, it does not describe one singular conversation, instead summarizing the gist of several dialogues. In each case, our mothers' beliefs were polar opposites. Mine was staunchly pro-life, while their mothers took pride in their pro-choice identity and baked their moral assumptions into the minds of their children.

> After some time debating the topic, in which she argued abortion was a human right for a host of reasons, one of which included compassion for the plight of abused children, I challenged my friend with blunt, biting questions.
>
> "If a mother can determine the worth of an individual's life, why can't that same individual make the precise same moral calculation? If my mother, who was indisputably abusive, could justifiably kill me to save myself from her torment, why couldn't I kill myself after birth to prevent the pain of life?"

She shifted in her seat, "Suicide," she said, "is not the answer. People shouldn't kill themselves to escape pain."

I countered, "You evaded the question. According to your logic, mothers have more control over people than individuals themselves. What gives mothers the sole authority to determine whether a given human life is worth living? Why can't the people who in fact endure life's pain make the same moral calculation?"

I watched as she averted eye contact and moved her head from side to side in search of an answer before she admitted, "I don't know. I don't have an answer." This response was profound, an admission most progressives would have refused to utter. But it was what came after that revealed the heart of her attachment to abortion dogma.

A moment of pause descended before she spoke. "There's another side to this though," she said, regaining her confidence. "My mother had an abortion before I was born, and she told me how important this was for her journey. 'If I had not had the abortion option, you would not be born. You should thank God for abortion, because without it, I would have one child, but that child would not have been you.'"

I searched her face as she spoke, the raw pain was palpable as she warred within herself.

The squinting of her eyes avoided tears, and compulsive hand movements self-soothed her disturbed spirit. Before me was the victim of an emotionally abusive mother who used her innocent child as a vehicle through which to justify her willful destruction of human life. Rather than question her mother's moral character, my friend lashed out with the natural, instinctual response, seeking to preserve the integrity of the mother-child bond.

"She was right to make that choice. She alone bore the consequences of pregnancy, and she is the only person with the ability to determine what children she brings into the world." Then, to preempt the obvious, she further protested in her mother's defense, "She is a loving, perfect mother. I couldn't have had a better mom, no one could ever love me better than her."

Alas, she protesteth too much. I backed off, aware that pushing the argument further was an exercise in emotional destruction, for the woman before me bore the lashes of her mother's emotional torment. I realized many of my female friends were not pro-choice because reason and logic dictated this response. Rather, they were pro-choice because the bond between themselves and their mothers depended upon their affirmation of abortion as a human right.

In this moment, I observed the miraculous nature of my own childhood musings and noticed how—despite the pain of abuse—the name "half-aborted" had presented me with an opportunity to recognize the harsh reality many avoid. I was no child prodigy, but it takes little brain power to recognize how abortion dogma stifles a child's ability to openly engage with the moral arguments regarding the equal worth of children in relation to their mothers. The tension between the twin claims of equality and the belief in abortion "rights" was written on the face of my distressed friend who—when faced with the difficulty of objectively evaluating the immorality of her mother's actions—retreated into the maternal womb—fearful of the consequences of questioning her mother/master.

These women are far from alone. Progressives, particularly progressive women, hold enormous power over the incentive structure children must navigate to safely live within Western culture. All mothers are women, most current and future educators are women.[48] In addition, most educators are progressive supporters of the "right to choose."[49] Those who craft curriculum are of the same ideological persuasion, as are the gatekeepers of all popular mediums of cultural power, from movies and music, to

---

48 Reeves, Richard. "Missing Misters: Gender Diversity among Teachers." American Institute for Boys and Men, February 27, 2024. https://aibm.org/research/missing-misters/.

49 Klein, Alyson. "Survey: Educators' Political Leanings, Who They Voted for, Where They Stand on Key Issues." Education Week, December 12, 2017. https://www.edweek.org/leadership/survey-educators-political-leanings-who-they-voted-for-where-they-stand-on-key-issues/2017/12. Izumi, Lance. "Why Are Teachers Mostly Liberal?" Pacific Research Institute, April 3, 2019. https://www.pacificresearch.org/why-are-teachers-mostly-liberal/.

journalism and beyond. Thus, children are inundated with messages from female authority figures who operate from the assumption that abortion is a human right only opposed by those in support of the oppression of women.

Abortion regulation, which has been a contentious issue in American political life for well over fifty years, is frequently communicated to children from abortion advocates who happily remind the public how activists labored in love for decades before celebrating the birth of the "right to choose" incoherently articulated in the Supreme Court's notorious 1973 *Roe v. Wade* decision.[50] Given the broad support for abortion within culturally elite spaces, children face relentless pressure to view human life as worthless until stamped with maternal approval.

Take the case of a child born to an abortion activist and imagine the costs the child would bear if she announced her commitment to the pro-life cause?

Such stories are not hypothetical. Abortion activist and—ironically—self-described "doula," Carly Manes wrote a children's book titled, *What's an Abortion, Anyway?* This book is designed to fill the gap in children's literature, which, to Manes's knowledge, did not include the word "abortion" for audiences thirteen years or younger prior to her book's publication. For Manes, this book provides families with "resources" to have "compassionate

---

[50] Reese, Thomas J. "Even RBG Thought Roe v. Wade Went Too Far. We Should Learn from Her Incremental Approach." *America: The Jesuit Review*, September 24, 2020. https://www.americamagazine.org/politics-society/2020/09/24/ruth-bader-ginsburg-abortion-roe-v-wade-catholic.

and nonjudgmental conversations about abortion care with the young people in their lives."[51]

According to Manes, children should not only learn about abortion from an early age, but should be taught there is no "good" or "bad" reason to utilize a procedure that cannot be successfully carried out without a human being's death.[52] Abortion activist Hannah Matthews took advantage of Manes's works, detailing how she read this "joyful" children's book to her young son, a medium she used to inform him she aborted his sibling, describing the procedure as "easy peasy, lemon squeezy," eliciting childish laughs while omitting the violence inherent to the destruction of a human body growing in utero.[53,54]

It is not difficult to imagine the struggle children taught by activists such as Manes and Matthews would have, should they grow up and begin questioning the moral underpinnings of the ethical conclusion taught to them by their primary caretakers from the earliest of ages. The relational damage done to the mother-child bond would be enormous, analogous to a child announcing a commitment to atheism to his devout Christian mother. The knowledge of this strain alone will undoubtedly enter the child's

---

51 Manes, Carly. "What's an Abortion, Anyway?" Kirkus Reviews, September 1, 2021. https://www.kirkusreviews.com/book-reviews/carly-manes/whats-an-abortion-anyway/.

52 "What's an Abortion Anyway?" The Abortion Project, accessed January 30, 2025. https://theabortionproject.com.au/shop/p/whats-an-abortion-anyway.

53 Matthews, Hannah. "I Read to My Baby about Abortion." *Electric Lit*, January 12, 2023. https://electricliterature.com/i-read-to-my-baby-about-abortion/.

54 "What's an Abortion Anyway?" The Abortion Project.

mental calculation. Furthermore, the ability to condemn one's own mother after learning she has had one or more abortions only compounds the difficulty involved in coming to a moral conclusion opposite that of the mother.

Indeed, even without age-inappropriate indoctrination tactics employed by zealous advocates, children intuitively know that supporting abortion scores social points while supporting life results in social sanctions. It is in the cultural air they breathe and the current of the cultural waters in which they swim. The burden of this choice is hidden but costly; they can either assert that all humans have equal value or accept subordination to their mothers in exchange for maternal love and social acceptance.

This choice is inescapable because the culture in which children are currently born unequivocally states abortion is a "human right," thus communicating to children that their moral status, indeed their right to exist, is entirely dependent upon the opinions their mothers held when their lives were at their most vulnerable. To hold culturally acceptable views of morality, children must accept a status inferior to their mothers. Failure to comply with this progressive moral doctrine results in social scorn, pejorative name calling, and the accusation that the child "hates" women, and more importantly, their own mothers.

In short, children are socially conditioned to accept abortion the way an abuse victim is conditioned to view physical punishment as appropriate. Children internalize an inferiority complex where they hold the worth of their mother as superior to their own. This complex is created under conditions of duress existing within a power structure that disfavors children because children, who are incapable of consent, are biologically wired to attune to the needs and desires of their mothers.

Long before children learn the word "abortion," they seek maternal love, affection, and care. This occurs without the child's consent, for they are bound by biological forces outside their control to desire the nurture of a specific woman. Thus, mothers and children exist within a unique relationship involving an inherent power imbalance where mothers possess a near limitless ability to shape their children's perceptions, experiences, and reality. Mothers driven by sociopathic tendencies have the power to psychologically manipulate their children in a manner no other human can replicate. Whether mothers assert this power is one matter, whether they hold it is incontrovertible.

Of course, not all mothers who believe the moral doctrine that abortion is a human right are sociopathic or void of empathy. But, over the course of decades, zealous pro-choice activists have birthed thousands of babies who undoubtedly learned their mother's ability to kill them was a "human right." It is said a picture is worth a thousand words, and one pro-choice activist vividly captured a child's dilemma when, in defiance of the *Dobbs* ruling, she stood outside the Supreme Court, proudly displaying the words "NOT YET A HUMAN" written in a circle around her visibly late term, pregnant stomach.[55] Imagine living as this child, with a perpetual, visual reminder of the lack of humanity afforded to her life before Mother God granted her value? A child in such a home has roughly the same odds of voicing her concerns

---

[55] "In Pictures: Americans React after Supreme Court Overturns Roe v. Wade." CNN, June 28, 2022. https://www.cnn.com/2022/06/24/politics/gallery/roe-v-wade-supreme-court-reactions/index.html.

with abortion as a gay child does living with his Westboro Baptist preacher father.

ABORTION AS PROTECTED, SEX-BASED VIOLENCE

Abortion is the quintessential example of female-perpetrated violence because, despite being a perpetrator of violence, the woman remains the primary recipient of compassion. The woman creates her child, kills her child, and yet demands society hold compassion for her because choosing to kill her child was a trauma to her own body. To avoid appearing callous toward women, many of whom are in admittedly bad circumstances when they choose to abort, society has failed to call female perpetrators to account.

This is because female-perpetrated violence is bound up in victimhood. It is easier to condemn violence when the perpetrator of harm is seen as strong and capable. Modern feminists prey on the cultural perception of women as victims, successfully conning society into viewing women as both empowered and traumatized by abortion. Thus, children, the ultimate losers in "abortion rights," are written out of the debate. Their pain is invisible, consumed by the destruction of the mothers who view them as property, nothing more than an extension of her body.

Musk is, unfortunately, correct. The left has destroyed the sacred, symbiotic relationship between mother and child, transforming mothers into masters and children into emotional slaves. The devouring mother, the archetype of female predation, preys on children, viewing them as property, not people. Fully dismantling the worst of progressive prejudice will not be complete until the relationship between women and children is healed, and this healing cannot begin until society can criticize women and hold them to account when they violate the rights of children.

Ironically, this need not involve the destruction of feminism, but rather reimagining feminism in its earliest, purist form. Although pro-life feminism is now culturally an oxymoron, this was not always the case. In fact, the first feminists, those who secured the modern woman's right to vote, faced oppression with an unwavering commitment to real justice. Feminists for Life of America highlights the courage of the original feminists, stating that despite living under laws that allowed marital rape and prevented women from controlling their finances or pursuing higher education, first-wave feminists understood that violence was no solution to their problems. Instead, they gave voice to the vulnerable, including the lives they created in their own wombs.[56]

Although the modern feminist impulse to destroy the beauty of the mother-child relationship should be resisted with an accurate historical narrative that highlights the anti-abortion beliefs of the earliest warriors of women's rights, the importance of rejecting the left's current belief in female supremacy is vital.

Here it is important to note the difference between the belief that abortion should not be criminalized and the assertion that it is a "right."

It is one thing to assert abortion should be legal, but asserting abortion is a "human right" places the procedure in a category separate from "actions which should be legal." Human rights are not merely actions that society should refrain from including in

---

[56] Foster, Serrin M. "'First Wave Feminists' Intro." Feminists for Life of America, accessed January 30, 2025. https://www.feministsforlife.org/firstwaveintro/.

criminal code or otherwise heavily penalizing. Instead, human rights are moral absolutes and are functionally treated as if they were spoken from the mouth of God Himself, and he who disagrees stands for injustice.

Most children, when confronted with the choice of either committing the social sin of condemning women—and by extension, their mothers—or accepting their own status as existing at the mercy of maternal power, will behave as my friend did, willingly accepting their own inferiority to prop up the power of their mothers. With this path comes the social benefits accompanying progressive praise.

Although the pro-life movement may represent a significant portion of American society, as discussed above those with pro-life views are nonetheless pariahs in progressive communities, which are disproportionately represented in elite cultural spaces. Children who aspire to careers in education, journalism, law, arts, entertainment, or corporate environments will undoubtedly experience harsh blowback for openly expressing pro-life views while watching their pro-choice counterparts be lauded for their efforts by nearly every national "women's" organization. The incentive structure for children is clear: Acceptance of the pro-abortion position makes it easier to climb the ladder of success by placing people in the position of "supporting" and "trusting" women.

The devouring mother will be defeated when women are no longer presumed to be morally pure, when the answer to the question "Do you trust women?" is a resounding "No." Trust in any individual or group should be earned, not granted based on sex. Nor should the interests of children, incapable of political emancipation, be held hostage by those who created the inconveniences they wish to kill. Indeed, in a hypothetical world in which children could exercise the right to vote and assert their worth regardless of maternal opinion, one can only wonder if the self-interested ballots they cast would lead to "a world that looked more like them,"[57] thereby exposing how progressive "liberation" rests on a foundation of innocent human blood.

[57] Greenspan, "Michelle Williams Makes a Passionate Plea for Abortion Rights in Golden Globes Acceptance Speech."

CHAPTER 2
Suicide

NEARER MY GOD TO THEE

By age ten, my life was as it had always been. Daily, I experienced my brother—a dutiful student of my mother—mercilessly degrading his half-aborted sister.

Abortion was death. It was also a joke.

"What is the result of a botched abortion?" my brother asked, before answering, "a human mistake!"

But the joke did not end there. According to his logic, if the house was set on fire, he would save every person and possession in the home before even thinking about coming back for me. Indeed, having to even *consider* saving me was offensive. "You shouldn't have been born," he jeered. "We would all be better off if you were dead."

Yet, the problem was deeper than his wounding words, for how could I blame him? Would I do any better had the birth order and maternal favoritism been reversed? Probably not. Thus, in the worst of times, even moral superiority was insufficient to prove my worth. Instead, I could only watch him debase me while my family either ignored his attacks or participated for their own delight.

As my intellectual maturity developed and circumstances remained unchanged, it became increasingly difficult to believe human life, including my own, was inherently good or worthy of the effort required for its sustenance.

Within this context, I first questioned the concept of mercy as a form of justice.

The story of Noah's Ark had been told to me more times than I could count, yet my ten-year-old mind, now fully consumed with death and pain, pondered the story as if I had never heard it before. Rather than revealing a God of judgment, what I witnessed was a God full of senseless mercy. An instantaneous rage built within me as I read how He allowed life to survive the flood.

"*How despicable!*" I thought. "*Why did He not complete His judgment?! Just a few more deaths and humanity would have ended. He could have wiped pain and death off the earth. Why would he* force people to live?"

I tried to tame the internal monologue, but it would not cease, for anger demanded immediate attention. I wondered whether God was like Mom, interested in keeping people alive to bask in their torment and shame.

"*His mercy is far worse than judgment.*"

My indignation over the outcome of Noah's Ark was symptomatic of my developing outlook on the value of life. Rather than invoking pain, I had come to view death with an aura of peace, beauty, and hope.

Among the first hints of this hope came in the form of an archeological discovery. One day, Dad and I were watching TV and saw a documentary about the *Titanic*. An archeological finding renewed the historical tale, and it was music to my ears. Unlike Noah's Ark, the lucky souls aboard the *Titanic* were spared the horrors of a long life.

Instead, as the ship sank to the bottom of the sea, the band played a rendition of the hymn, "Nearer My God to Thee." Death, it seemed, brought with it the promise of a closer proximity to God—and by proxy—goodness itself. The dying souls, singing this hymn as they perished, would soon move into whatever life exists after death...a world where pain ceased, one that could be accessed through no medium other than physical demise.

I felt my soul come alive as I celebrated the fate of the ship's occupants. This beauty was followed by a deep envy, which led me to obsess over the story. For some time, I collected books and facts about the *Titanic*'s rise and fall, information I used to meditate on the beauty of death and the hope of joy after earthly expiration.

As I collected and pondered, a single question played on a loop in my mind: "*Why shouldn't* I *get to die?*" I wasn't sure. It seemed to defy fairness that some people were allowed to die while I had to go on living. So, the question stayed in my consciousness like a hamster on a wheel, each fiber of my intellect working overtime in a vain attempt to find an answer. Alas, a definitive conclusion remained out of reach.

Until one day, the words of an abortion supporter exposed a rift within my troubled spirit.

Coexisting alongside my disdain for life was a dissatisfaction with the hypocritical conditions under which the right to death was accepted. Earlier, I had encountered the term "forced birth," which is commonly[58] used by abortion supporters to describe what they view as the indignity of requiring women to carry a child to term when she would prefer an abortion.

However, I was immune to their marketing. Instead, the term filled me with indescribable fury.

"*The* mother *is the one undergoing forced birth?!*" I thought in mockery. "*What child ever consented to being born? If anyone endures 'forced birth,' it is children, not women. What is nine months in comparison to a lifetime?*"

My dissection of the term had only just begun, for soon I internally articulated another obvious truth:

> *Why is abortion good, but suicide is bad? If mom can kill me, why can't I kill myself? If she killed me, her decision would have been celebrated, but if I even try to kill myself I will be labelled mentally ill, removed from society, and placed in a ward with "crazy" people.*

The inconsistency of the world's moral standards left me maddened and perplexed, to the point of internal defiance. I vowed no one, neither the God of the Bible nor the Goddess of the women's movement, had the authority to force me into a life I did not want to live.

---

[58] The concept of forced birth is common in feminist dialogue. A basic understanding of the concept can be found here: DeSanctis, Alexandra. "The 'Forced Birth' Falsehood." Ethics and Public Policy Center, May 5, 2022. https://eppc.org/publication/the-forced-birth-falsehood/.

PROGRESSIVE CONTRADICTIONS AND COGNITIVE DISSONANCE

My childhood epiphany, birthed from silent suffering, highlighted an ongoing hypocrisy within progressive thought: the simultaneous embrace of abortion and rejection of suicide.

Abortion and suicide both result in the termination of a human life, and arguments for both often rest on the idea of preventing excessive suffering. The phrase, "Don't like abortion? Don't get one," can just as easily apply to suicide. Still, society consistently champions one while stigmatizing the other.

This distinction is highlighted in the Supreme Court's pre-*Dobbs* disparate treatment of abortion and suicide. When abortion hung in the balance, the Court searched diligently through invisible "penumbras" of the Constitution to find—by any means necessary—a woman's "right" to kill human life growing in utero.[59] However, when the Court was asked to recognize a fundamental "right" to assisted suicide, the penumbras granting privacy rights in individual medical decisions led them to deny the request.[60]

Thus, for nearly fifty years, all people were told their right to bodily autonomy is inherently less important than the corresponding right of their mothers. But those who commit suicide harm *only their own* body, while those who have abortions sacrifice

---

59 "*Roe v. Wade*, 410 US 113 (1973)." Justia US Supreme Court, accessed January 30, 2025. https://supreme.justia.com/cases/federal/us/410/113/.

60 "*Washington v. Glucksberg*, 521 US 702 (1997)." Justia US Supreme Court, accessed January 30, 2025. https://supreme.justia.com/cases/federal/us/521/702/.

a growing human being in various stages of bodily development for their own convenience, comfort, and/or perceived well-being.

This highlights how, despite what adherents to progressive values sell, their worldview requires its believers to hold cognitive dissonance surrounding the nature of human dignity, including regarding who has the right to define what dignity means. It is difficult to argue all humans have an inherent right to dignity—as defined by the ability to choose or terminate life—while simultaneously granting women the right to destroy the growing human body within them and denying the choice of death to those who suffer the lifelong weight of trauma.

This dissonance is passed on to vulnerable people whose pain is ignored, trivialized, or otherwise treated as insignificant; in particular, unwanted children. Their confusion is *compounded* by a culture that explicitly tells them pre-birth death would have been preferable to life while reminding them that—because birth occurred—committing suicide would be morally wrong.

Law and culture can either affirm all life as valuable, and thus worthy of protection, or accept that some lives can be justifiably ended. The progressive proclivity to give women who do not bear the permanent consequences of a forced life the right to end that life while denying those who could never consent to birth the ability to choose death is morally and logically incoherent.

SELLING DEATH AS A SOLUTION TO SUFFERING

Despite the badge of compassion worn by progressives, the foundation of the worldview they advance sells death as a solution to suffering. Their belief regarding the nature of human dignity asserts human life has absolute value and should be preserved in some contexts—such as suicide, or murder outside the womb—while being absolutely worthless at its earliest stages.

This cognitive dissonance represents the culturally dominant worldview of the present era, in which progressives routinely frame abortion as a fundamental right yet fail to address this philosophy's implications in other arenas. Take Vice President Harris's remarks at the April 2023 Fighting for Reproductive Rights event at Howard University, where she equated abortion access with American ideals. There, she announced "fundamental freedoms" are under attack,[61] and to respect America's traditions, students should "fight for the ability of all people to be who they are and make decisions about their own lives and their bodies."[62] For, "[w]hen you love something, you fight for it, and we will fight for the ideals of this country."

Despite progressive feel-good rhetoric showcasing their self-described empathy, as progressive ideas permeate culture, the belief that death is preferable to life has expanded. Abortion has moved from "safe, legal, and rare," to "shout your abortion" and free, celebratory abortions outside the Democratic National Committee Convention for the nomination of their party's

---

[61] Sanders, Larry J. "Vice President Kamala Harris '86 Provides Remarks at Reproductive Rights Event at Howard University." *The Dig*, April 26, 2023. https://thedig.howard.edu/all-stories/vice-president-kamala-harris-86-provides-remarks-reproductive-rights-event-howard-university.

[62] Sanders, "Vice President Kamala Harris '86 Provides Remarks at Reproductive Rights Event at Howard University."

presidential candidate.[63] Unfortunately for society, the idea that there is "no such thing as a bad abortion" has implications that move beyond the immediate context of women killing their offspring for convenience, or access to sexual gratification.

Progressive moral consistency would expand the conditions under which death is deemed acceptable.

What would society look like if the progressive predicate—expressed through abortion—that holds life has no inherent value were consistently applied in other contexts involving questions of human dignity?

There are theoretical and practical examples of what such a world would look like. Philosophers and other thinkers who support the "right to choose" have expressed the disconnect between the arguments championed by confused progressives. Rather than starting from the premise that all human life has inherent value, these intellectuals begin their analysis from the *opposite* proposition.

Peter Singer, a controversial but well-known and consistent, utilitarian philosopher, wastes no time making incoherent arguments. Instead, he readily accepts that life in utero is a human being, then undercuts the core of the pro-life position by simply stating, "The belief that mere membership of our species, irrespective of other characteristics, makes a great difference to the

---

[63] Feurer, Todd. "Planned Parenthood Offers Free Abortions, Vasectomies at Mobile Clinic near DNC." CBS News, August 20, 2024. https://www.cbsnews.com/chicago/news/planned-parenthood-mobile-clinic-abortions-vasectomies-dnc/.

wrongness of killing a being is a legacy of religious doctrines."[64] Therefore, in his view, whether or not a developing fetus is a human being is irrelevant to the abortion debate.

Unwilling to hide the harshness of his logic, Singer evaluates the moral worth of severely disabled babies with clarity, saying, "Killing a disabled infant is not morally equivalent to killing a person. Very often it is not wrong at all."[65] Instead, he contends the conditions under which a disabled infant's suffering becomes unbearable should be judged by parents, not the state, a position that allows parents with little interest in incurring the inconvenience required to raise a disabled child a morally acceptable reason to recommend that child's death.[66,67]

There is a satisfying consistency in the honesty of the Singers of the world. Instead of pretending that mutually exclusive beliefs can co-exist, he clearly states what morality and justice looks like in a world that has abandoned a belief in humanity's inherent worth. According to Singer's logic, it is justifiable to kill children

---

64 Singer, Peter. "The Value of Fetal Life." In *Practical Ethics*, 3rd ed., 135. Cambridge University Press, 2011.

65 Singer, Peter. "Life and Death Decisions for Disabled Infants." In *Practical Ethics*, 3rd ed., 167. Cambridge University Press, 2011.

66 Singer, "Life and Death Decisions for Disabled Infants."

67 Similarly, the historian Yuval Harari contends the idea of human life having inherent worth is rooted in the Christian idea that humanity is made in the image of God. To cling to this idea is to cling to religion, thus his rejection of the divine causes him to similarly jettison the dignity progressives—inconsistently—claim humanity holds. TEDx Talks, "Bananas in Heaven | Yuval Noah Harari | TEDx Jaffa." YouTube, December 8, 2014. https://www.youtube.com/watch?app=desktop&v=YZa4sdIwV04&ab_channel=TEDxTalks.

in utero, infants, and adults with sufficient suffering if their deaths reduce overall human suffering.[68]

Despite the callousness of Singer's views, he carries the predicate on which pro-choice logic rests to its natural conclusion, describing some classes of humans as unfit for life and admitting his worldview advances the idea that the intense and profound suffering some people experience may cause their lives to have negative value, which justifies killing them.

CHANGING ATTITUDES TOWARD SUICIDE

In practice, as Western society has moved in a direction more closely aligned with progressive values, death is increasingly embraced as a positive good. This emerging reality can be observed in social beliefs, laws, and attitudes surrounding abortion and euthanasia.

First, regarding abortion, children with Down syndrome—one condition among many that can be diagnosed with a high degree of accuracy in utero—are aborted at a rate of 60 percent to 90 percent, dwarfing the 18 percent of abortions performed to kill "normal" children.[69]

---

[68] Singer, Peter. "Involuntary Euthanasia." In *Practical Ethics*, 3rd ed., 158–167. Cambridge University Press, 2011.

[69] United States Joint Economic Committee. "Down Syndrome and Social Capital: Assessing the Costs of Selective Abortion." Social Capital Project, March 18, 2022. https://www.jec.senate.gov/public/index.cfm/republicans/2022/3/down-syndrome-and-social-capital-assessing-the-costs-of-selective-abortion#:~:text=Misconceptions%20about%20people%20with%20Down,all%20pregnancies%20ending%20in%20abortion.

Additionally, the economic toll of caring for a child with a disability, an age-old justification for abortion long recognized by honest pro-choice advocates, is, in some jurisdictions, a necessary predicate for filing wrongful birth or wrongful life lawsuits. These suits may be filed by parents or children, and are a subset of medical malpractice claims. In a wrongful birth lawsuit, parents argue that a medical professional was negligent by failing to inform them about a birth defect in their child prior to birth.[70] Because of this negligence, parents are forced to carry the financial burden of a child they would have otherwise chosen to kill. Similarly, in wrongful life lawsuits, children may sue medical professionals for failing to disclose conditions that would have resulted in their abortion.[71] Currently, these lawsuits generally limit recovery to economic damages and are limited to plaintiffs who were born with severe disabilities, or their parents.

Yet, despite the fact that the legality of abortion is a necessary predicate for the existence of such lawsuits, and despite the clear message they send regarding the worth of disabled people relative to their non-disabled counterparts, progressives have failed to broadly discuss the obvious systemic prejudice issues these lawsuits raise.

---

70 "Wrongful Birth Lawsuits." Justia, October 2024. https://www.justia.com/birth-injuries/wrongful-birth/#:~:text=Compensation%20in%20Wrongful%20Birth%20Claims&text=If%20they%20were%20not%20properly,the%20professional%20standard%20of%20care.

71 Lee, Curtis. "What Is a Wrongful Life Lawsuit?" Nolo, August 3, 2022. https://www.nolo.com/legal-encyclopedia/wrongful-life-lawsuit.html.

As discussed in the previous chapter, attitudes surrounding abortion have, particularly in younger generations,[72] moved from the view that abortion is inherently tragic to the view that it is a positive good for humanity. This belief is summed up by activists, such as Katha Pollitt, who argue for "abortion without apology." Pollitt describes abortion as beneficial to society because it prevents women or society from bearing the burden of unwanted children.[73] For this reason, "there is no such thing as a bad abortion," a statement, that, if true, implies that even the most trivial reasons for seeking an abortion—for instance, the baby is projected to be born at an inconvenient time of year—are morally sufficient to justify death because the growing life has no value except that assigned by its mother.[74]

ASSUMPTIONS IN SOCIETIES THAT ACCEPT SUICIDE

What would society look like if suicide were treated as a morally beneficial solution to human suffering in the same manner?

Canadians seem determined to find out. In Canada, medical assistance in dying (MAID) was legalized in 2016, though access was initially limited to individuals suffering from terminal

---

[72] Cox, Daniel. "There's a New Age Gap on Abortion Rights." FiveThirtyEight, June 1, 2022. https://fivethirtyeight.com/features/theres-a-new-age-gap-on-abortion-rights/.

[73] Ronan, Alex. "'There's No Such Thing as a 'Bad' Abortion.'" *The Cut*, October 13, 2014. https://www.thecut.com/2014/10/theres-no-such-thing-as-a-bad-abortion.html.

[74] Ronan, "'There's No Such Thing as a 'Bad' Abortion.'"

illnesses.[75] Then, in 2021, access to MAID expanded to people with incurable—but not necessarily terminal—diseases.[76] Currently, individuals who wish to end their life based solely on suffering from a mental illness are ineligible under a temporary pause that is set to expire in 2027.[77] Additional liberalization effects, supported by Canada's justice minister, would allow "mature minors" to access assisted death.[78]

The Liberal Party of Canada, its progressive party, wants to proceed with the expansion, only agreeing to a temporary pause in eligibility expansion until all Canadian provinces are assessed as ready to implement changes.[79] Following news of the expansion's temporary pause, two Independent senators, Pamela Wallin and Marie-Françoise Mégie, and Liberal Stan Kutcher spoke against the pause at a press conference, arguing that denying eligibility to those who seek death due to mental illness is a form of discrimination and denies them equal access to Charter rights. This argument is also supported by the Canadian Psychiatric Association, which states that excluding people who seek MAID services

---

75 "Canada's Medical Assistance in Dying (MAID) Law." Government of Canada, July 31, 2024. https://www.justice.gc.ca/eng/cj-jp/ad-am/bk-di.html.

76 "Canada's Medical Assistance in Dying (MAID) Law."

77 Baxter, David. "Medically Assisted Death for Mental Illness Delayed until 2027: Minister." Global News, February 1, 2024. https://globalnews.ca/news/10265616/maid-expansion-delayed-2027/.

78 Paperny, Anna Mehler. "She's 47, Anorexic and Wants Help Dying. Canada Will Soon Allow It." Reuters, July 15, 2023. https://www.reuters.com/world/americas/shes-47-anorexic-wants-help-dying-canada-will-soon-allow-it-2023-07-15/.

79 Baxter, "Medically Assisted Death for Mental Illness Delayed until 2027: Minister."

solely for mental illness creates a false dichotomy between mental and physical health that only increases stigma against mental illnesses and discriminates against psychiatric patients "solely on the basis of their disability."[80]

These perspectives provide only a peek into norms in a society where arguments for the right to "autonomy" and individual "dignity" are applied both in the context of suicide as in abortion. In a society that fully goes down this route, the barriers to accessing "health care," including assisted death,[81] would be perceived as intolerable, oppressive restrictions on the exercise of a fundamental human right.

Indeed, even common arguments presented to those in the throes of suicidal ideation would be viewed as coercive in the same manner as pleas to carry pregnancy are viewed as the improper imposition of private moral or religious precepts onto women. For, in both instances, the individual is asked to sacrifice for the future of another. A woman considering abortion is told her temporary pain and discomfort will bring a valuable human being into the world. This individual, full of potential, can bring joy, love, and beauty to the world. They could make valuable contributions to society—if given the chance—and those who desire to see this individual flourish are denied the opportunity if the child is aborted. Similarly, the suicidal person is asked to look

---

[80] Tasker, John Paul. "Liberal Government Promoting a 'Culture of Death' with Medical Assistance in Dying Law, Conservative MP Says." CBC News, March 6, 2023. https://www.cbc.ca/news/politics/culture-of-death-medical-assistance-in-dying-mental-illness-1.6769504.

[81] Baxter, "Medically Assisted Death for Mental Illness Delayed until 2027: Minister."

externally for a reason to choose unwanted life. Loved ones, they are told, would mourn their death, and their potential in life is cut short by a "permanent solution to a temporary problem."

In a society that views suicide and abortion as human rights, these sorts of statements, said from a place of care, love, and respect for life, would have no place.

Is this the kind of society we want to live in?

RENAMING DESTRUCTION AS "HEALTH CARE"

Most people would answer the above question with a resounding, "No." Even those who are pro-choice do not necessarily favor second and third trimester abortions. Public support for abortion goes down from 69 percent to 37 percent when individuals are asked about their support of the procedure from the second to the third trimester of pregnancy.[82] This places mainstream progressive, Democratic viewpoints well outside the public's Overton window. Recall, neither Harris nor other prominent Democrats can verbalize a single restriction they believe should be codified on abortion.

In true devouring mother fashion, the leftist view of human dignity commodifies the body and fights for destruction under the guise of compassionate care. Of the ten states that allow medical assistance in dying, most are Democratic strongholds such as California, Hawaii, Oregon, New Mexico, and the District

---

[82] "Where Do Americans Stand on Abortion?" Gallup, July 7, 2023. https://news.gallup.com/poll/321143/americans-stand-abortion.aspx.

of Columbia.[83] Many of the same states are featured on a list of the nine states with no gestational limit on abortion.[84] Lastly, the Democratic Party has transformed the unnecessary medicalization of children into an issue of "rights."

The ability to ensure children have access to puberty blockers, that is, medication that stunts and halts normal biological development, is the subject of a lawsuit at the Supreme Court.[85] Left-wing activists argue the state of Tennessee's ban on medical procedures that alter, remove, or otherwise change a child's physical appearance to enable a child to live in accordance to an identity contrary to the child's sex violates the equal protection clause of the Fourteenth Amendment and the right of parents to make medical decisions on behalf of their children.

Issues related to transgender "care," particularly in relation to minor children and the presidential election, are discussed in subsequent chapters of this book. However, when taken as a whole, the progressive view of abortion, assisted death, and treatment for transgender individuals, particularly minors, reveals a desire to transform "care" into control under the guise of compassion. Rather than respecting life as having innate value that should be preserved, those on the left view human life as clay that can be created, destroyed, or molded, not respected.

---

83 "States Where Medical Aid in Dying Is Authorized." Compassion and Choices, accessed January 30, 2025. https://compassionandchoices.org/states-where-medical-aid-in-dying-is-authorized/.

84 "State Bans on Abortion Throughout Pregnancy." Guttmacher Institute, accessed January 2, 2025. https://www.guttmacher.org/state-policy/explore/state-policies-abortion-bans.

85 "*L. W. v. Skrmetti*." SCOTUS Blog, accessed January 30, 2025. https://www.scotusblog.com/case-files/cases/l-w-v-skrmetti/.

All these issues also share destruction in common. In abortion, a woman kills the human being she created. In assisted death, an individual destroys his or her life to avoid suffering. In the case of child transgenderism, children are encouraged to destroy the natural development of puberty in service of an ideological belief that individuals can be "born in the wrong body." In each case, the natural human state of being is pathologized. Abortion destroys the symbiotic bond between mother and child, dehumanizing the growing child as a "parasite." Assisted suicide tells those who face overwhelming suffering that death is preferable to the pain that is all too often innate to the human experience. However, attempts to alter the bodies of children is particularly repugnant to the public because it forces children—incapable of consent—to shoulder harms they cannot possibly understand.

This is an open and notorious fact. One of the early leading transition doctors, Marci Bowers, observed that of children hormonally blocked from ages nine to eleven, none were able to experience orgasm.[86] Bowers expressed her concerns to journalist Abigail Shrier, the author of *Irreversible Damage: The Transgender Craze Seducing Our Daughters*, stating her concerns regarding ideological capture of her field, acknowledging it was "naivete on the part of pediatric endocrinologists who were proponents of early [puberty] blockade thinking that just this magic can happen, that surgeons can do anything."[87]

---

86 Stanton, Glenn T. "Leading Trans Docs Admit Experimenting on Children." *Daily Citizen*, September 8, 2022. https://dailycitizen.focusonthefamily.com/leading-trans-docs-admit-experimenting-on-children/.

87 Stanton, "Leading Trans Docs Admit Experimenting on Children."

Stories of transgender youth experiencing sexual dysfunction are increasingly common, but one of the most well-known comes from reality star Jazz Jennings.

Teen Vogue profiled this famous male to female minor transition story. In an awkward exchange where Jennings speaks openly about her sex drive with her own parents, it comes to light that she has a suppressed libido and has not experienced orgasm, which she imagines is similar to sneezing.[88] Jennings, of course, is a victim in this experiment. However, whether she will be capable of acknowledging the ways she has been harmed remains unclear; after all, it is immensely difficult to recognize and face maternal and paternal abuse. Instead, Jennings states she speaks of her sexual dysfunction to normalize her experiences. "Someone has to do it in order to get the education out there."[89] Although under her moral framework her advocacy is a net benefit to the movement, the words of Jennings's father reveal how speaking of such intimate issues undermines the transgender movement. While listening to his child describe her sexual function, he was so distressed that he admitted to having a desire to "cover my ears."[90]

For a movement that ridicules religious communities for creating unnecessary shame around sexuality, the left has an enormous blind spot when it comes to transgender issues. There are undoubtedly religious communities that have caused harm

---

[88] McNamara, Brittney. "Watch Jazz Jennings Talk to Her Parents About Orgasms." *Teen Vogue*, July 5, 2017. https://www.teenvogue.com/story/jazz-jennings-talks-to-parents-about-orgasm.

[89] McNamara, "Watch Jazz Jennings Talk to Her Parents About Orgasms."

[90] McNamara, "Watch Jazz Jennings Talk to Her Parents About Orgasms."

to children by demonizing sexual activity and presenting sexual desires as inherently sinful. However, even the worst of Christian fundamentalism does not remove, much less glorify the destruction of, an individual's ability to physically experience sexual pleasure.

These attempts to normalize morally destructive medical practices as forms of health care present problems for progressives because human nature does not change, and normal people are innately disgusted by attempts to claim forms of death and destruction are "compassionate" or "caring." Having empathy for those in adverse circumstances, from women who conceive during a difficult season of life to children facing the pain of gender dysphoria, is understandable, but the Democratic position on these issues is neither moderate nor popular. Abortion used as a form of birth control is stigmatized because people see it as immoral to recklessly create and destroy human life. Similarly, Jennings's parents may view suppressing their child's natural sexual development as morally acceptable; however, most voters view this as appalling.

Increasingly, Americans are asking themselves, "What kind of world do we want to create and leave for future generations?" The answer involves rejecting the moral underpinnings derived from the faux compassion of the destructive force birthed from the devouring mother.

CHAPTER 3
Homicide

ONE WOMAN'S PROPERTY

By age twelve, the cloud of despair haunting my mind and spirit had only grown. An unabating yearning for death lurked in the shadows of my mind, where I internally debated the meaning of life. Oscillating from hope to despondency, I observed adults navigate the world of choice while I watched from the fishbowl of a lonely existence.

Many unfortunate occurrences took place between the ages of twelve and thirteen, yet two experiences seared into my soul, encouraging an intensifying skepticism of social messages surrounding gender roles, assault, and the justified use of violence.

The typical feelings teens describe accompanying the onset of puberty barely registered as concerns. I found myself internally struggling to relate to the feelings I was told everyone experienced. My mind was too preoccupied to contemplate sexual feelings, particularly given the unavailability of the opposite sex. Besides, I observed men as neither pleasurable nor dangerous. Rather, my chief anxiety were the prying eyes and predatory hands of women.

In the presence of men, there was an assumed safety because an invisible social barrier stigmatized bodily touch or unseeming voyeurism. I knew if a man attempted to lay hands on me, watch me as I undressed, or even speak of my body sexually, his behavior would be universally condemned. This social condemnation meant I had a level of power in relation to men because, should any man engage in such actions, my words would at least carry weight. After all, for a practice to be scandalized, it must be known, and the potential for men to engage in predatory behavior toward women was so common it had become cliché. Given these social norms, circumstances where I was concerned someone of the opposite sex would touch or look at me inappropriately without the possibility of facing severe consequences never occurred.

The same was not true of women. The inability to avoid the female gaze, grope, and grasp suffocated my spirit. Masked by social propriety, the growing awareness of puberty brought a sense of dread, an unspeakable form of unease that evaded articulation. Social norms told me female spaces were safe—after all, men were banned—yet the melody of reality sang the opposite song. *Something* I could not speak told me the safety of female spaces was an illusion.

Although obtaining the linguistic tools to put my experiences into words would not come for well over a decade, two experiences described below, spaced approximately one year apart, opened my eyes to abuses most never contemplate and thus fail to see or believe.

The first occurred at age twelve when I developed a vaginal infection. In hopes I could avoid the stifling impulses of maternal care, I ignored the condition, believing time would solve the problem. Such hopes were in vain because my mother, who strictly controlled the household chore of laundry, became suspicious and demanded to inspect my body.

Soon, I found myself in the urgent care waiting room, wishing I could flee, yet knowing there was no form of escape. After being ushered into the doctor's office where an appropriate prescription to treat the infection was swiftly identified, the doctor informed my parents it was his responsibility to ask me some questions. At this time, my father was led out of the room, but my mother was allowed to stay.

I watched as the door closed behind my father before making eye contact with my mother. In her eye was the familiar, authoritative gaze, telling me that one wrong word would lead to severe retribution.

The doctor asked a series of questions about whether my genitalia had been touched. If such touching had occurred, how often? And, lastly, in the event this had occurred, what *male* was responsible? Initially, when he posed the question of whether a man had touched me, I said, "No." He then asked if a boy had done so. Again, I said no. Now, he hesitated, but asked if I had brothers. I answered truthfully, "Yes," already well-aware he would follow this question by asking if they were responsible for my condition. Truthfully, I again responded no, for they had never touched me. The same held true for my father.

The conversation was brief, and soon I was back in my parents' van, riding to the pharmacy to pick up the prescription to treat the rash. We walked into the door and I caught my reflection in a mirror. I observed my slender body, adorned in a blouse, tucked into a knee-length brown skirt with matching boots. My face was downcast. I felt as if I were looking at the image of a painting. I shared no emotional connection to the person in the reflection.

Instead, my mind was far away:

Why did the doctor only ask me about men? Do women not have hands? Do their hands not cause infections? He did not ask about my sisters or my mom. What made him assume the source of the problem had to be a male?

I struggled to understand his logic. In fact, I had been scared he *would* ask about women. Such a question would have put me in a bind because my mother would not have been comfortable with an honest answer.

Dad had to leave, but mom stayed. The doctor can't think women are physically incapable of touching me? No...he must think like most people do...that men are predators, while women are pure.

I was sullen on the drive home, still unable to understand the source of my suffering. Mechanically, I walked to my room, preparing to apply the medication to the infected area. As usual, my mother followed close behind, and, before I could process what was happening, my attempt to take the prescription to the bathroom for self-application was swiftly thwarted. Instead, in a display of power and control, I watched as my body was treated as an extension of her own. I was reminded that, from growth in utero until age eighteen, I was one woman's property.

Deep within, duality raged, for I wanted to fight despite the battle's futility. Instead, I looked upward, fixating on the ceiling room fan. The blades spun on the lowest setting, allowing me to catch faint, distorted reflections that mirrored the confusion residing within my mind and spirit. From a place of primal pain, my defilement cried out for justice…yet I knew the truth would not prevail.

There is no use, she can use you as she pleases.

The treatment lasted only two weeks, but its effects created an unseen rift within my being. Given my inability to articulate my grief and the unavailability of a lending ear, the pain I experienced moved to the recesses of my mind, where it was stored among the thousands of other humiliating, debasing experiences.

Out of habit, I hoped to crush the memory through the combined forces of will and time, yet the future held different plans.

Approximately one year later, my appendix ruptured. I did not experience the traditional symptoms of a rupture, leading doctors to believe my fever and pain were caused solely by an insignificant urinary infection. They were unable to discover the rupture until antibiotics to treat the urinary infection failed and a CT scan showed the true cause of my illness.

At the hospital, doctors once again removed my father from the room to ask routine questions regarding sexual contact.[91] Whether these questions were standard protocol or derived from the initial urinary infection diagnosis remains a mystery. I also cannot recall with specificity whether my mother was removed from the room. Regardless, I was too weak to speak on my behalf. I already knew the doctor was only interested in male behavior, and soon my suspicion was confirmed. The questions were nearly

[91] I cannot recall whether the questions were asked before or after the surgery. If I were to bet, it was before, during the admission process, but there is no way to verify the accuracy of this claim, thus I am attempting to avoid its inclusion in the text.

identical to those asked a year prior, and all assumed exclusively male contact.

Still, the seriousness of my predicament only dawned on me immediately following the release of the CT scan. Doctors rushed into my room, administered anesthesia, and wheeled me out of the room after explaining my appendix had ruptured and required emergency surgery.

As I swallowed the pill and drifted off to sleep, I prayed—with the sincerity of a saint—that I would never wake, and hoped these would be my last moments on earth. I observed my surroundings and found the setting to be serene. It was not the perfect place to die, but sufficiently far removed from familial rejection to give at least the façade of peace.

Alas, I awoke and my nightmare resumed.

My mother, unwilling to loosen her iron grip of control, fawned over me while staff praised her for her "doting" nature. I was sickened and struggled to sleep, fearful of my mother's stifling touch, a force I could neither dispute nor repel. I spent approximately one week in the hospital in recovery where I was unable to physically care for myself. Typically, nurses came into my room to help me shower when I was capable of bathing, but, at least one or more times, this function of their job duties was passed to my mother, whose active involvement in my care gained the trust of the hospital staff.

As I was passed to her for care, familiar feelings washed over me, and my spirit and flesh felt as if they separated. I knew I could not question her care, for I was a slave to social norms that echoed the same message communicated the year prior.

Men are predators, women are pure.

Once again, my bodily violation silently screamed for justice, but this time I began to consider whether violence was a reasonable solution to my predicament. For years, I had seen suicide as the only viable solution to the incessant torment of life, but this assumption began to break under the weight of pain and the irrationality of the principles I saw championed by culture.

Why can't I fight back when she uses my body as her own? Why are children required to serve an eighteen-year prison sentence before having the right to bodily autonomy? She owns my body, and, rather than receiving judgment, she is praised. If she doesn't leave visible scars, she can use my body in any way she wants.

She could have killed me before I was born, even though I only limited her bodily autonomy for just nine months. But she can use my body like a rag doll for years and I can't fight back without being seen as immoral and cruel. Why shouldn't I fight back?

WHEN IS KILLING OKAY?

My teenage predicament exposed some of the practical problems progressive philosophy encounters. Issues surrounding the gender assumptions at play will be discussed in subsequent chapters, but a philosophy that denies the inherent value of all human life faces rational questions surrounding the conditions under which killing human beings is appropriate.

Is it just to accept the proposition that growing life in utero is less valuable than the life of a rapist? Or should it be easier to kill the rapist than the unborn? And, specifically in relation to maternal abuse, if mothers can kill their children in utero *or* force them to live, should children who suffer at maternal hands possess a corresponding right to terminate their abusive makers? If not, why?

These are all rational questions, none of which are seriously grappled with in progressive cultural spaces.

GYPSY: MURDERER OR MARTYR?

The case of Gypsy-Rose Blanchard highlights the difficulty that accompanies assessing the morality of killing in a paradigm where innate human worth is not assumed.

Gypsy became nationally famous following her participation in a scheme to kill her mother, Claudine "Dee Dee" Blanchard. From birth until the age of twenty-three, Gypsy faced relentless abuse from her mother, who manipulated the medical system to ensure her daughter was completely dependent on her care.[92] Dee Dee invented fictitious disorders, claiming her daughter suffered from epilepsy, leukemia, muscular dystrophy, vision/hearing impairments, and other physical ailments.[93]

These lies caused Gypsy to be forcibly wheelchair bound and kept on a feeding tube, resulting in numerous surgeries, including procedures on her stomach and the removal of her salivary glands.[94] To prevent others from discovering her nefarious

---

92 Smith, Jenner, Joseph Diaz, and Alexa Valiente. "How a Young Woman Forced to Used [sic] a Wheel Chair, Treated for Several Illnesses Ended Up in Prison for Her Mother's Murder." ABC News, January 4, 2018. https://abcnews.go.com/US/young-wheelchair-bound-woman-treated-illnesses-ended-prison/story?id=52138979.

93 Ibid.

94 Ibid.

scheme, Dee Dee kept Gypsy isolated and changed physicians whenever suspicions regarding her behavior were raised.[95]

Despite knowing she could walk and eat, Gypsy, like many victims of abuse, was afraid to disobey her abuser. Attempts at rebellion were met with severe consequences, including physical abuse and the withholding of life necessities, like food.[96]

After decades of abuse, Gypsy formed an online relationship with a man named Nicholas Godejohn. The two carried on a virtual romance for years without Dee Dee's knowledge. When Gypsy took the step of introducing her mother and lover, Dee Dee ordered Gypsy to abandon the relationship.[97] Unwilling to do so, Gypsy hatched a plan with Godejohn to kill her mother, believing this was her only route of escape.

This belief was not necessarily ill founded. In over twenty years, Gypsy had seen at least 150 doctors. Of those doctors, only one, Dr. Bernardo Flasterstein, reported concerns about Gypsy's welfare. Child protective services opened an investigation, only to swiftly close it after making a home visit and finding no obvious signs of abuse.[98]

Gypsy's one attempt to run away from her abuser's "care" resulted in physical assault, with Dee Dee chaining Gypsy's arms to her bed, placing bells on her door and telling those whom Gypsy knew to notify Dee Dee if they noticed Gypsy doing anything without maternal approval.

---

95 Ibid.

96 Ibid.

97 Ibid.

98 Ibid.

Given the severity of the abuse and the inability of the adults around Gypsy to notice the problematic nature of Dee Dee's care, it remains unclear whether Gypsy could reasonably have escaped her nightmare without resorting to physical violence. And violence was the unfortunate outcome of Gypsy and Godejohn's scheme. Their plan culminated in Godejohn stabbing Dee Dee in her bed while Gypsy sat shaking in fear in her adjacent childhood bedroom.

BODILY AUTONOMY AS A JUST REASON TO KILL

Gypsy's case is extreme, but it shows the disparate treatment society grants to mothers and their children. Despite the chronic and extreme forms of abuse, when ABC Network's *20/20* interviewed Gypsy and she expressed she believed murder was her only way out, the interviewer asked incredulously, "But, killing your *own mother*?"[99] Gypsy was also asked why she did not simply walk up and leave, since she knew she was capable of walking.

But if, as in the progressive view, human life has no innate worth and ongoing violations of bodily autonomy are sufficient reasons to end human life, Gypsy's plot to kill her mother is not obviously immoral. Why should Gypsy be forced to sustain an unknown period of bodily abuse to spare her abuser's life? After all, the bodily autonomy violations perpetrated against Gypsy were extreme and, as mentioned above, there was no clear way for her to stop these violations without the use of violence.

---

[99] Emphasis added

Still, Gypsy agreed there was no excuse for killing her mother, stating, "It may seem like every avenue is closed off but there is always another way. Do anything, but don't take this course of action."[100] Despite the decades of abuse, and feeling freer in prison than in her childhood home, Gypsy still misses her mother, and hopes her mother still loves her and knows she is "so sorry" for her role in Dee Dee's death.[101]

Had this story broken while I was a teenager, I would have viewed Gypsy's words as weakness. In fact, I would have seen Gypsy and her lover as heroes who fought against the machinations of an evil tyrant.

This is because the authority Dee Dee exercised over Gypsy was clearly unjust. And, given the practical constraints of the world in which she lived, Gypsy had no higher authority to whom she could appeal for help. Perhaps she could have prayed for an exit, but this was neither compelling to my young mind, nor a viable option in a secular moral framework. Instead, decades of experience proved that God, to the extent He existed, was not coming to her immediate aid, and human authority figures outside the home were more than willing to accommodate Dee Dee's behavior while showing no concern that Gypsy may be the victim of her mother's cruel game.

---

[100] Darby, Margaret. "An In-Depth Timeline of Gypsy Rose Blanchard's Childhood, Murder Case, Release from Prison and Pregnancy." *Deseret News*, January 8, 2024. https://www.deseret.com/u-s-world/2024/1/8/24024249/gypsy-rose-blanchard-timeline-murder/.

[101] Smith, Diaz, and Valiente, "How a Young Woman Forced to Used [sic] a Wheel Chair, Treated for Several Illnesses Ended Up in Prison for Her Mother's Murder."

Under these circumstances, Gypsy could either live as a slave until her mother's death or fight against the violence her mother perpetrated against her with violence of her own. I would have seen Gypsy's revolt as no different in principle than a slave in the antebellum South slaughtering a plantation owner to escape to the North in search of freedom. What's more, I would have seen anyone who assisted in such a killing as an accomplice for good. Why should Godejohn be condemned for releasing Gypsy from the torture she endured?

To hear a Christian condone the court's sentencing of both Gypsy and Godejohn would have irritated me, but hearing a self-proclaimed progressive justify the same result would have caused rage. The Christian perspective was off-putting yet consistent, while the progressive stance was irrational and incoherent.

THE SLIPPERY SLOPE OF "BODILY AUTONOMY" ARGUMENTS

Who are you to judge?

This sentence ran through my mind many times as a teenager when I contemplated a hypothetical dispute regarding the morality of my own murderous desires with a typical secular progressive. This anger was directly related to a selective, discriminatory importance attached to bodily autonomy, one that places the worth of children beneath that of their mothers.

Why does her body matter more than mine? Aren't you concerned with bodily autonomy? Who gives you the authority to judge me for killing someone who uses my body as her personal toy?

Thankfully, my childhood rage, while understandable, eventually gave way to the Christian ethic, and it is this ethic that underpins Western law, including laws against murder.

Rightly, under our current legal standards, Gypsy's plot to kill her mother is wrong because using deadly force against another human being is limited to narrow circumstances, such as self-defense. But, for self-defense to apply, the harm must be imminent.[102] Future harms are insufficient; the person acting in self-defense must reasonably believe she is in threat of immediate danger, death, or serious bodily harm.[103] Additionally, self-defense must be proportional, meaning the person acting in self-defense can only exert the force necessary to remove the threat.[104] Thus, if the threat is not deadly, the response may not be deadly.[105]

The threats to Gypsy were not deadly and could physically have been removed without the use of force. Despite the obvious psychological barriers, it is *physically* true that Gypsy could have walked away, called authorities, or attempted other means of escape before resorting to killing.

Although Gypsy presents a sympathetic case, there are valid reasons to support the murder charge she faced. Among many reasons is the necessity of bright-line legal rules. If the law broadly recognized ongoing bodily autonomy violations as a sufficient

---

[102] "Imminent Danger Definition and Citations." The Law Dictionary, accessed January 30, 2015. https://thelawdictionary.org/imminent-danger/.

[103] "Imminent Danger Definition and Citations," The Law Dictionary.

[104] Taylor, Daniel. "Is It Legal to Fight Back If Someone Hits You First?" FindLaw, March 21, 2019. https://www.findlaw.com/legalblogs/criminal-defense/is-it-legal-to-fight-back-if-someone-hits-you-first/.

[105] Taylor, "Is It Legal to Fight Back If Someone Hits You First?"

reason for people to kill one another, the homicide code would unravel. First, bodily autonomy is not easily defined, particularly not when coercion and psychological abuse—both enormously important in cases of abuse, including Gypsy's—are part of the equation. Furthermore, even if bodily autonomy could be defined with sufficient precision, how many bodily autonomy violations should someone sustain before resorting to killing? Must these violations be chronic? If so, what constitutes "chronic"?

Legal reasons aside, this ambiguity shows how difficult it is to assess a "just" killing under a moral framework where the emotions of a victim are used as the benchmark for determining the morality of taking human life. As I knew personally, it's easy for victimized people to justify the use of violence as vengeance against the wrongs they have experienced, but that doesn't make committing acts of violence moral.

If the right to terminate human life were applied to born life as it is to unborn life, the state's ability to prosecute murders would be significantly hamstrung because the available defenses to murder would drastically expand, as would the cultural impulse to empathize with perpetrators of deadly violence. The current bright-line legal rule prohibiting the murder of born individuals may cause sympathetic victims like Gypsy to face an unfortunate sentence, but it also protects society against the possibility of unjust killings. Unfortunately, identifying an abuser is, generally, not an easy task. Neither is making a determination of whether someone's bodily autonomy rights are being violated, either in the context of adult/child or adult/adult relationships.

The inherent subjectivity involved in abusive dynamics is a major barrier to victims identifying their circumstances as abusive. And, depending on the ideology of an abuser and his or her skill in manipulation, disclosing abuse may not result in belief. This was highlighted in the infamous #MeToo movement, where stories of abuse ranged from violent assault to drunken sexual encounters. For obvious reasons, some took a broad view of "abuse," while others saw a need to distinguish between unpleasant sexual encounters and "abuse."

Allowing individuals to kill others on the grounds that the victim of murder engaged in abuse or violated the murderer's bodily autonomy opens a can of worms no human person or regulatory body is prepared to adjudicate. This, perhaps, is why the use of bodily autonomy as a sufficient justification for taking human life is primarily limited to the abortion debate. Unlike cases involving malicious abusers, bodily autonomy is indisputably implicated, can be readily regained through killing, and the voiceless victims of abortion can be easily dismissed, removed from society's eye, and dehumanized as lacking full humanity.

IS MALICIOUS HUMAN LIFE MORE WORTHY THAN INCONVENIENT LIFE?

The implications of devaluing the inconvenient more than the intentionally malicious are not limited to the abortion context. This is because all schemes of human value come at a cost. The cost of believing all human life has inherent worth places Gypsy in a sympathetic, unfair position, even if it does not justify the use of deadly force. The progressive stranglehold on using their framework of values when assessing how to treat humanity is crumbling. Among the most obvious examples of this is the issue of immigration. Harris—not Trump—appeared callous and uncaring when the truth came out that Georgia college student Laken Riley's murder could have been prevented if her administration had adopted different immigration policies.

Whose benefits should be prioritized—that of the immigrant or the American citizen? Progressives and Democrats frame this issue around basic human rights, accusing their opposition of failing to care for the "least of these." However, because the rights and interests of different people always conflict, the progressive increasingly appears to be selectively outraged. This reduces the power of progressive messaging regarding human rights and compassion. Trump flipped the progressive script by highlighting those harmed by "compassionate" Democratic policies.

This worked, because the public can increasingly see how progressive values highlight specific types of pain while ignoring and dismissing others. The leftist emphasis on human rights—particularly without honesty regarding the tradeoffs involved—reveals itself as an attempt to redistribute power for political advantage. As mentioned above, the progressive view of bodily autonomy creates a bifurcated sense of human worth where the intentionally cruel and malicious are granted more rights than the inconvenient. Generally speaking, preborn human life is deemed to have no value unless such worth is conferred onto the human being through maternal desires. Thus, it is just to kill a human being who is inconvenient, but not malicious, while it is considered immoral and illegal to kill a human being who is intentionally destroying the bodily rights of another.

Thus, our current political and cultural landscape is ripe for understanding how progressive beliefs erode the view that innocent life should be protected. Those who speak of human rights should be able to explain how and why their policies may justly harm some humans while valuing others. After all, among the most common arguments for abortion is that it is moral to weigh the woman's bodily autonomy over the life of the unborn child because the child in utero is not yet conscious. Thus, killing the child kills nothing of value.

But, problems with this view arise. First, children in utero are not developmentally capable of consciousness. Thus, to kill them as they develop the capacity for consciousness is arguably no different than pulling the plug on a coma patient with a 99 percent chance of conscious recovery.

Imagine Dee Dee had not died from the stabbing attack, but instead had been rendered unconscious in a coma from which she had an almost certain chance of recovery. Anyone who moved to end Dee Dee's life, despite her lack of consciousness and her track record of utter depravity, would rightfully be labeled a murderer.

Second, unlike children in utero, abusers such as Dee Dee *are* fully conscious and intentionally using their consciousness to destroy the bodily autonomy of others. The child in utero exists precisely where they should be based on natural biological development. They develop at a biologically appropriate rate and limits the bodily autonomy of one person, per biological protocol, for a finite period. On the other hand, Dee Dee intentionally stunted the natural development of her child, physically violated her bodily autonomy for twenty-three years—well over twenty-three times the short period of gestation—and left Gypsy with lifelong trauma that will undoubtedly plague her physical senses until death.

As currently structured, our society argues abortion is a just taking of human life because of the sacred right to bodily autonomy, while legally categorizing Gypsy as a murderer for ending twenty-three years of physical and psychological torture. This is a culture where hypocrisy and confusion reign.

Indeed, if the homicide code were updated to include as many reasonable exceptions based on cases where homicide was understandable from an empathetic human perspective, the murder code would look like Swiss cheese. In reality, people have many rational reasons choose to kill, yet, our laws and culture reflect the belief that, even relatable murders are immoral, with one wide-open loophole: abortion.

MATERNAL ABUSE: UNCOMMON OR UNSEEN?

As with most cases where violence can easily be justified, there are underlying societal problems that, if addressed, would resolve abuse victims' rational desire for violence. However, social biases in favor of women obscure the existence of some victims. In Gypsy's case and my own, the ability of culture to perceive and reject the maternal abuse of power and control would have relieved the pain placed on its victims.

Although I no longer question whether I should have killed my mother (of course, I should not), my teenage insight regarding how maternal compassion can serve as a convenient cloak for power still rings true.

In fact, although rarely discussed, there are disorders, almost entirely experienced by females, by which people weaponize compassion and love in service of abuse. Munchausen syndrome by proxy, also known as factitious disorder imposed on another

(FDIA),[106] is the condition Dr. Flasterstein believed Dee Dee suffered from. Those with this condition are caregivers, usually mothers, who fabricate, exaggerate, or cause a child's illness to get medical care and attention for themselves, not the child.

Generally, known examples of this phenomenon are extreme, and for good reason. Subtle manifestations of such disorders are virtually impossible to establish. Accurately assessing the frequency of this disorder is frustrated by the enormous barriers associated with identifying its existence.

In the first place, victims like Gypsy must overcome significant hurdles to recognize they are victims of abuse. Long after she knew she could walk and eat, Gypsy still believed she had leukemia and seizures, because untangling the complex web of lies spun by her mother was a Herculean task.

Second, the structure of Munchausen syndrome by proxy can be applied in non-medical contexts, making its identification even more difficult. The scenario I faced with my mother was similar to Gypsy's ordeal, but lacked the medical component. Instead, my mother created a "disorder" for me through the term "half-aborted," giving her the internal justification necessary to engage in forms of control and abuse toward me that otherwise would have been clearly unacceptable. By segregating me from society, siblings, and even my father, her behavior flourished unchecked; she was well aware society was not going to question her or come to my aid.

Now, once one is willing to accept that the structure of Munchausen syndrome by proxy may be applied to issues of

---

[106] Smith, Diaz, and Valiente, "How a Young Woman Forced to Used [sic] a Wheel Chair, Treated for Several Illnesses Ended Up in Prison for Her Mother's Murder."

emotional and psychological well-being, the potential scale of abuse explodes. Despite societal stereotypes that frame men as predators and women as innocent and pure, women, who are responsible for the majority of childcare, also represent the majority of known, much less unidentified, child abusers.[107]

THE FALLIBILITY OF HUMAN JUDGMENT

In a culture where the inherent value of all human beings is not assumed, children facing circumstances such as Gypsy's—or my own—have every reason to question why they cannot kill their abusers. Yes, especially their mothers. Yet, ultimately, the reasons why maternal child abuse victims should resist embracing the authority to kill is the same reason mothers should not have the right to abort their offspring. No human being has the knowledge necessary to justly mete out the judgment of death or the gift of life. The ability to accurately assess the value of human beings transcends the limitations of the human mind and no amount of adverse circumstances grant any people group the just authority to kill on command.

Why we should doubt humanity's capacity for perfect judgment is best explained by the wise words of J. R. R. Tolkien, one of the few fiction authors to have a dramatic impact on my understanding of philosophy and life. In a scene between Frodo and Gandalf from *The Lord of the Rings: The Fellowship of the Ring*, Frodo, distraught over the machinations of the creature Gollum,

---

107 "Child Abuse in the US - Perpetrators 2022, by Sex." Statista, December 9, 2024. https://www.statista.com/statistics/418470/number-of-perpetrators-in-child-abuse-cases-in-the-us-by-sex/.

consumed by fear that Sauron will find him because of Gollum, declares in anger, "What a pity that Bilbo did not stab that vile creature, when he had the chance."

Gandalf, the wise wizard of Middle Earth, replies:

> Pity? It was Pity that stayed his hand. Pity, and Mercy: not to strike without need.... Many that live deserve death. And some that die deserve life. Can you give it to them? Then do not be too eager to deal out death in judgement. For even the very wise cannot see all ends.[108]

When circumstances are difficult, death can appear to offer a solution to the senseless suffering experienced daily by millions of people. Yet, this wisdom remains relevant and true in situations where people contemplate killing as a swift answer to intense, unabating pain. For the wisest man "cannot see all ends," and even when it may seem as if "every avenue is closed off" there is always a way out that does not involve the shedding of blood.

---

[108] Tolkien, J. R. R. 2004. *The Lord of the Rings: The Fellowship of the Ring*. Houghton Mifflin Company.

CHAPTER 4
Amorality

My skepticism of acknowledging a human right to kill, through abortion, suicide, or murder, faced stiff competition, both practically and philosophically. My warring desires resulted in a near-constant internal discussion in which I oscillated between justifying a secular versus sacred ethic. Similarly, I vacillated between justifications stemming from emotion and logic.

This internal battle led me to understand the futility of separating the heart and mind in pursuit of truth. Given the finite nature of the human mind, I knew that those who claimed to have "rationally" selected an ethic from a thorough analysis of all competing truth claims were mistaken, and I knew my chosen worldview could not rest on rationality alone.

THE INNATE IRRATIONALITY OF HUMANITY

No one is born in a vacuum. All people are products of a complex interplay between the past, present, and future. Furthermore, all are subjected to cultural forces that deeply influence their views of the various gods who war for their allegiance. To pretend as if family history and geography—both within the world and within a nation or state—play no role in the development of one's moral beliefs is to deny reality.

No man, or woman, is capable of rationality, because perfect rationality would require complete knowledge, and anyone claiming such omniscience seeks the status of a deity. God is all-knowing, and if He is not real, then "all-knowing" is a fiction rendering comparative human value judgments nearly impossible. For, without a reference point of perfection, how are humans to assess the comparative validity of moral values?

My understanding of this derived from my mother's emphasis on mathematical rigor in moral thought, and from the Protestant critique of reason summarized in the Latin phrase *incurvatus in se*, or *cor curvum in se*, or a "curving in" toward oneself.

My mother's mathematical precision focused heavily on the necessity of "givens." To successfully complete her math curriculum involved rigorous Euclidean geometry. Prior to using theorems, it was necessary to write out cumbersome proofs, all of which began with a set of established "givens," or statements assumed to be true. My mother used this as an opportunity to show the necessity of holding to specific "truths" when thinking. For, without a foundation of truth claims, moving through a rational analysis was rendered impossible. Mathematics itself, highly revered within the Giuliano home, showed the finite nature of the human mind and reinforced the necessity of living as if some claims are true despite the human inability to perfectly prove said claims.

Martin Luther's critique of reason appeared to contain essentially the same idea, expressed philosophically and religiously rather than mathematically. He uses the idea of "curving in" to describe the frailty of the human condition, specifically highlighting the ease with which individuals can justify self-serving passions, desires, and ideas when they serve as both judge and jury of morality.[109]

It serves as a reminder of the essential nature of "givens," "presuppositions," or foundational principles: As with mathematical proofs, an error in moral input naturally causes a corresponding error in behavioral output.

AUTHORITY OR AMORALITY?

As I began to seriously consider the moral foundation on which my adult life would rest, I began to sense a deep tension between choosing to follow an authority—whether secular or religious—and a desire for acting out an amoral ethic, one that I could construct, mold, and manipulate according to my unique needs, desires, and sensibilities.

There was no obvious way to resolve this tension because, as previously mentioned, I knew the finite nature of the human mind. Aware of the limitations of the human condition, I struggled to justify amorality, yet I knew that if I rejected a belief in the God of the Bible, there was no human authority, man or woman, to which I would willingly submit. Taking this path would necessitate accepting a form of amorality, because if God were not real

[109] This idea is not novel, and has been communicated by thinkers across the ages, but, among the most relevant and influential to the author is Bonhoeffer's expression of this idea. *See,* Bonhoeffer, Dietrich. "The Transcendental Endeavour." In *Act and Being*, 19–28. Harpers & Brother, 1961.

and I rejected a belief in the validity of human authority, I would effectively be asserting myself as a god unto myself. Given the impossibility of achieving omniscience or omnipotence, such a statement would lead to what is colloquially called "amorality," or the lack of a belief in any form of morals.

As I grappled with whether to accept authority or amorality, I encountered two opposite answers to questions of life and death, each of which illuminated the implications of each choice.

THE TWO PETERS

These encounters came through the philosophical works of two Peters that represented warring sides in a battle between secular and faith-based ways of thinking. Peter Singer, the well-known and controversial utilitarian philosopher stood on the side of the atheist, while Peter Kreeft, a prolific Catholic writer and professor of philosophy, fought for the values of Christendom.

Both tackled the question I believed was foundational to determining whether a system of belief was moral or immoral, a question that strikes at the heart of whether human beings have innate dignity: Do some humans have the just authority to assign negative or positive value to specific human lives to determine whether those specific humans live or die?

Singer answers this question with a resounding yes. Under his worldview, some human lives are more valuable than others and human assessment of people's worth should be used to determine who lives and who dies. Kreeft argues the opposite, holding to the belief that all human lives possess equal value and no human being has the just authority to determine who lives and dies.

Ultimately, I chose to embrace a Christian worldview. The secular critique of God, particularly on moral grounds, rang hollow to me because within the context of my specific life, there stood an undeniable truth: Under progressive values, my life was less valuable than the lives of my peers because it was characterized by the type of suffering that is used as a justification for abortion.

Unshackling oneself from divine authority clearly does nothing to alleviate the individual and collective burden of living out coherent moral and ethical worldviews. And, if all authority is ultimately manmade, a Pandora's box of unfortunate possibilities is opened.

Unfortunately, rather than focusing on finding a way to create a coherent communal morality from the ground up, many atheists spend almost all their time debunking what they already believe to be fiction.

This appears not only in the atheistic impulse to use rational arguments as an attempt to debunk the idea of God's existence, but also in atheist philosophical efforts to reimagine morality by undercutting the Judeo-Christian ethics of the Western world.

SELECTIVELY DEVALUED

The tendency to critique Christian ethics often manifests in subverting the character of the Christian God, a deity who is often described as callous toward human life, casting people into eternal "hell" for trivial reasons.

I found it necessary to run a similar critique of atheist figures who cloak their ethical ideals in the language of compassion. Support for abortion as a positive good, infanticide, and euthanasia have all gained ground in recent decades and are justified primarily on the basis that they reduce overall human suffering. This places a burden on intellectual rivals. After all, who *supports* suffering?

As explored in Chapter 3, despite the increasing popularity of movements explicitly advancing the circumstances through which innocent human suffering can be alleviated via untimely death, there is no corresponding call for a reexamination of murder code, or an expansion of the conditions under which capital punishment is allowed.

This shows the narrow and nonsensical ways in which human suffering is handled by popular secular society. The typical argument for death as a solution to human suffering has been discussed in earlier chapters, but it almost exclusively involves advocating for the ending of the lives of people who live under the weight of a pain they *did not cause* and *that they cannot control.* Unborn children, and those with disabilities, chronic illnesses, mental illness, and childhood trauma, have grown accustomed to watching as their pain is used as a justification for death.

"Are *these* lives *really* worth living?" is the implicit rhetorical question underlying the dogmas accepted as axiomatic in progressive culture.

I searched for Singer's justification of expanding the murder code to ensure victims of violence were afforded greater rights in destroying the direct cause of their human suffering, yet found no such viewpoint expressed. There was no ethical examination of how to reduce human suffering through the devaluation of malicious human actors; only the innocent and weak fell under Singer's moral microscope.

Of course, one man does not speak on behalf of all secular, progressive culture. Still, there is nonetheless an undeniable trend in left-wing thought: Suffering caused by human actors is viewed with sympathy and forgiveness while suffering innate to human existence, such as disability or poverty at birth, is viewed with pity and scorn.

For example, pro-choice advocates are no strangers to underscoring the perceived negative economic impact of banning abortion. In the wake of the *Dobbs* ruling, prominent figures, such as Federal Reserve Chair Janet Yellen, pointed out the correlation between the birth of unplanned children and poverty rates.[110] And, in Iceland, Down syndrome has nearly been "eradicated" through selective abortions. In 2017, an unborn child diagnosed with Down syndrome in utero stood a nearly 100 percent statistical likelihood of prenatal death.[111]

On the other hand, violent criminals create millions of victims, and according to recidivism rates, a significant portion of these criminals compound human suffering by reoffending.[112] While it is difficult to uncover the causal impact of violent crime, it undoubtedly leads to an enormous amount of human pain. This

---

[110] Guida, Victoria. "Yellen: Banning Abortion Would Be 'Very Damaging' to US Economy." Politico, May 10, 2022. https://www.politico.com/news/2022/05/10/yellen-banning-abortion-damaging-to-economy-00031339.

[111] Quinones, Julian, and Arijeta Lajka. "'What Kind of Society Do You Want to Live in?': Inside the Country Where Down Syndrome Is Disappearing." CBS News, August 15, 2017. https://www.cbsnews.com/news/down-syndrome-iceland/.

[112] "Recidivism among Federal Violent Offenders." United States Sentencing Commission, May 9, 2022. https://www.ussc.gov/research/research-reports/recidivism-among-federal-violent-offenders.

suffering is imposed on the innocent against their will, and society foots an enormous bill sustaining the lives of the incarcerated, including those justly placed on death row. Yet, when it comes to determining which human lives can be assigned a price tag, progressive culture inverts compassion. The general principles of the progressive restorative justice movement encourage people to value the lives of those who *create* suffering on the basis they have the possibility, even if remote, of redemption. Simultaneously, the principle of abortion and the "right" to suicide incentivize the devaluation of human lives lived under conditions where suffering is innate to existence.

Thus, the unborn child faced with poverty, abuse, or other adversity, brimming with the potential to positively contribute to society despite inevitable pain, is worth less than the violent felon who lashed out at the world, intentionally choosing to create, rather than alleviate, human suffering.

THE APPEAL OF AMORALITY

As a teenager, I grappled with how the concealed defect of half-aborted would impact the perception of my human worth in a culture governed by progressive thought, should I choose to disclose this to others. Unfortunately, since college was my next destination in life, I was guaranteed to walk away from a family that saw me as a necessary nuisance toward a culture that would, passively or actively, wish I did not exist at all.

Under these circumstances, I flirted with amorality. Why extend a gracious hand to those who would have encouraged my mother to abort me as a mechanism of "saving" me from pain?

As I searched for evidence of the goodness of humanity, a self-evident truth to many, all I saw was the individual and collective attempt by the powerful to exploit the weak. The notion that this sprung from humanity's religious impulse was a weak analysis in my mind, for the ideological forces most likely to view my life with a mixture of pity and scorn were decidedly anti-religion.

Belief in humanity—like love or God—appeared to amount to nothing more than false hope.

The reality of the cards I had been dealt, either by the divine or through the cruelty of coincidence, left me questioning whether I wished to participate in life as a functional sociopath, willing to treat others as a mechanism for the advancement of my own desires. Did I prefer to live as a god unto myself, to submit to human or divine authority, or kill myself and opt out of the game of life entirely?

My options were limited, unsavory, yet clarifying and stark. As I continued to contemplate the path I would choose as a consenting adult, I turned to another foundational question: Was I going to submit to the authority of man (even if only myself), or that of God?

CHAPTER 5
Relationship

PROGRESSIVE PREACHER

Among the many fixed realities of my childhood was the knowledge that college was the only escape route from home. In my household, education was for the purpose of attending a university and alternate career paths were not merely discouraged, but intentionally foreclosed.

Because of this, I had the benefit—and drawback—of being able to juxtapose my personal identity against two set, definable cultural contexts. The first was the culture of my family, which included our limited church engagement. The second was the culture of academia.

Knowing that the collegiate world would be the first community I would inhabit as an adult gave me an incentive to pay close attention to the biases, prejudices, beliefs, and practices of universities generally, and the University of Oklahoma in particular.

It was no secret that the culture I was destined to enter was, broadly speaking, secular and progressive in philosophic and political orientation. Thus, as a baseline, I could safely assume that my public persona was the embodiment of what this culture disliked, making it likely those around me would seek to transform me in their own image.

Many factors pointed to this reality, but two were impossible to avert. First, my parents' decision to homeschool and make outward, albeit superficial, displays of conservative religious devotion, played into common progressive stereotypes—specifically, the belief that homeschoolers are brainwashed victims in need of a white progressive savior to enlighten them by introducing the uninitiated to the ways of the world.

I had observed progressive proselytization efforts deployed against my siblings, who were placed in the unenviable position of attempting to solidify their adult identities without succumbing to the immense pressure exerted from the warring cultures around them.

Second, I was aware my own life story came with unique relational complications. The distinguishing factor between my journey and that of my siblings who traversed the halls of the academy before my entrance was my unique title: half-aborted. This marker of shame brought with it the hard choice of either hiding or revealing a vulnerability the world would be quick to exploit.

Two weeks into my collegiate career, I encountered the prejudice of my surroundings.

I slipped into the auditorium fifteen minutes before the lecture began. The topic, feminism and equality, combined with the verbiage of the flyer's advertisement, clearly signaled the progressive leanings of the lecturer.

Before the speaker approached the lectern, she was introduced as a decades-long advocate for women's equality, rights, and empowerment. I couldn't help but notice how this introduction mirrored that of a pastor introducing a guest preacher to the pulpit. The atmosphere created in the room told the audience this was a righteous woman whom they should admire.

She approached her pulpit where she sermonized about the importance of young women placing career ambition before family formation, the need for roughly equal gender representation in corporate board rooms, and the difficulty of achieving "equality" in cultural spaces with values opposed to her personal preferences.

As with all feminist messages, her proselytization would have been incomplete without a passionate defense of a "woman's fundamental right" to abortion. She alleged this right is necessary for women to have equality, personhood, and dignity. In essence, she argued that, without the right to create and destroy human life on a whim, women are not fully human.

This was a bold claim, one that was stated as if it were self-evident. Like a pastor explaining the importance of the virgin birth, she spent no time defending this idea against reasonable countering positions, instead assuming either the audience would agree with her assertion, or that those who disagreed deserved no explanation. In this setting, she knew her dogma was *presumed* to be true.

But not every audience member was a true believer. Curious to understand the reasoning behind her beliefs, I stood in line following her presentation for the chance to ask her questions about her stance on abortion.

As anticipated, most questions she received were friendly, ranging from praise for her work to practical questions from students eager to spread her message in an "oppressive" red state. Given the positive nature of her exchange with students, I was unsurprised, yet deeply satisfied, by the visible disappointment in her eyes when she heard my question.

"You describe abortion as a human right," I said. "Do you believe the fetus is a human being?"

"Yes, the fetus is human," she replied.

This was a helpful admission, for many in the pro-choice community are incapable of such an honest response.

"So, if the fetus is human and women have a right to kill fetuses, do you believe women have the just authority to determine which human beings live or die?"

Tension built as I awaited her reply, observing her demeanor shift as the uncomfortable reality of her advocacy was unexpectedly challenged.

"Yes, women have that right," she said. But, as the words escaped her mouth, her hands shook and her confidence broke. "This," she said "is more complicated than you realize. Unwanted children suffer immensely. Children with severe disabilities, those who live in extreme poverty, and children subjected to gross abuse. It is cruel to force them into such circumstances."

Astounded, yet pleased with her honesty, I asked one last question.

"Do you believe children who will suffer greatly, such as those abused or who experience other forms of extreme pain, are better off dead?"

Without hesitation she replied, "Yes."

I gazed into her discomforted, stoic eyes one last time, searching for an observable hint of the inhumane character she verbally espoused. But, reminiscent of the TV commentator from my youth, there was no overt sign of the darkness she harbored. She had covered her dehumanization of those who suffer under the guise of female empowerment, and for this, society had championed her as a saint. There was no incentive for her to understand the brutal nature of her worldview.

The hubris hung in the air as I overheard the following students gush over the presenter's accomplishments on behalf of their gender. Silently, I left the auditorium, wondering how many abuse victims internalized her dehumanizing message, viewing their lives as unworthy because of circumstances beyond their control.

> *"How many women become killers because society grants them the unearned 'right' to serve as the arbiters of human value? And how many children bow before the altar of maternal power, convinced their submission to Mother God is necessary to obtain love and live as a good and righteous member of Her society?"*

Although I knew these questions had no obvious answers, I pondered the cultural prominence of the prejudicial waters in which I swam. I could not make peace with people whose fundamental philosophical beliefs informed them I should be dead.

A SILENT SOCIAL EXPERIMENT

Thus, it was clear, my best course of action would be to hide.

As detailed above, common progressive prejudices paired with superficial politeness shattered the illusion that genuine, love-based relationships between myself and philosophically progressive people were possible. Such relationships would require a blind faith in their moral character and an asymmetrical relational risk I was unwilling to bear.

Still, I was curious to explore how pro-choice progressives viewed the worth of those who face severe earthly suffering. Since abortion as a "human right" represents the default setting for most progressive women, particularly those who champion "women's rights," I began to confront various classmates with an anonymous telling of my own life story.

Since no one on campus had knowledge of my nickname, half-aborted, or my status as an unwanted, abused child, this was a simple task. For the entirety of my freshman year, when conversing with a female classmate who established a passion for women's rights, female empowerment, or reproductive rights, I would ask a series of questions involving the potential suffering of hypothetical children.

The disabled and abused children were almost always the first on the chopping block.

"Why bring people into the world only for them to suffer?"

These college students, self-proclaimed compassionate, bleeding hearts, failed to understand that those who suffer may prefer life to death. Birthed in the cradle of American privilege, many feminists spoke of various forms of privilege without a practical understanding of their own bigotry.

The dehumanization of unwanted children was profound, and I was both fascinated and terrified of their capacity to drink the drug of denial. Out of sight, out of mind took on new meaning, for once they could see a human being physically, these women expressed a form of care, represented by their widespread rejection of suicide as a solution to suffering. Yet, when a human being was mere months from visibility, they were comfortable butchering her to prevent future pain.

Many times during these exchanges, I mentioned a "friend" of mine who had been gravely mistreated. This friend, I explained, had been called half-aborted by her mother. Throughout her life she was isolated, abused, and terribly mistreated. Then I would ask, should my friend wish she had been aborted? If time travel were possible, should her mother reverse time and kill her to avoid the pain she now experienced?

When confronted with a detached human experience, the cruelty of their worldview was swiftly laid bare. No pro-choice progressive woman spared my life. When half-aborted was discussed, she was universally condemned to death. All admitted to pitying this friend's existence. In their eyes, her humanity was tainted by pain, and the suffering she experienced overshadowed her worth.

"It is sad to say, but I pity your friend."

"That's awful, *and I'd never say this to her face*, but she would have been better off aborted."

"Your friend's story is a great example of why abortion should be legal."

"This is why women should always abort unless they are 100 percent ready for children."

With each encounter, I was reminded of the impossibility of living authentically within progressive culture. In their eyes, my life was a mistake, my existence a tragedy, and my human worth devalued by senseless suffering.

In the eyes of the culture I navigated, suffering was synonymous with human reduction. Children born into a life of love, comfort, and ease were innocent, while those born into adversity were tainted and stained, making them unworthy of protection.

This was a culture where the predominant worldview had added a condition to the child-centric teachings of Christ. Where Jesus said, "Let the little children come to me and do not hinder them, for to such belongs the kingdom of heaven," the secular progressive made subtle changes: "Let the little children, *whose suffering is likely to be sufficiently small*, come to me and do not hinder them, *unless they suffer extreme abuse*, for such belongs the kingdom of women."

RELATIONSHIPS AND RELIGION

My collegiate experiences aligned with the practical implications of adhering to progressive beliefs. Although there are a few outliers,[113] most of the progressive culture is characterized by an allegiance to the axiomatic belief that women possess an innate authority to judge the value of human life. This belief leads to an inability to see, understand, and contextualize female forms of malevolence, instead placing women in a unique authority role once reserved only for God.

As discussed in the previous chapters, I was well-aware of the profound nature of this claim. Whether verbally acknowledged

---

[113] "Who Are We?" Progressive Anti-Abortion Uprising, accessed January 30, 2025. https://paaunow.org/who-we-are. "Mission and Vision." Secular Pro-life, accessed January 30, 2025. https://secularprolife.org/mission/.

or not, the pro-choice argument that abortion is a human right, is, at its core, a deeply philosophical claim. That the claim does not involve the Bible is irrelevant, because it fundamentally alters the nature of human relationships. Ironically, despite feminist rhetoric, the belief in abortion as a human right grants women more rights than men. For, at no time in human history have men claimed a universal, God-given right to kill their offspring.

In progressive culture, women hold a status *above* men. Thus, the hierarchy operates with women's interests at the top, below which are the interests of children (to the extent such interests are not in conflict with women), Then, at the bottom of the totem pole are the interests of men.

This awareness of how feminist dogma affected my own human dignity played in my mind in my teenage years as I struggled to determine my philosophic identity. Ultimately, I could not justify the relational power imbalance granted to women advanced by a secular progressive model of justice.

UNWORTHY YET MORALLY SUPERIOR

The first commandment God handed to the Israelites was clear and direct: "Thou shalt have no other Gods before me." This claim presumes that God speaks as someone worthy of absolute devotion and obedience. The Christian conception of morality assumes Christ, the Godhead, is worthy of humanity's undivided love, devotion, and worship. He deserves this devotion because He is the embodiment of good. Without Him, humanity would neither know nor experience anything good.

When assessing the claim that women possess a human right to abortion, one must assume either that human life is trivial or that women possess a superior character worthy of determining who can live and die. Additionally, one must be comfortable with affirmatively asserting that a child's identity is inherently bound up in maternal assignment of value.

This reorients the mother-child relationship. Where once women owed a duty of care to their children, now the child lives for the pleasure of the mother. In a deeply profound way, the mother tells her child, "I am your God. I had the right to kill you, and you would not know goodness without me."

What struck me about the two models of belief was that one could operate under the rules of equality while the other could not. Under the Christian religion, if I rejected Christ, I was treated the same as any other sinner. I had been born and given a chance to accept Christ for the duration of my lifetime. According to the rules of the religion, rejection of Christ was a rejection of a relationship with him. And he honored the request by withholding his affection and casting me into hell.

But, under the rules of secular progressive dogma, I was both unworthy of life while simultaneously possessing a higher degree of moral authority than my fellow man.

I was unworthy of life because, if given the chance, secular progressivism would almost certainly assume my life, riddled as it was with suffering and abuse, was better off extinguished before birth. However, since the ideal option was no longer available, I was now a *woman*, someone with the right to create and kill on a whim. I could create a human being with the sole purpose of intending to cause them the excruciating pain of in utero death, and, according to the prevailing moral belief, such an action is acceptable, something only religious fanatics would dare to judge.

As the next chapters will explore, the incoherence of the beliefs of the secular world caused me immense confusion, particularly among those who claimed to advance human rights against "oppressive" religions while championing a woman's right to kill her children as among the most sacred of human rights.

Nearly every New Age atheist (with notable exceptions, such as Christopher Hitchens,[114] who did not support elective abortion) argued against the existence of God on the grounds of His cruelty while supporting the establishment of a belief system that rendered children nothing more than the playthings of their maternal overlords.

The absolution of the mother's ability to kill her children at will repulsed me throughout my youth, and it made me deeply skeptical of the moral claims of leftwing, progressive culture. This culture offered power, but at the cost of the human soul.

FEMALE EMPOWERMENT AND EMBITTERMENT

This deformity of the human soul leads to confusion in human relationships, particularly between men and women. Culture simultaneously speaks to women as if they were victims *and* conquerors, making modern female identity appear bipolar and confused. By rooting empowerment in the sex-based right to kill on command, social conversations about sex and gender fail to address the radical change in relational authority women wield.

---

[114] Hitchens, Christopher. "A Left-Wing Atheist's Case Against Abortion." *Crisis Magazine*, December 5, 2019. https://crisismagazine.com/opinion/a-left-wing-atheists-case-against-abortion.

Instead, efforts to analyze the disparate power between men and women remain locked in the past. Abuses of women from prior decades and even centuries are used as evidence of a victimhood feminists have no intention or incentive to ever abandon.

Because social discourse about women's issues assumes women exist in a perpetual state of victimhood, many struggle to distinguish between genuine attempts to understand female-perpetrated abuse and the hatred of women.

Even commentators sympathetic to the plight of young boys bombarded with messages encouraging them to view a fundamental aspect of their humanity as irredeemably "toxic" express sympathy for the motivations of women. Jordan Peterson astutely observed the dilemma women face when attempting to distinguish between competence and dangerous aggression in men.[115]

Many women, Peterson states, have had no positive relationship with masculine men. Not only are their relationships with men not positive, but women often experience a string of negative relational experiences with men. Understandably, after numerous iterations leading to poor outcomes, a man's display of competence or confidence is easily miscategorized as an attempt to exercise unjust control or power.

Despite being the subject of significant controversy, Peterson's commentary regarding the female dilemma is relatively benign. It is unlikely many would argue with his statements and the relational dynamic of an abusive relationship where the woman is powerless

---

[115] Response Ability. "Why Women Get Into Bad Relationships - Jordan Peterson JRE #1933." YouTube, January 31, 2023. https://www.youtube.com/watch?v=Ns8MDeTihas.

against a domineering man is expressed across in enough cultural mediums to reach the status of cliché.

Now, contrast this with his professional interpretation of the psychological literature regarding female-driven forms of aggression. Journalist Anne McElvoy questioned Peterson's assertion that men struggle to relate to female bullies because the use of force against women, unlike men, is socially prohibited.[116]

When answering McElvoy's questioning, Peterson referred to such women as "completely out of control." In response, McElvoy sarcastically asks, "What is an out-of-control woman? What is this creature, how do we know when we have met one?"

This question is more profound than it appears on the surface. Behind the query is an uncomfortable truth: Society has no idea what an out-of-control woman is because confronting female bullies requires identifying and understanding the malicious traits of females.

To engage in such an analysis involves violating two social norms. First, one must be willing to view women as morally equal, rather than superior, to men. And, second, one must be able to competently distinguish between valid criticisms of pathologies generally expressed by women versus critiques of women rooted in ignorance, prejudice, and hatred.

Unfortunately, failing to understand the dark side of femininity obscures the negative experiences of both men and women who have had few, if any, positive relational experiences with women. Society understands why women may lash out at men,

---

[116] Intelligence Squared. "Anti-Social Behaviour in Men and Women - Jordan." YouTube, December 7, 2022. https://www.youtube.com/watch?v=Fx4DJ21B-3M.

but there is no corresponding comprehension of a man's motive when speaking negatively of women.

Under current norms, culture is incapable of facing the reality, and corresponding implications, of female-perpetrated forms of relational harm. This is observed in both political and social contexts and has been an ongoing problem for decades.

Political examples of this phenomenon are legion, but most easily observed in the heightened sensitivity surrounding the use of perceived or real male-driven sexism.

In Chapter 3, the observation that society views men as predators and women as pure is helpful in understanding how culture frames disputes between the sexes. It also explains why it is acceptable to make opposite, but equally sweeping, generalized statements about the nature of men and women. Women who speak negatively about experiences with men are never asked to soften their language or carefully craft their words for fear of offense. Similarly, when someone makes a generalized statement about the purity of women, for example, "Women don't lie about sexual assault," the statement raises no eyebrows.

Even well-meaning attempts to placate women often backfire. In 2012, Mitt Romney's bid for the White House arguably ended when he referred to the "binders full of women" he requested when seeking to hire more women to positions of power traditionally held by men.[117] Just five years later, the phrase #BelieveAllWomen became a rallying cry of the #MeToo, a cultural movement designed to highlight the sexual assault of

---

[117] Madison, Lucy. "Fact-Checking Romney's 'Binders Full of Women' Claim." CBS News, October 18, 2012. https://www.cbsnews.com/news/fact-checking-romneys-binders-full-of-women-claim/.

women. Questioning the absolute nature of the phrase led to cries of sexism, internalized misogyny, and other similar insults.

Although nearly all mainstream cultural discourse surrounding sex and gender starts with the axiomatic belief in the truthful nature of females, the 2018 confirmation hearings of Supreme Court Justice Brett Kavanaugh offer a textbook example. During an otherwise smooth confirmation process, Kavanaugh was accused of sexually assaulting Christine Blasey Ford while both were in high school.

Immediately following the allegations, commentators and journalists rushed to use the accusations as a vehicle through which society could better understand general relations between the sexes. In true progressive fashion, the press cast Kavanaugh as the villain while Ford was presented as courageous and incapable of moral impurity.

Time magazine featured an article discussing how the accusations "showed why the myth of nice girls and tough guys persists."[118] *The New Yorker* ran a commentary describing Kavanaugh's confirmation in the wake of Ford's allegations as evidence that the "Republican mindset" is infected with "the enduring influence of sexism, misogyny, and privilege."[119] *Teen Vogue* even jumped into the fray, eager to inform young girls and women

---

[118] Edwards, Haley Sweetland. "The Kavanaugh Hearing Showed Why the Myth of Nice Girls and Tough Guys Persists." *TIME*, September 28, 2018. https://time.com/5409351/christine-blasey-ford-brett-kavanaugh-gender-dynamics/.

[119] Cassidy, John. "The Senate Republicans' Less-than-Human Treatment of Christine Blasey Ford." *The New Yorker*, September 28, 2018. https://www.newyorker.com/news/our-columnists/the-senate-republicans-less-than-human-treatment-of-christine-blasey-ford.

of the "sexist double standard" evidenced by those supporting Kavanaugh's confirmation.[120]

Aside from the political motivations and biases of those who opposed Kavanaugh's confirmation to the Supreme Court, there was a fundamental assumption underlying the widespread belief in Ford's testimony. This assumption asserted that women simply do not lie about sexual assault. Those who questioned Ford risked the appearance of victim blaming.

The timing and cultural tides certainly favored Ford, who delivered her testimony the year after the #MeToo movement went viral and mere months after NPR described the phrase "believe all women" as the #MeToo "rallying cry."[121] Perhaps this explains why Kavanaugh's infamous high school yearbook was meticulously analyzed while Ford's credibility-damaging high school past was largely ignored.[122] Despite being scrubbed from the internet, Ford's yearbooks could have been featured in Republicans' questioning during her Senate testimony. However, Capitol Hill watchers, always concerned with public backlash,

---

[120] Filipovic, Jill. "Brett Kavanaugh and the Sexist Double Standard of Being Held Accountable for Your Actions." *Teen Vogue*, September 18, 2018. https://www.teenvogue.com/story/brett-kavanaugh-sexist-double-standard-being-held-accountable-for-your-actions.

[121] @NPR. "'Believe All Women' Has Been the Rallying Cry of the #MeToo Movement - a Mantra Embraced by Some but Dismissed by Others as Naive. The Tension Over the Credibility of Women Is Nothing New, Especially in Rape Investigations - https://t.co/AoIiFivaG4." X, February 7, 2018, 5:37 PM. https://x.com/NPR/status/961277626986868736.

[122] Sperry, Paul. "Suppressed Blasey Ford Yearbooks Reveal Fast Times at Holton-Arms." Real Clear Investigations, September 27, 2018. https://www.realclearinvestigations.com/articles/2018/09/27/blasey_ford_yearbooks.html.

cautioned that attacking Ford's reputation could lead to backlash against Republicans.[123] Given the kid-glove treatment Ford received, it seems these fears were heeded.

Sadly, the truth of Ford's testimony was irrelevant to the social and political discourse surrounding Kavanaugh's confirmation. Instead, Ford and Kavanaugh were avatars for their respective genders. And, if nothing else, the hearings served as a reminder that the character of men, particularly their propensity to engage in predation, is subject to a public examination in a manner unbecoming of women. Kavanaugh moved from a man accused of sexual assault to a gang rapist overnight.[124] The allegation of gang rape turned out to be a dud,[125] but the political theater that was Kavanaugh's confirmation hearing accomplished Ford's goal of placing an "asterisk" next to his name.[126]

While there are many lessons to glean from the Kavanaugh debacle, it is evident that society understands predation as male-driven behavior while assuming women operate as morally pure

---

[123] Sperry, "Suppressed Blasey Ford Yearbooks Reveal Fast Times at Holton-Arms."

[124] Hutzler, Alexandra. "Brett Kavanaugh Accused of Drugging Women, Participating in 'Gang Rapes' by Michael Avenatti Client." *Newsweek*, September 26, 2018. https://www.newsweek.com/brett-kavanaugh-gang-rape-avenatti-julie-swetnick-1139745.

[125] Eustachewich, Lia. "Third Kavanaugh Accuser Backs Away from Some of Her 'Gang Rape' Claims." *New York Post*, October 2, 2018. https://nypost.com/2018/10/02/third-kavanaugh-accuser-backs-away-from-some-of-her-gang-rape-claims/.

[126] Crowe, Jack. "Blasey Ford's Lawyer Admits Client Wants 'Asterisk' Next to Kavanaugh's Name When He Rules on *Roe*." *National Review*, September 4, 2019. https://www.nationalreview.com/news/christine-blasey-fords-lawyer-admits-client-wants-asterisk-next-to-kavanaughs-name-when-he-rules-on-roe/.

victims. It was easy to cast Kavanaugh as the villain and Ford as a saint because our collective consciousness implicitly understands this story.

A simple thought experiment elucidates this point. Imagine if, during the confirmation of Justice Ketanji Jackson, she was accused of sexual assault by a high school male classmate. This man approaches the podium to deliver testimony and displays visible signs of holding back tears. Many, in the press and public alike, would undoubtedly be taken aback. A small minority may immediately believe such an accusation, but this accuser would be unlikely to receive a chorus of praise. On the contrary, many would express confusion. How, precisely, would a man fall victim to female assault?

Under current cultural norms, this response is rational. Legitimate critiques of past abuses and negative stereotypes imposed on women are ubiquitous. However, these norms are not without their flaws. Why must past social flaws and the existence of sexism quash society's ability to grapple with the dark side of femininity?

COMPLEMENTARY BUT DISTINCT

For decades, common feminist talking points focused on negating any inherent differences between the sexes.

However, this shallow analysis fails to respect fundamental, nature-driven differences between men and women, and does not address both the positive and negative tradeoffs of attempting to make men and women relationally interchangeable. This hyperfocus on rights and refusal to address responsibility also creates its own gender stereotypes by forcing women in the role of victim while assuming masculine men are incapable of anything other than acquiring and wielding power.

In reality, true equality need not be at war with reality. Women do not face a binary question of accepting the dogma of feminism or returning to the 1950s. Peterson's observation that men and women run a different playbook when engaging in malicious behavior should be welcomed, not because it advances a political or social agenda, but because it is true.

Men and women are not identical; the tradeoffs they face in society are different, and the virtues and vices they are prone to embody are complementary, but distinct. Perhaps there is a legitimate fear that understanding how the virtues and vices of men and women differ will make it difficult to identify those outliers who do not conform to gender stereotypes. But such a concern is of little consequence because gender stereotypes are, to some degree, inevitable. Society will always be prone to imposing a limited understanding of the human condition onto both sexes, but this is no excuse for failing to deepen cultural awareness of reality.

Recent examples help understand the limitations of a form of feminism that views men and women as interchangeable.

Take the controversy surrounding Ballerina Farm. *The Sunday Times* feature story covering social media influencer Hannah Neeleman generated passionate debates surrounding the benefits and drawbacks of the new "tradwife" lifestyle gaining steam as a niche lifestyle choice made by women interested in focusing their efforts on nurturing and homemaking rather than pursuing economic opportunities outside the home.[127]

The story follows Neeleman, a talented ballerina who left the prestigious Juilliard School to marry a wealthy Mormon man. The two own a homestead in Utah where Neeleman publishes content sharing her life as a homesteader and mother to eight children. Contrary to progressive messaging regarding tolerance, the author of the article, Megan Agnew, judges Neeleman, questioning whether her decisions are genuine or coerced. This concern arises from Agnew's interview with Neeleman, which she states was derailed by Neeleman's husband and children, making it difficult for Agnew to know Neeleman's independent thoughts on her life.

This narrative, however, is disputed by Neeleman who stated she was "taken aback" after reading the article, one she believes inappropriately portrays her as oppressed by her husband. Neeleman says Agnew's conclusions, far from reality, are a predetermined projection of the reporter's own biases. Furthermore, despite being known as a tradwife, Neeleman does not view her choices as traditional. Instead, she said she views her lifestyle as "paving a lot of paths that haven't been paved before."[128]

---

[127] Agnew, Megan. "Meet the Queen of the 'Trad Wives' (and Her Eight Children)." *The Times*, November 18, 2024. https://www.thetimes.com/magazines/the-sunday-times-magazine/article/meet-the-queen-of-the-trad-wives-and-her-eight-children-plfr50cgk.

[128] Aguirre, Kimberly. "Ballerina Farm Influencer Slams 'Attack' on Family. What to Know About 'Tradwife' Controversy." *Los Angeles Times*, August 2, 2024. https://www.latimes.com/entertainment-arts/story/2024-08-02/ballerina-farm-controversy-explained-tradwife-article-hannah-neeleman.

Online reactions to the controversy show the ease with which choices can be glorified or demonized based on prior ideological convictions. Voices across the spectrum projected their personal opinions about gender roles and motherhood onto Neeleman's life, reading her as either empowered or victimized based on their orientation toward feminism, not the facts.

Interestingly, the progressive *Sunday Times* view of Neeleman is remarkably narrow. Neeleman said it best when she observed that her life is neither oppressed nor traditional. Instead, it mixes tradition with trailblazing, a combination that is foreign to the progressive mind. This is because, under the rules of modern feminism, values of the past are, by definition, oppressive. This is why Agnew viewed Neeleman's choices under the assumption that her interests were contrary to her husband's.

In her commentary on the Neeleman's relationship, Agnew writes:

> Daniel wanted to live in the great western wilds, so they did; he wanted to farm, so they do; he likes date nights once a week, so they go (they have a babysitter on those evenings); he didn't want nannies in the house, so there aren't any. The only space earmarked to be Neeleman's own—a small barn she wanted to convert into a ballet studio—ended up becoming the kids' schoolroom.[129]

[129] Aguirre, "Ballerina Farm Influencer Slams 'Attack' on Family. What to Know About 'Tradwife' Controversy."

Neeleman, the individual actually living within the marital union, disagrees, stating the couple's objectives and interests are aligned: "We are co-parents, co-CEOs, co-diaper changers, kitchen cleaners and decision makers.... We are one."

Her view is confusing to progressives because the concept of cooperation, rather than competition, between the sexes is not part of their paradigm of reality. Under the Democratic worldview, women exist in a cosmic struggle with men to ensure their basic human rights—including the right to kill their offspring—are not impeded. Harris's campaign ads made this overt, pitting women against men by showing wives hiding their transgressive vote from borderline abusive, Republican men.[130]

The tradwife trend reveals the impoverished embitterment of modern feminism because it reveals the limitations of the ideology. Rather than celebrate the unique combination of values derived from various generations, that is, traditional gender roles with entrepreneurship fueled by modern technology and social media, the progressive instinct is to look under every rock for the oppressive man who held a woman back from independence and empowerment, a state of being women cannot achieve without engaging in economic output traditionally seen as "masculine."

---

[130] McCammon, Sarah. "Meet the Conservative Women Who Are Keeping Their Votes for Kamala Harris a Secret." NPR, November 4, 2024. https://www.npr.org/2024/11/03/nx-s1-5159978/republicans-for-harris-women-voters-secret-votes-quiet-voters-2024-election-trump.

THE FINAL TABOO

Americans are growing weary of the progressive attitude, both because it is hypocritical for the self-proclaimed "tolerant" to diagnose marital abuse over Instagram, and also because progressive viewpoints are increasingly detached from reality. The tradwife trend attempts to solve a longstanding problem facing modern women, namely the difficulty associated with attempting to give adequate attention to a career while raising children. Physical realities dictate women bear a far greater economic cost when navigating pregnancy, childbirth, and postpartum. Is it not commendable to find creative solutions to this problem by leveraging modern technology that facilitates freelance, contract work that can be accomplished from any location?

Furthermore, by denigrating the decision to raise children in lieu of pursuing a typical nine to five, progressives reveal their participation in the "anti-child" culture J. D. Vance was criticized for observing. *Someone* has to raise children, and what does it communicate to children when their care is seen as the worst possible occupation, a role reserved for oppressed women incapable of contributing to society through more respectable ways? Childrearing, when done well, is of infinite value. One obvious example of this: Children who grow up in nurturing, loving homes are far less likely to interface with the criminal justice system.[131]

---

[131] Wyrick, Phelan, and Kadee Atkinson. "Examining the Relationship Between Childhood Trauma and Involvement in the Justice System." US Department of Justice | Office of Justice Programs, April 2021. https://www.ojp.gov/library/publications/examining-relationship-between-childhood-trauma-and-involvement-justice-system.

In the 1990s, Michele Elliott, a child psychologist, edited the book *Female Sexual Abuse of Children*. The book, written by numerous professionals and abuse survivors, received backlash due to a perception that it was "anti-female."[132] This perception, Elliott states, comes from a fear developed by some that "even talking about female abusers" is "treason to the cause of feminism."[133] Given the cultural disconnect between feminism and exploring female predation, the book devotes a chapter to a feminist viewpoint on female perpetrated abuse, exploring the question of why it is so hard to believe women initiate sexual abuse.[134]

Now, thirty years after the book's publication, it is arguably just as taboo to discuss female-perpetrated sexual assault of children. After all, isn't such a conversation a distraction from the danger of men?

Ironically, social assumptions about women cloud society's collective vision, making it difficult to believe victims who do not fit the narrow understanding of power, oppression, and victimhood articulated and controlled by progressive, feminist beliefs dominating institutions of cultural influence.

This problem can be solved, but only if society is willing to approach human equality from the vantage point of both rights *and* responsibilities.

---

132 Elliott, Michele. "Introduction." In *Female Sexual Abuse of Children*, 1. The Guilford Press, 1994.

133 Elliott, "Introduction."

134 Young, Val. "Women Abusers - A Feminist View." In *Female Sexual Abuse of Children*, 100–115. The Guilford Press, 1994.

Therefore, if equality is the goal, it will not be achieved when board rooms reach gender parity, but when it becomes socially acceptable to answer a simple question: What is a predatory woman?

CHAPTER 6
Worldviews

HEART OF DECEIT

As a high school student unsure of what I believed, I was concerned with the possibility of adopting religious beliefs out of parental pressure. However, I was equally concerned that I would be tempted to adopt my philosophical beliefs through cultural osmosis by allowing trendy ideals into my moral map without considering their consequences.

Given the ideological predisposition of the collegiate culture I was destined to inhabit, I was particularly concerned that my prior religious, homeschooled upbringing would make me a prime target for progressive proselytization and emotional exploitation. Determining my worldview before college was a way for me to avoid being pressured into beliefs I did not hold through the inundation of progressive values that would inevitably come from professorial lectures and propagandized peers.

Unfortunately, there was no way to avoid all external influences before making a decision. However, my unique home life gave me an advantage. Outwardly, I could present as my parents desired and, because our social circles were essentially nonexistent, I was guaranteed years of time to think through my decision before acting publicly on my beliefs.

This time could not be squandered.

Although I had always been interested in issues of morality, the intensity of my mental ideation began to steadily grow. Questions surrounding vengeance and violence combined with a verse from the Biblical book of Jeremiah: "The heart is deceitful above all things, and desperately wicked; who can know it?"

The concept described in this verse cuts to the core of common moral arguments, both religious and philosophical. For, if the heart *is* deceptive "above all things," then the process of understanding oneself and the surrounding world with any degree of clarity is severely undermined.

That this verse flew in the face of modern conventional wisdom was, to me, as self-evident as it was sad. My first encounter with the "follow your heart" messaging promoted culturally to children left me repulsed. Years prior, I had entered the Barnes & Noble children's section with high hopes only to find what I believed to be shallow content. The characters in this particular book were learning to "follow their hearts," but there was nothing relatable about their desires, all of which were benign, and, in my view, superficial.

"*This isn't realistic*," I thought. "*None of the children want to do anything wrong. What are the kids in this story supposed to do when their heart tells them to steal, cheat, or kill? Why is the author of this book acting like children only want good things?*" I swiftly solved my problem by exiting the children's section in search of books worth reading. But, years later, I still felt far away from answering whether Jeremiah was right about the deeply depressing nature of the human heart.

To test the heart's deception, I began to analyze my deepest desires. This required distinguishing between normal, daily feelings and the expression of closely guarded emotions. Among the countless desires I examined was recurring yearning to use suicide as a weapon of retribution.

This fantasy revived itself in dreams each Christmas season for years. Each year the dream began and ended identically. First, I wrote notes to select members of my family, attached to personalized stocking stuffers. These notes would detail my perception of the long list of grievances enacted against me. After stuffing the stocking, I killed myself, leaving my body for my family to find on Christmas morning, a discovery that I knew would change the course of their lives. From the safety and privacy of my dream, I could finally assert control over those who tormented me.

Each day, after I awoke, I contemplated my dream, wondering if there was a possibility of turning it into reality. But the risk was too high. If a note was found before the process was complete, or I was found with a knife in the act of ending my life, I knew my life would drastically change. Punishment would be nothing short of severe. What if my parents rescinded their promise to send me to college? I could barely conceive of a worse fate than living in my parents' home until I died. Thus, even the smallest risk of losing access to a college degree was nothing short of terrifying. Instead, the dream I had continued to burn in the back of my mind. Sometimes it faded into oblivion, only to return in time for the celebration of Christ's birth.

I analyzed the structure of this fantasy. Did I yearn for this dream *only because* it could exist nowhere but in the realm of my imagination? Would I dare go through with the plan if it were possible? Would I even want to? There was no way to know the answer to these questions, yet they revealed an important tension between belief and action, one that was highly relevant to the question of worldview plaguing my mind.

The difficulty distinguishing between my own desires and the realities of my life was laid bare. Was my desire for revenge literal or metaphorical? Was it self-serving or indicative of an internal cry for pain? Did I want to kill myself or was this a mere mental manifestation of a chronic sense of rejection? My inability to ascertain my own motives was reasonable and deeply painful. I knew the actions I took while living with my family were not a genuine expression of myself. My life revolved around the ever-changing emotional waters of my mother's spirit. Undetectable to the five senses, this spirit controlled my responses to stimuli. I observed how over the years I had learned to understand when her temperament changed, and how to morph to avoid emotionally drowning in the wake of her tidal wave.

Still, what occurred within my mind was beyond her reach. Or, was it?

One day I would walk through the door of adulthood. Either my actions and beliefs would converge to create a strong foundation for consent, or they would diverge, leading to dissonance, pain, and the possibility of a chronic victimization characterized by a confused mind, unsure of how to acquire wisdom.

I knew living as myself within my biological home was never going to be possible. But, one day, I would exit that home. And...

what then? After years of having no agency, what would become of me? Would I continue the pattern of adapting my being to the environment in which I existed? This thought brought a cocktail of emotions, ranging from disgust and rage, to active rebellion.

"*Whatever choices I make in the future, as an adult, I will make them based on what I believe, not based on the opinions of those around me.*"

This was a lofty goal, one I knew would require a healthy awareness of my inherent limitations. Thus, the idea of reviewing all available worldviews before determining what I believed was an attractive fiction. Instead, I focused my analysis on the most fundamental question underlying any worldview: "Is God real?" This, I reasoned, would allow me to choose between atheism and Christianity. The limitation to a binary choice was strategic.

I was well-aware of my youth and the possibility that further exposure to ideas and worldviews would lead me to reject my decision in the future. To account for this possibility, I promised myself I would make a determination as to my acceptance of the atheistic or Christian worldview by the time I entered college. Furthermore, I planned to commit to faithfully living out this worldview for ten years. After a decade, I would then reassess my worldview by analyzing the degree of integration between my beliefs and actions between my heart and mind. This, I believed, could assist me in pinpointing deficiencies in the motivations driving my beliefs and actions.

The limitation of place made it more reasonable to analyze the Christian God against an atheistic perspective. I had limited time and resources at this initial stage of worldview development and these were the two worldviews with which I was guaranteed to routinely interact.

However, even if I accepted a different philosophy after my period of reassessment, this worldview was guaranteed to hinge on the question of God's existence. Of course, I knew a broad definition of God did not necessitate the reality of the God described in the Bible, but He represented the foundation of the moral and ethical systems of the civilization into which I was born. He was not merely the God of my mother, He was the father of the world in which I lived, and the author of the historical conception of human rights.

Despite their animosity, even atheists borrowed from the morality laid out in His word. Like lukewarm Christians, they cherry picked the morals of their choosing. Most did not argue for the *opposite* of biblical morality, but rather for the rejection of aspects of its morality that constrained their own desires. The commandment to "love thy neighbor," for example, caused no offense.

My initial impression of atheism was skeptical. I was attracted to this system of thought, but only if a logical interpretation could be enacted without devolving into tyranny.[135]

ATHEISM

The attraction of atheism is easy to understand. Humanity's desire to usurp just authority and live as God is universal and

---

[135] Tyranny here is intended to convey the broadest use of the term, that is, any unjust form and/or use of force regardless of legal or political structure.

explored culturally through many worldview lenses. For example, many critiques of political figures focus on—often justified—fears related to the unjust acquisition of power. The idea that political figures, such as Trump, should not be above the rule of law, presumes the existence of a just authority to which all men and women should submit.

Thus, those attracted to atheism as a means of escaping the need to follow all forms of authority must reject the most common, popular manifestations of atheistic philosophy in favor of a more brutal, yet logical atheistic system championing anarchy rather than social order.

GOD IS GOOD

In vogue during my youth was the new atheist movement, popularized by figures such as Sam Harris and Richard Dawkins. These atheists passionately argued that goodness and morality are separate from God. To be good, one need not believe in God.

I was puzzled both by this assertion and what appeared to be a strong emotional commitment to a disbelief in all forms of God. Firstly, in my mind, the claim was absurd because it hinged on conflating the concept of God with the specific nature and character of the God described in the Bible. Rejecting Jesus as Lord appeared unrelated to the question of whether any form of God—supernatural or not—existed. Secondly, there was the structural similarity between the competing religious and secular arguments for morality and goodness.

The concept of God as the author of goodness need not involve a personal deity of the character described in the Bible. The deistic beliefs of many of America's most influential founding fathers suggest as much. They viewed God as a creator, not necessarily a savior. God was the "watchmaker,"[136] the One who caused all other effects. Was He more than that? Unclear. Many deists rejected the authority of the Bible. This is historically represented by Thomas Jefferson's infamous personal "Bible." He created the document by cutting all references to miracles from the New Testament, attesting to the characteristics of the Christian God he was unable to accept.[137]

Although the nature of God is unclear, the debate over his existence and the extent to which the idea of God is necessary for a coherent moral system will persist into perpetuity. This is because it involves assessing ambiguous, abstract evidence, and engaging the totality of the human person. Simply put, it is an endeavor that defies absolute physical proof, making it reasonable for people to doubt all possible answers. The man who seeks an answer to the God question must accept the necessity of using both intellectual and emotional reasoning because the consequence of belief—or disbelief—clearly involves the embodiment of beliefs rather than mere intellectual assent.

Thus, approaching the question from a different angle yields more direct answers. Rather than asking whether God is necessary for morality, it is more useful to ask whether morality can be rationally grounded in man. Examples of the debate exist

---

136 Kidd, Thomas S. "Reconciling Deism and Puritanism in Benjamin Franklin." Yale University Press, May 12, 2017. https://yalebooks.yale.edu/2017/05/12/reconciling-deism-and-puritanism-in-benjamin-franklin/.

137 "The Jefferson Bible." The Jefferson Bible, accessed January 30, 2025. https://thejeffersonbible.com/.

throughout history, but well-known modern examples of this intellectual dispute include new atheist Sam Harris and Canadian psychologist Jordan Peterson.

Both participated in a 2016 debate on this issue, where Harris argued God is irrelevant, while Peterson argued atheists bow before a God they refuse to name.[138] Peterson observed how atheists borrow from the wells of religious wisdom when constructing their philosophical and ethical stances. He also criticized the dissonance between an atheist's beliefs and actions, noting how—practically speaking—atheists live *as if* God were real. This is seen through the atheist's willingness to follow codes or morality and goodness.

For, just as God either exists or does not, so too the concept of "goodness" is either valid or invalid. In religion, God *is* good, meaning he defines goodness itself. In an atheistic system, good *is* God, meaning the philosophical system being defended defines the parameters of goodness, supplanting what traditionally was viewed as a sentient entity, that is, "God," with an abstract, non-sentient concept, that is, "good."

An easy way to see the structural similarity in religious and secular thought processes is to observe "God is good" as if it were an equation. It would read as A = B. And A = B is synonymous with B = A. Thus, at a structural level, the atheist who argues for goodness without the need for a religious God argues for a distinction without a practical difference. Score one for Peterson.

---

[138] Pangburn. "Does God Exist? Jordan Peterson vs Matt Dillahunty." YouTube, May 5, 2018. https://www.youtube.com/watch?v=FmH7JUeVQb8&t=2552s.

This is easy to identify by observing the consequences of each man being wrong. The first man, Adam (pun intended), is religious. If he is wrong, and there is no God, his earthly attempts to live according to goodness limited him to pursuing only one path of possible goodness, namely that path defined by his fictitious God. Now, imagine Andrew. He is far more enlightened than Adam and rejects God, instead stating he can either define or discover goodness without the need for a mental crutch like religion.

If Andrew is wrong, he rejects God, and with Him, goodness, leading to eternal pain in which he experiences a reality devoid of anything that can be defined as good. His being now wars with reality by acting as if his internal definition of good can replace God. However, if Andrew is correct, and goodness can be defined or discovered without God, he accepts the rule of man. This is true because the atheist does not argue that the need for morality, justice, and goodness is absolved if God is not real, rather that it *should* be constructed purely by man rather than subject to flawed texts written by our ancestors on the assumption their words had divine inspiration.

To legitimize secular morality, the atheist first attacks religion as nothing more than a man-crafted system of rules and laws. Then, he seeks to subvert manmade religious systems with man-made philosophical systems that, functionally, operate identically. Non-religious philosophical belief systems, after all, are used to justify rules and enforce laws in accordance with the values defined as "good" under the moral framework of the philosophy's adherents.

Now, again assuming the atheist is correct, and there is no God, how can God, or religion, be routinely blamed for the actions of men? If He never existed, is it not man—rather than God—who is to blame for the evil and pain caused? In essence, if the atheist is correct, whether God as traditionally defined is real or not is wholly irrelevant to the pursuit of morality. For all such pursuits are, by definition, creations of man. And if man constructed what atheists believe is the destructive force of religion, would it not stand to reason he would construct other equally malicious philosophical forces through which to perpetrate harm?

The existence of destructive, non-religious philosophies, notably communism and eugenics, serve as reminders that man need not use a traditionally religious conception of God as sufficient justification for perpetrating heinous acts of harm against his fellow man. He is perfectly capable of engaging in genocide and psychopathology through moral foundations void of religious justifications.

Furthermore, if the atheist is correct, and religious conceptions of God are fictitious, from a day-to-day perspective, this matters little to the men and women bound by the morality of the society in which they live. According to atheism, whether one lives under the moral code of Mao's communism or the medieval Catholic church, he is required to bow before the moral orthodoxies of an imperfect system with which he does not necessarily agree.

Thus, *why*, precisely, anyone should respect man-made philosophies, but not respect man-made religions, remains a mystery the atheist is rarely asked to answer.

EQUAL CAPACITY FOR EVIL

Attempts to critique the religious definition of God are often presented as a rejection of unjust authority. However, as discussed above, the rejection of God does not lead to the rejection of authority, morality, or justice. Instead, the rejection of God leads to competing definitions of "good." Eventually, one definition will win and serve as the predicate of culture's governing moral system. Relativism may seek to solve the power struggle, but it is destined to fail because embracing the ability of each person to define and live out their own personal versions of morality comes at an unbearable cost.

UNDER ATHEISM, MANMADE AUTHORITY IS INHERENT

The classic critique of godless belief systems, namely that "without God all things are permitted," is a tough question for atheists to confront, not because all men who reject religion necessarily become psychopathic murderers, but because, under purely manmade philosophies, there is no sufficient justification for *commanding all people* to refrain from becoming psychopathic vipers.

Some men will, by virtue of their conscience, refrain from such behavior. But in the absence of laws *binding* men from psychopathic behaviors—however defined—chaos reigns. This is easily observed by the reality that all societies, whether ruled by religious or irreligious men, are governed by legal codes and cultural norms. There are no truly free societies, certainly not under a definition of "free" that requires the absence of an authority structure.

If atheists are correct, the implications of this reality are inherently and irredeemably bleak, for it requires each person to accept that some men should rule over others, with no grounding in any form of justice aside from power. At best, this involves imperfect moral calculations that lead to justice that can never be corrected (for the perfect justice rendered at the seat of judgment is mere fiction), and at worst, it involves utilizing power as a privilege through which to enhance their own self-interest, even if this harms those under their rule.

As it turns out, atheistic concerns with the injustice of the alleged fictitious "God" or "gods" of religion are equally applicable to the man-made authority established by godless belief systems. Which is what one would expect, since if religion is fiction, it was created by man. Thus, any evils perpetrated by God are really nothing more than the machinations of His "creation." This is why the atheistic tendency toward displaying anger to an unreal God while espousing that man—freed from the strict confines of religion—would become "good" is logically incoherent.

In reality, the atheistic worldview suffers steep hurdles to justifying any definition of morality. First, under atheism, where inherently limited, finite, and flawed creatures reign, defining good and evil is an ongoing group project that cannot be completed. Since good and evil are assumed to exist, yet impossible to perfectly define or practice, man is forever at war over the foundation of what constitutes "good and bad," and "right and wrong." Amid this ambiguity, society must enforce some type of order to effectively restrain the worst impulses of human ideation and action. If this is not restrained, life on earth spirals into nothing more than a brutal power struggle where survival and pain avoidance are the best possible outcomes of existence.

ATHEISM FAILS TO ADVANCE EQUALITY

Thus, while the ongoing, impossibly complex debate over what constitutes good and evil wage, man constructs moral philosophies that are, for all practical purposes, indistinguishable from religion. Within this system, and ironically as an outgrowth of the civilizational soil nurtured by the Christian religion, is a belief in human equality. The equal dignity of each person is often used as reason to embrace relativism, that is, the belief that morality can be defined by each person based on the unique circumstances of their beliefs and experiences.

Under an atheistic reality, this makes sense because, without an entity like God, who possesses just authority to judge humans and their behavior as good or bad based on His innate superiority, it is difficult to justify why men should serve beliefs and values they do not hold.

However, in practice, relativism guarantees higher degrees of cultural conflict because the conditions under which each man or woman will be compelled to fight to defend deeply held values fractures, leading to confusion that breaks down the foundations of relational peace, which is based on clarity and trust. Individuals have disparate abilities to define their value structures internally, much less communicate them effectively to others, particularly when conflict arises.

Thus, the problem with atheism at scale is that, if it is "nothing" as some of its adherents describe, it possesses no ability to create shared cultural and communal coherence and therefore no mechanism to prevent the spread of evil behavior. And, without a shared system of morality, "evil" can be defined in nearly infinite ways, thus causing deep social rifts between mutually exclusive philosophical beliefs.

And when evil cannot be defined, identified, and constrained, people with psychopathic tendencies are often emboldened. This is why vengeance is perceived as rational, and in many cases, difficult to condemn.

This is because living in an atheistic society is structurally the same as living under a religious system. Killing God does nothing to extinguish the demands men and women face to obey laws, and cultural norms in accordance with society's moral beliefs. While there are reasons to obey moral codes, these reasons are structurally similar to the rules of religion. Obedience to shared cultural morality brings peace, and an orderly system that metes out justice systemically, according to well-defined rules and norms crafted by men, even if it means there will be circumstances where the pain of victims is never avenged.

At the same time, it is rational for individuals to question obedience, both to religious and philosophic "gods." Barring people from seeking vengeance through violence, killing, and other forms of pain and punishment after sustaining an unjust injury is always difficult to explain, but more so under an atheistic view of morality.

ATHEISM'S ANARCHY PROBLEM

If the assumption that God is not real is true, then the atheist must contend with the logical implication of this claim, specifically the inability of defining goodness. Instead of a common, fixed definition, "good" would be synonymous with individual—or cultural— preferences. Thus, if the atheistic worldview were logically applied, anarchy would be its most reasonable expression. Legal systems and cultural norms would give way to individuals and factions seeking to actualize their preferences. These preferences *could* be expressed through laws, cultural norms, and the like, but to endow preferences through the permanence of tradition would be senseless.

Under such conditions, life would be a game of power because, when definitions of "good" clash, only those with the ability to enforce their preferences would win. An authentic expression of atheism turns the phrase "might makes right" into an axiomatic truth.

Anarchy, it seemed, was nothing more than the definition of hell offered by the Christian religion.

In Christianity, hell is the permanent separation from God, or, in secular terms, goodness. To be cast into hell is to be removed from the presence of this goodness. Thus, a godless world is a place where "good" cannot be experienced; instead, its residents' lives are filled with destruction, pain, and betrayal. If heaven is real, then escaping pain is possible. But, the absence of heaven does not destroy hell, it merely transforms earth into the dreaded pit of fire.

This transformation is a natural consequence of the human quest for power. If man is the measure of goodness, and no one definition of "good" is objectively binding, then individuals are incentivized to assert their own will in a quest to avoid subjugation. The pursuit of power begins in the mind, where individuals wrestle with competing conceptions of goodness. Since every person is a complex combination of rationality, emotion, and experience, different theories of "God" appeal to various aspects of the individual. This poses an internal problem; if there is no objective morality, then a person could hypothetically pursue mutually exclusive moral beliefs.

However, while people can live with some cognitive dissonance, an individual would go mad if they sought to act out numerous conflicting beliefs. Indeed, schizophrenia—hardly an enviable state of mind—is characterized by emotional responsiveness and the disintegration of thought. To avoid insanity, people internally follow one concept of goodness. They may live with some degree of cognitive dissonance, or become hypocrites who routinely fail to follow their god, but they do not live as if morality is relative.

Thus, after internally bowing before some concept of goodness, the individual in a state of anarchy must now defend his god against those who compete for power. This competition for power is inevitable because people living with conflicting definitions of good will struggle to maintain peace. Anyone raised in a home with parents whose divergent beliefs caused routine conflict can attest to this reality. Both parents, convinced of the superiority of their beliefs, view themselves as the victim and their spouse as the aggressor.

Such homes are characterized by power, not peace. Of course, some parents can compromise to maintain a relatively orderly home, and the same is true for society. However, the larger numbers of people and beliefs seeking to live together are guaranteed to break down the social cohesion of any given geographic region. This is why anarchy is unsustainable.

Yet, despite atheism's implications, aside from a small community of anarchists espousing a range of political philosophies, atheistic voices fail to contend with the logical outcome of their beliefs. Rather, numerous atheistic philosophies have emerged, each seeking to systematically define morality. But, again, this side steps an obvious question. What is the purpose of developing a flawed man-made philosophy of morality to replace existing flawed man-made religious systems? Why would someone follow the moral teachings of Immanuel Kant, Jean-Jacques Rousseau, or Ayn Rand, but scoff at the idea of following Jesus? Indeed, is there any functional difference between adhering to philosophy instead of religious teachings?

Under an atheistic system, the sociopath is no less moral than the saint, yet this conclusion flies in the face of civilization itself. I can find no historical precedent for a culture void of moral standards. Even communist regimes that persecute unapproved religious teachings have their own standards of goodness. The state may usurp the divine, and when it does, brutally enforced totalitarian order, not anarchy, reigns.

Totalitarian regimes often rise under conditions necessary for anarchy to exist, that is, when there is an absence of structure. Napoleon rose to power following the chaos and bloodshed of a French Revolution fought to upend hierarchies to bring equality to the people. Similarly, although fictitious, George Orwell's *Animal Farm* follows a revolutionary movement that leads to an abuse of power. The animals of Manor Farm conspire to overthrow their oppressive humans. Not long after their successful revolution, Napoleon (based on Russian dictator Joseph Stalin) becomes what he once proclaimed to hate. Napoleon's transformation is complete when he—and other pigs in the ruling class—embody the discordant philosophy "all animals are equal, but some animals are more equal than others." This degradation of the mind becomes physical when Napoleon and his ruling class of pigs take on human form by walking upright, drinking whiskey, and smoking cigars. Their transformation is complete when common animals are unable to distinguish their leaders from the human rulers they fought to defeat.

Although unsavory, the truth of the human condition renders attempts to destroy the absolute authority of God futile. Anarchy leads to absolute power, not paradise.

As I was contemplating the flaws of atheism, I was confronted with a choice that would force me to publicly profess, or reject, faith.

COERCED BAPTISM

By sixteen, I was still far from a final determination of how my worldview interacted with my life, leaving me deeply indecisive. I oscillated daily between accepting and rejecting Christianity. At this point in my decision-making process, I hyperfixated on suicide—whether it was moral, or if not, if it was at least a forgivable sin. Of course, assuming God was real, completing the act would answer my questions, but it remained unclear whether the answer would render premature death beneficial or purely destructive.

Amid this indecision, I was forced to make a public profession of faith. Long before I was born, my parents attended several churches with their children before withdrawing from congregations entirely. Some of these churches practiced infant baptism, others did not. As a result, only four of their seven children were baptized. One day, my brother, the oldest of the three unbaptized, approached my parents and told them he intended to pursue baptism in our Presbyterian church. I heard the news from my father who informed me that my sister and I would be baptized as well so the entire family could join the church together.

This news was distressing because I was neither a Christian nor willing to announce my apostasy to my family, especially my mother. At nine years old, I had observed my mother emotionally torment my eleven-year-old sister for the sin of questioning Christ. My sister made the mistake of telling my mother she felt far from God relationally, was unsure He existed, and was worried about obeying rules she did not understand, one of which was the command to obey your parents. Instead of contextualizing my sister's concerns and offering appropriate encouragement, my mother saw an opportunity to manipulate.

"You are like a worm in comparison to God," she said. "He can see everything, you can barely see what is in front of you, and he prepares a feast for you while you are content eating dirt. You will never understand God's plans or purposes. All you can do is obey."

I was initially amused by this overt attempt at manipulation, until I saw the distress this brought on my sister.

"I'm like a worm?!" she asked. "But worms don't have brains. Why would He let me question if He didn't want to give me answers?"

"He does," Mom replied. "He could kill you if He wanted, but instead, He blessed you with a loving family." She continued, "Why are you doubting God? You are worthless, like all people. None of us deserve His grace or anything good. Still, He provides for us, and you respond by questioning His commands? All He asks is that you obey. Those who don't are punished in hell. Do you want to go to hell?"

My sister, always prone to pleasing and deeply unwilling to face eternal torment, swiftly doubled down on her commitment to obedience, causing me to further bury my emotions, for I had no intention of creating the conditions that would give rise to a lecture about my worthless, wormlike nature.

The lesson I took from this impromptu childish Bible study was that questions about God's goodness are best processed alone. To the extent I have questions, I thought, they should be framed to avoid any appearance of questioning the Almighty.

Fortunately, this was a small practical barrier, because it was not hard to reword questions into a format that would satisfy Mom. For all her faults, the woman genuinely cared about providing her children a good education and, as a strict mathematician, understanding God syllogistically was encouraged. Thus, she made it easy for me to mask my disbelief under the guise of wanting to understand how to answer a Devil's Advocate.

This made accessing nearly any competent perspective from authors of philosophy, atheism, apologetics, and theology easy. And for years, this arrangement worked perfectly. By strategically choosing content from perspectives ranging from politically conservative authors such as Sarah Palin and John McCain to secular ones like Karl Marx and Peter Singer, I was able to hide my internal confusion, giving me open access to any content I desired to explore.

Now, with the announcement of baptism, I was faced with the prospect of blowing my cover. Rejecting baptism would require me to state my beliefs; after all, I was sixteen, well past the age of childish confusion and perfectly capable of determining the status of my orientation towards God. However, I knew honesty was guaranteed to raise mom's ire, and I had to remain at home for over two years before college. Telling the truth could cut off the free flow of information I had worked so hard to cultivate and, instead, I would be forced to argue with my mother for years.

At the center of my concern was consent. How would this impact my ability to determine what *I* believed? How would my desires, for or against God, be manipulated by this cunning woman whose sole purpose was to control her children by forcefully projecting her desires onto them?

I searched the depths of my memories for any positive experience when engaging in conflict with Mom. I came up empty handed, and I decided to sleep on my thoughts before determining whether telling the truth was a risk worth taking.

Sleep brought additional reminders of the dangerous predicament in which I had been placed. In particular, my reflective dreams focused on some harrowing experiences with my mom after my appendix surgery.

Attempts to regain agency post-surgery were difficult. Mom enjoyed my temporary state of helplessness because it gave her an outlet to care for me as if I were an infant, satiating her perverse desire to never live without a small child. For weeks my dignity evaporated as she insisted on thoroughly bathing me despite my need for only minimal assistance.

After falling asleep, a particularly jarring incident replayed in my dreams. As if in a flashback, my dream replayed how she delighted in the predicament, reminding me of the control she possessed over my body.

"It's nice to have a baby to take care of again," she said cheerfully.

I tried to gently avoid infantilization. "I don't really need help anymore, the scar is protected," I said, pointing to the water-resistant plastic she had placed around my incision to prevent infection. "I can wash my own hair."

She rebuffed my attempts, grabbing my arm and reaching for a container to pour water over my head. I considered lying down to avoid her, but my core was too weak to sit back up, and this risked leaving me even more vulnerable.

I pushed her arm away. "I can bathe myself, Mom!" I said forcefully, making strong eye contact to indicate my ability to carry on alone.

In an instant, her demeanor changed and her eyes flashed with the same intensity they had when I attempted to thwart her application of the therapeutic cream a year prior.

"Leslie, you are too weak and could hurt yourself. You won't be able to get up without help."

"I can call you when I need to get up," I replied.

But my luck had run dry.

"No," she said, "*I* will help you."

This process dragged on for days as I waited for the drain to close and the stitches to be removed from my incisions. As quickly as possible, I tried to regain independence even if the pain was acute and had not subsided. Days blurred into one another as I felt my body slip away. As I struggled to maintain emotional control, I actively tried to distance my mind from my body to dull the sense of indignity that comes from this unique type of violation.

"*It's just a temporary body. It won't go with you when you die,*" I told myself. "*Even if God isn't real, your body will eventually decay. All that will remain are your bones. Your mind and spirit are all that can possibly live on, and she has no control over either. Your mind is a distant home, the door is locked and you hold the only key. It is your job to never let her in.*"

With each bath, I could feel her touch less, and by the third bathing, I barely noticed she had touched me at all. My conscious efforts to dissociate were effective.

However, they came at a cost. For days I found myself uncommonly distraught. Eating and sleeping were nearly impossible. I routinely crawled behind the dresses in my closet to weep, strategically scheduling these sessions while my mom and sister were busy with school. When the closet was unavailable, I walked acres deep into the backyard to cry until I could compose myself and return to the house.

I convinced myself the feelings would eventually dissipate after my physical health returned. Once I was independent again, Mom would have no excuse to touch me. For some time, this process worked until I made a critical error.

The next portion of the dream moved to another humiliating incident during my recovery. One evening, my attempts to bury my emotions failed and I noticed I needed to cry. However, before I could find a safe location, tears began to flow. Mom heard me and I fled to my room, but she caught me as I tried to slam the door.

"What's wrong?" she asked, wrapping me into a bear hug.

I struggled to free myself, causing her to squeeze tighter. I pushed her away, but she refused to leave the room. I found a corner between the bed and nightstand and curled into a ball.

Her tone shifted from concern to command. "I'm not leaving until you talk to me," she said.

Years of experience taught me this was literally true, and I was depleted of energy, unable to fight with her for the hours it would take to escape the situation without revealing anything I wished to hide.

I tried to avoid the situation by refusing to speak at all, but this only caused her to approach me, wrap her arms around me, and refuse to release me from her grasp. Now, in a weakened emotional state, I tried to repress the feel of her body, but failed. My heart rate increased, and I began to gasp for air.

"What is it, baby?" Mom asked in a loving tone.

"Baby?!" I cried in anger. "*I am not your baby*! I am fourteen years old and you refuse to let me grow up. You won't even let me control my body when I can bathe on my own. I'm not your perpetual infant!"

My body shook as I sat, pushing my arms against her attempt at a hug, shaking and glaring into her eyes.

"Let go of me. I don't want a hug."

"No," she said forcefully. "You need a hug, even if you don't want it. And it is my job as your mother to comfort you."

I rolled my eyes. "Is this what comfort looks like to you?"

Angered at my rejection, she lashed out. "You mock me today, but one day you will have children and then you will understand," she retorted.

"When did I ever say I planned on reproducing?" I asked.

"You will change your mind," she declared, "and then you will regret how unfairly you have treated me. As your mother I deserve better."

This filled me with rage. "You deserve nothing! Remember, 'You are a mere mortal deserving God's wrath and eternal judgment.' When did He say you deserve a daughter who loves you even when you try to destroy her independence?"

Immediately, I sensed my attempt to hurt her was effective. "How dare you speak to your mother like that!" she cried. "You have always been insolent, and you will pay the price. From birth you were only half-human, with a fraction of a soul...half-aborted. I knew it as soon as I held you."

I glared and pushed her away. This time she willingly released her grasp.

"I always knew you would have a hard life," she said, changing her tone from that of an angry tyrant to a callous, calculated teacher. "You may see yourself as a victim, but that won't serve you. The resentment will only hurt you further. You can either accept everything that has happened to you or slide into cynicism, in which animosity will crush your soul. The choice is yours, you can either grow strong or self-destruct."

With these final words, she arose and left me to ponder her words.

As the story came to its conclusion, I awoke in a fright and shot up to a seated position, staring at the wall in front of me. Quickly, I got dressed and threw shoes on before retreating to the backyard as quickly as I could. I wanted to be as far away from home as possible, so I rushed to a tree. I sat with my back against the trunk and settled in to contemplate my dream's meaning and the choice I was forced to make.

A verse from the Bible provided essential guidance. In Matthew, Jesus warns His disciples of persecution, stating, "Behold, I am sending you out as sheep in the midst of wolves, so be wise as serpents and innocent as doves."[139] This, however, should not give rise to anxiety or dread. "[D]o not fear those who kill the body but cannot kill the soul," He said, "[r]ather fear him who can destroy both soul and body in hell."[140]

I knew there were worse sentences than physical death. My mind must be guarded at all costs to preserve my soul from self-destruction.

"*If Mom reacted with so much anger to me repeating religious beliefs she holds, how much more will she emotionally torment me if I declare I am not even a Christian?*" I pondered. "*The answer to this is obvious. Our relationship will spiral into new depths of hell not yet reached.*"

Then, I posed the important question. "*What will this do to my decision-making process? If I want to determine what I believe before college, how can I accomplish this when all my emotional energy will be spent arguing with someone I hate about the most important questions of my life?*"

After years of laborious reading, I already knew I had previously, and inappropriately, conflated Mom's behavior and teaching with biblical principles. Although this was understandable,

---

[139] Matthew 10:16 (ESV) *The Holy Bible: English Standard Version.* Wheaton, IL: Crossway, 2016.

[140] Matthew 10:28 (ESV) *The Holy Bible: English Standard Version.* Wheaton, IL: Crossway, 2016.

it was an impediment to making an informed individual choice. The answer to whether I would lie and declare a faith I did not hold became increasingly obvious.

"*If I am locked in a war with Mom, I will probably reject Christianity out of spite,*" I realized. "*That's the obvious danger.*" Knowing my decision-making process and ability to continue to explore my faith would be so severely impeded, I traded the truth for the opportunity to make my own decision. Still, I knew it was far from ideal.

"*Lord, if you are there, forgive me. I would rather try to know you than reject you out of anger and spite,*" I reasoned. "*I trust this is not a choice you would have forced upon me, but why can't you rid me of this madwoman and let me live in peace?*"

In an ideal world, honesty would be incentivized, but reality is far from perfect. In the real world, avoiding the truth, or even telling lies, is the easiest way to avoid trouble. The value of deception increases when emotional manipulation is normalized.

CHAPTER 7
Liberty

CONSENT ACCEPTS CONSEQUENCES

Although suicide was a rational option under an atheistic framework, there were other possibilities. Unable to remove the functional need for a ranking of values, I was aware that continued rejection of God was the equivalent of serving an external or internal human master in his place. I easily recognized this as Christianity's definition of idolatry, which states no other God or concept of "goodness" should be placed before Christ. Doing so indulges pride, the root of all sin.

Unfortunately, avoiding the concept of idolatry was impossible. Rejecting Christ was not rejecting the concept of God; rather, it was removing Jesus from the list of gods available to worship. Devotion, it seemed, was not easily avoided. Even if I chose to live life as if it were a gambling game, worship would move from the external to the internal. Choosing this path would fulfill my own needs, and my desires would take precedence above all else. Why should it not? Aside from avoiding authorities with more structural or technical power—for example, law enforcement or judges—why should I live on anyone's terms but my own?

An answer to this question came from an unexpected source.

Most of my childhood pastimes revolved around either acquiring knowledge about history, philosophy, and theology to gain a better understanding of the adult worldview I would inhabit, and annoying my mother. My favorite activities combined both endeavors, and it was at the intersection of these two that I found an answer to pressing moral and ethical concerns.

Music, although focused on the emotive, offered a wealth of knowledge from which I could glean important lessons about the human condition. It was also a medium my mother sought to highly control, thus giving me an opportunity to provoke her through intentional rebellion. For most of my childhood and adolescence, I was locked in a cold—sometimes hot—war over what musical content I could consume. For years, my mother tried, in vain, to limit my musical choices to the genres of Christian and classical.

Despite her best efforts, my mother was unable to enforce her ban on non-conforming melodies. Ironically, the music I sought out was not risqué, at least by modern standards. Instead, they were old, the most modern dating back to the 1970s. This was because my interest in music was tethered to lyrical substance, not emotion. With few exceptions, my taste did not align with popular music from the 1980s onward because I viewed it as overly focused on sex, fleeting hedonistic pleasure, or, in the case of the emo/punk genres, concerns of first-world, privileged, performatively "rebellious" children.

The themes of modern songs, except for country, failed to resonate with my experience. However, certain artists from the revolutionary period of the 1960s and 1970s spoke to my concerns. Whether I intellectually agreed with the artists was irrelevant; I was far more interested in analyzing the content, for it was useful in understanding how the same philosophical and theological ideas were represented across the dimensions of human identity, ranging from syllogistic thought and fiction, to poetry and lyrical expression.

Among the songs I routinely meditated on was The Supremes 1968 hit, "Love Child." As lead singer, Diana Ross sang the story of a child born out of wedlock, and described an experience causing the protagonist to develop a cautious sexual ethic that placed concerns with the possibility of passing her shame to the next generation above immediate gratification.

Ross details the hardships her character experienced growing up, including material deprivation and a pervasive need to hide her condition from her friends, fearful they will see the guilt consuming her soul.

Now an adult, the child wrestles with her desire to provide her lover physical affection without abdicating the responsibility she bears to a child who would inherit the consequences of an unplanned birth.

The profound consequences of reckless sexual encounters are contemplated and the high cost of creating human life is a sufficient reason for the song's protagonist to avoid sex.

The song was an exploration of genuine reproductive justice. It did not shame sexual desire, instead recognizing sex as love's appropriate expression. However, because love creates life, listeners are reminded of the weighty implications associated with recklessly reproducing in the throes of passion. Such decisions place the burden of stigma on the shoulders of unwanted children. These children sense their inferiority and live under an unearned weight of shame.

Long before I was a Christian, I was profoundly impacted by the message of these lyrics. Its effects cut so deeply that I could not emotionally connect with the idea of pursuing sexual desires outside the security of a publicly committed relationship. Importantly, it was not a religiously motivated desire; rather, it was rooted in the fear of passing harm to children who had no voice in the matter of their existence or the unfortunate circumstances of their conception.

Because of these lyrics, I began to question the secular dogma surrounding sexual ethics in culture. I already viewed most cultural expressions of secular progressivism as hypocritical because the philosophy concerned itself with protecting society's marginalized while advocating for the "human right" to kill humanity's most vulnerable members.

Now, I applied the same skepticism to sexual ethics. Broadly speaking, it was undeniable that progressives took a liberal view of sexual behavior, generally speaking positively of sex outside of marriage, and viewing the ethics of whether to engage in sex—whether casually or within a relationship—as involving no parties other than the two sexual partners. This was clearly expressed in the widespread claim that the morality and ethics of all sexual activity is predicated only on the consent of the adults involved in the sexual acts in question.

After considering the possible negative implications of sex on those who could not consent to the act's consequences—that is, the next generation of children—I viewed the above claim as an ill-thought-out slogan that failed to grapple with obvious, objective aspects of reality.

If secular progressives cared about the vulnerable, they would advocate a sexual ethic consistent with Christian norms, even if they embraced these ethics for an entirely separate set of reasons. Yet, instead of advocating for caution in sexual relations, progressive culture ran in the opposite direction, encouraging adults to indulge temporal pleasures without considering the costs they were passing to the next generation of children who would either die in abortion procedures or be born into instability created by their negligent parents.

Internally, I mused, "*Why are those who reject God while priding themselves on their protection of victims so quick to turn a blind eye to the needs of children? What is it about children that progressives unconsciously hate so much?*"

LIBERTY AND LAW

The tension between rights and responsibilities is a fundamental fault line in the competing definitions of liberty that war for culture's allegiance. Generally speaking, those who are concerned with responsibilities focus on the implications an individual's actions have on others, while an emphasis on an individual's rights is primarily concerned with allowing people to self-actualize in more diverse ways by expanding the universe of socially acceptable choices.

However, the degree to which someone's analysis focuses on expanding individual choices versus considering the needs of others is governed by their commitment to an underlying worldview that defines moral values. This is one reason why culture wars are fought by people who view those with whom they disagree as hypocrites. Both sides claim the values of freedom, equality, and a commitment to human dignity, but they differ regarding when it is appropriate to emphasize an individual's right to self-actualize versus when people should refrain from engaging in specific conduct due to its potential consequences to others.

Obvious examples abound. Many on the left view Jack Phillips, a devout Christian, with scorn for his decision to self-actualize by adhering to his religious convictions and refusing to bake cakes in celebration of same sex weddings. LGBTQ champions contend Phillips's responsibility to prevent harm to members of a historically marginalized group should take precedence over his commitment to his beliefs. According to a value system that heavily punishes conduct that may offend individuals in marginalized communities, Phillips's refusal to celebrate the identity that once brought these people social shame is a form of selfishness, perhaps even malignant bigotry.

Ironically, secular commitment to the vulnerable does not factor into discussions of how the perpetual battle between the sexes impacts the lives of children. Although the song "Love Child" is now decades old, it advances—from a secular standpoint—a view of sexual ethics consistent with Christian values generally subject to social scorn. Using story, the lyrics present a more powerful argument for the wisdom of sexual caution than most sermons I have heard. It effectively undercuts the idea that a temporal, self-centered view of sexual decision-making by calling the listener's attention to the impact such instant gratification has on unwanted children.

These questions at the heart of what leftists call "reproductive rights" are fundamentally questions of freedom, equality, and dignity. Disputes over these idealistic concepts have existed since the American experiment—created to secure and protect the God-given rights to "life, liberty, and the pursuit of happiness"—began. Currently, in the sexual context, secular, progressive cultural spaces view liberty as licentiousness, because it is characterized by a commitment to the freedom to pursue individual happiness, *even if* it results in the destruction of human life.

This attitude toward life is essential to uphold the lowest common denominator of shared meaning our relativistic, fractured culture can produce. With the breakdown in cultural norms, to the extent American society has a shared definition of morality, it almost exclusively concerns itself with maximizing an individual's ability to self-actualize any desire they choose.

"Do as you please unless your actions harm others," sounds good in theory, until several minutes of self-reflection bring the wise words of John Adams to mind. In a letter to the Massachusetts militia, Adams stated the US constitution was "made only for a moral and religious People." The document, he opined, is "wholly inadequate to the government of any other."[141] While Adams is no longer able to provide clarifying commentary on his remarks, there is a self-evident truth to his statement. For, without a shared

[141] "From John Adams to Massachusetts Militia, 11 October 1798." National Archives | Founders Online, accessed January 30, 2025. https://founders.archives.gov/documents/Adams/99-02-02-3102.

understanding of what is "good," how is society able to accurately discern what constitutes "harm"?

In the sexual realm, licentiousness triumphed over life causing our collective mind to live according to a fiction that declares liberty and equality are compatible with a sex-based right to kill.

OVERREACH IN THE PURSUIT OF EQUALITY

Champions of women's rights have long advocated for the interchangeable nature of men and women. Social norms created by patriarchal oppression of women, they argue, account for most differences across the sexes. Although this belief is misguided, it was once understandable. However, cultural changes over the course of the twentieth and twenty-first century increasingly expose how detached the patriarchy narrative of feminism is from reality.

There was a time when political systems universally and indisputably favored men. During the same period, conception had not yet been tamed and abstaining from marriage was a woman's only reliable form of birth control. Thus, nature, law, and culture made women's equal participation in educational and employment opportunities impossible. Additionally, it is true that opponents of gender equality have historically used differences between men and women to make sexist arguments, concluding women are inferior to men or ineligible to participate in public life.

That being said, the reality of sex relations in 2024 bears no resemblance to the gender dynamics of 1924. Assumptions, beliefs, and biases have radically changed. Simply put, the patriarchy narrative takes the structure of past cultural prejudices and assumes that those prejudices are a fixed element of the human condition across history.

This is not true and it leads to a simplistic and binary analysis of the complex interplay between men and women. Although feminism is often framed as nothing more than the belief women should have a choice in whether to pursue educational or career success over family formation, in practice, the movement focuses on controlling outcomes of reproductive choices that have already been made.

And, by tying the dignity and worth of women to the right to destroy their children, pro-abortion feminism severed the sacred bond between mother and child. As a consequence, our culture has spent fifty years in a social experiment where the best interests of women and children are at war. Despite the vast relational changes caused by abortion, this experiment has occurred in the public eye with virtually no commentary on its wide-reaching relational consequences.

This increased power produced predictable results. Women have obtained a power greater than men, but at the price of their conscience. In 1973, women sold their souls by trading the lives of their children in exchange for access to power. Now, fifty years later, the effects of this decision are clear and affirm fundamental aspects of human nature described by philosophers, theologians, novelists, and poets across centuries.

The damaging effects on children should be clear. When J. D. Vance was criticized for accusing the left of harboring anti-child sentiment, I was somewhat surprised this was controversial.[142]

---

[142] "JD Vance Suggests Top Democrats Are 'Anti-Child.' Hear Pete Buttigieg's Response." CNN Politics, August 11, 2024. https://www.cnn.com/2024/08/11/politics/video/sotu-buttigieg-reacts-jd-vance-interview.

Growing up, it was common for people to question why my parents had seven children. The further to the political left people were, the more likely they were to react with disgust at the number of children my mother birthed. I always wondered how many kids they wish my mom had aborted, and which children, precisely, should feel guilty for existing.

Of course, there is nothing wrong with the choice to have no children or to have a small family. However, the idea that there are no individuals—predominantly on the left—repulsed by the thought of having a large family is laughable. As discussed in Chapter 5, the feud between feminists and tradwives touches on this exact topic. Additionally, anyone who spends years on college campuses can attest to the judgment that befalls women who delay completing their degrees or place their career on hold to birth an unplanned or unwanted child.

This brings us to another cultural taboo created by progressive ideologies: childcare. Taking care of children is presented as among the worst human endeavors. A recent movie, *Nightbitch*, perpetuates this mindset, presenting postpartum as mind numbing, soul crushing, and psychosis inducing. There appears to be little to no concern that such caricatures are deeply damaging to postpartum women, many of whom have quite positive experiences, while further communicating to children their status as burdensome beings whose existence comes at the price of their mother's sanity.

While the tradwife trend has its own set of cultural defects, its rise is a sign that there is increasing opposition against the progressive impulse to portray traditional feminine pursuits as an oppressive cage rather than a natural and powerful aspect of humanity.

THE STRUCTURE OF FEMALE-CREATED SYSTEMS OF INEQUALITY

Assessing the causal relationship between ideas and movements in culture is a notoriously difficult task, but it should come as no surprise that philosophies derived from feminism have come to govern the social relations of modern culture.

One such foundational feminist philosophy is intersectionality. As the brainchild of gender studies feminists, intersectionality is an inherently ideological system of study. Originally created by Kimberlé Crenshaw[143] in an attempt to demolish social hierarchies, intersectionality now refers to a sociological method that explores the overlapping or intersection of various forms of discrimination[144] against people with historically marginalized identities, including sex, class, and race. In a nutshell, intersectionality posits that people experience discrimination differently based on their unique identities. For example, racial minorities experience the world differently based on both their gender *and* race.

The academics who advance this methodology are not fully homogenous in their philosophical views, but they do share some fundamental beliefs. The variances in their worldviews are analogous to the differences within protestant denominations: Fierce

---

143 Coaston, Jane. "The Intersectionality Wars." Vox, May 20, 2019. https://www.vox.com/the-highlight/2019/5/20/18542843/intersectionality-conservatism-law-race-gender-discrimination.

144 "Intersectionality." Merriam-Webster, accessed January 30, 2025. https://www.merriam-webster.com/dictionary/intersectionality.

infighting over esoteric theological beliefs does not negate the shared values that unite the faith.

One shared value is the idea that hierarchies are inherently unfair and must be demolished. There's just one problem: Achieving the goal of demolishing hierarchies is impossible. As limiting and flawed as hierarchical structures can be, the world will never exist without competition between identity groups. Crenshaw's own theory offers no explanation for how to cease all forms of identity-based competition.

She critiques court cases that refuse to create protected classes based on intersectional identities, such as "black women." In one case, the court addressed the impracticability of implementing intersectionality in law by observing that the creation of new protected minority classes would open a Pandora's box of new identities with no obvious limiting principle.

Crenshaw argued the court's ruling is an example of the "conceptual limitations of...single-issue analyses" when considering overlapping identities. The problem is the limitation Crenshaw complains of has no remedy, and the court correctly identified why: It incentivizes the creation of endless new identity groups and fosters pointless competition between them.

This fundamental problem is exemplified in a scene from an episode of the television series *Modern Family*.

In the show, Cameron and Mitchell, a gay couple, arrive at an interview to place their child in an elite school. When sizing up the competition, Mitchell nervously notes their competitor's marginalized identities, nervously saying, "single white mother with a black child." To calm his husband's anxiety, Cameron rebuts with their credentials, "Lily's Asian, we're gay. In the school admissions poker game, we're the winning hand." This was just the build-up of the joke; the punchline is delivered when the single mother's disabled lesbian partner enters. In disbelief, Cameron describes the school admission's royal flush: "Disabled interracial lesbians with an African kicker?!" to which his husband replies, "I did not see that coming."[145]

Jokes aside, in practice, attempts to rid society of competing identity hierarchies are dangerous because they transform human pain into social currency, thus commodifying suffering for the purpose of redistributing social power. This incentivizes people to identify (or invent) new, novel identities to acquire the currency that flows from having experienced multiple forms of social discrimination. It should come as no surprise that never-before known genders and novel mental disorders are emerging for the first time in history during the height of identity politics' social utility.

Identity characteristics measured by degrees of real—or perceived—social oppression are increasingly relevant to an individual's social status and power. Then-presidential candidate Mitt Romney played this game in 2012, through his misguided attempt to elevate women to positions of power by collecting a binder of women.[146] By 2020, then-presidential candidate Joe Biden took a more overt intersectional approach to Supreme Court

---

[145] Packerpride66. "Cam Pretends to Be Indian." YouTube, October 13, 2011. https://www.youtube.com/watch?v=1RB1Gh7H3NQ.

[146] Madison, "Fact-Checking Romney's 'Binders Full of Women' Claim."

nominations by making a campaign promise to select a black woman to the nation's highest court if he won the White House.[147]

Additionally, the same principles are used to determine who should have access to compassion, and in what amounts. This finite social resource is distributed unequally based on the perceived marginalization of its recipient. Greater degrees of marginalization result in higher compassion payouts. On the flip side, those perceived to exist in a group that currently or historically discriminated against those with protected identities are disqualified from accessing social sympathy.

This structural reality permeates society. In the gender and sexuality context, cultural critiques of men are common, while criticism of women is intentionally misrepresented and scorned. For example, when Republican vice-presidential candidate J. D. Vance addressed what he described as the rise of anti-child rhetoric on the political left by sarcastically referring to a subset of women in positions of power as "childless cat ladies," he was chided for not apologizing to those he may have offended. The flood of criticism Vance received generally failed to engage with the social issues he addressed, instead focusing on the perceived sexism in his comments.

Notably, the premise of his commentary was correct. There is a noticeable rise of anti-child sentiment from subsets of the left.

---

[147] Kapul, Sahir. "Biden Pledged to Put a Black Woman on the Supreme Court. Here's What He Might Have to Do." NBC News, May 6, 2020. https://www.nbcnews.com/politics/2020-election/problem-biden-s-pledge-black-woman-justice-n1200826.

Some use nakedly derogatory terms like "breeding" to refer to reproduction and "breeders" to refer to larger families.[148]

While the decision to be child-free is case-dependent, a CNN article profiling women who plan not to procreate opened with a predictable story. Dyanna Volek never saw herself as a mother, an absent desire that may have been driven by watching her mother "sacrifice her dream" to raise her children.[149] Other concerns women cited included fears of adopting responsibility and the process of pregnancy.[150]

Before growing into men and women, boys and girls navigate childhood. For decades, young girls have been flooded with increasingly strong messages encouraging them to view pregnancy as a life-ending event and children as a depressing burden. Ironically, in a progressive, feminism-saturated culture, pregnancy, childbirth, and childrearing are lesser endeavors. In feminist terms, female success is measured according to career aspirations. Abortion rhetoric makes that link clear, hence why

---

148 Talbot, Margaret. "J. D. Vance and the Right's Call to Have More Babies." *The New Yorker*, August 5, 2024. https://www.newyorker.com/news/daily-comment/j-d-vance-and-the-rights-call-to-have-more-babies. Vanderhoof, Erin. "The Ballerina Farming of America: How JD Vance, Elon Musk, and the Entire GOP Want to Trigger Mommy Mania." *Vanity Fair*, October 1, 2024. https://www.vanityfair.com/style/story/ballerina-farm-jd-vance-babies. Del Valle, Gaby. "The Far Right's Campaign to Explode the Population." Politico, April 28, 2024. https://www.politico.com/news/magazine/2024/04/28/natalism-conference-austin-00150338.

149 Kaur, Harmeet. "Why More Women Are Choosing Not to Have Kids." CNN, September 25, 2023. https://www.cnn.com/us/childfree-by-choice-women-birth-rate-decline-cec/index.html.

150 Kaur, "Why More Women Are Choosing Not to Have Kids."

the "right to choose" as the foundation of women's equal participation in society is invoked by the left in nearly every discussion of the issue.

While the rise in childlessness is multifactorial, it is the logical outgrowth of grounding women's rights in an act of violence against children. Abortion is now unironically referred to by some commentators as pro-family. *New Yorker* staff writer, Margaret Talbot, describes abortion as nothing more than a benign way to allow individuals to "build the families they envision, at points in their lives when they are able to take care of children."[151] Family formation created through the strategic use of death is now considered a positive social good by a sizable portion of the American population.

The growing cohort of a demographic of middle-aged, childless Americans is undoubtedly tied to the increasingly pessimistic view of procreation. Attempts to decouple this pessimism from the rise in normalization of abortion are misguided, particularly given the overlap between the childless demographic and those who seek abortions. Statistically, abortion is driven by young, unmarried women. Centers for Disease Control and Prevention (CDC) data from 2021 shows 57 percent of abortions were sought by women in their twenties, and 87 percent of women who had abortions were unmarried.[152]

---

[151] "Margaret Talbot." *The New Yorker*, accessed January 30, 2025. https://www.newyorker.com/contributors/margaret-talbot.

[152] Diamant, Jeff, Besheer Mohamed, and Rebecca Leppert. "What the Data Says About Abortion in the US." Pew Research Center, March 25, 2024. https://www.pewresearch.org/short-reads/2024/03/25/what-the-data-says-about-abortion-in-the-us/#what-are-the-demographics-of-women-who-have-had-abortions.

This rise in anti-child sentiment can also be seen in public policy. Nine states and the District of Columbia have no gestational limits on abortion.[153] A bill introduced in Congress during the 2021–2022 legislative session would have federally protected abortion through viability and placed no gestational limit on abortion when "good-faith medical judgment of the treating health care provider" determines the pregnancy poses a risk to the mother's "life or health."[154] This effectively allows for abortion throughout pregnancy. Similarly worded legislation failed due to backlash against its extreme nature. For example, a 2019 Virginia bill sought to remove restrictions on abortions deemed necessary for mental health purposes through the third trimester.[155] This bill failed to pass subcommittee, but not before its sponsor testified that her proposed legislation would legalize abortion for mental health concerns alone, even after a woman began labor.[156]

FEMINISM'S OBJECTIFICATION OF CHILDREN

Implicit in the female-created structures of human relations is the belief that children are objects of maternal desire. Their existence has no inherent meaning, and their bodies are justly sacrificed and

---

[153] "State Bans on Abortion Throughout Pregnancy." Guttmacher Institute, accessed January 2, 2025. https://www.guttmacher.org/state-policy/explore/state-policies-abortion-bans.

[154] Women's Health Protection Act of 2022. Bill (2022).

[155] The Republican Standard. "Kathy Tran Presents Virginia Third Trimester Abortion Bill in Committee." YouTube, January 29, 2019. https://www.youtube.com/watch?v=OMFzZ5I30dg.

[156] Diamant, Mohamed, and Leppert. "What the Data Says about Abortion in the US."

abused to benefit their makers. Children, biologically designed to seek maternal care and socialized to accept women as categorically safe caregivers, are not in a position to fight against the female-created systems that objectify their bodies to either prevent women's pain or maximize their pleasure.

Instead, the authors of their subjugation hide behind social authority and the widespread disbelief in female forms of malevolence. Despite the social belief in female moral purity, women are the majority of child abuse perpetrators.[157] And disorders involving the objectification of children's bodies, such as Munchausen syndrome by proxy, the disorder Gypsy-Rose Blanchard's mom likely had, are almost exclusively perpetrated by female caregivers, particularly mothers.[158]

This disorder, one in which the body of a child is used as the playfield of a woman, is moving from obscurity into the mainstream, fueled by the rise in gender dysphoria among today's youth. Urban Dictionary now has a term, "Trannyhausen-by-Proxy," describing a parent who projects an emotional agenda onto their child through the use of the child's body.[159]

---

157 "Child Abuse in the US - Perpetrators 2022, by Sex." Statista, December 9, 2022. https://www.statista.com/statistics/418470/number-of-perpetrators-in-child-abuse-cases-in-the-us-by-sex/.

158 Abdurrachid, Nuzhat, and João Gama Marques. "Munchausen Syndrome by Proxy (MSBP): A Review Regarding Perpetrators of Factitious Disorder Imposed on Another (FDIA)." *CNS Spectrums* 27, no. 1 (2022): 16–26. https://doi.org/10.1017/s1092852920001741.

159 "Trannyhausen-by-Proxy." Urban Dictionary, December 15, 2020. https://www.urbandictionary.com/define.php?term=Trannyhausen-by-Proxy.

As previously discussed, the identification of Munchausen syndrome by proxy faces enormous hurdles because behaviors characterizing the condition are often indistinguishable from typical caretaking. This is because the disordered behavior exists in the unseen realm of the emotive and relational, not the physical. Unlike male-driven forms of abuse, overt physical aggression sufficient to provide visual evidence is rarely present. The victim has no bruised images to display or semen to collect. Therefore, without significant relational information gathered across years in context-dependent settings, understanding which behaviors are abusive is a remarkably difficult task.

Instead, female forms of abuse and objectification are subtle and can hide behind compassion, empathy, and other virtuous character traits. Like all human pathologies, perverse forms of female relational dynamics have existed as long as people have walked the earth. Yet, in modern times, any discussion of corrupted feminine traits is taboo and readily erased by vilifying victims' voices as "anti-woman" or "misogynistic."

Examples of this erasure often emerge in the shadows, through admissions too honest to publicly speak. One of the many conversations I had with an avid pro-choice woman reveals one of the ways in which women justify the objectification of their offspring.

In the safety of solitude, a friend discussed her genuine motivations from transitioning from a pro-life to pro-choice stance in her early collegiate years. She admitted her socially sanitized talking points masked a desire for easy access to temporal bodily pleasure and control.

After having unprotected sex and becoming fearful of an unplanned pregnancy, she knew abortion had to be available as an option to avoid the destruction of her life's ambition. A baby would have "ruined" her plans, and giving up sex wasn't realistic because doing so would make her "miserable." She converted to a pro-choice belief out of a desire for absolute control, not compassion. Behind the slogans and emotionally sensationalized stories of sexual violence are darker, but quintessentially human, motivations for supporting abortion. I could not help but immediately recognize how she justified her moral position out of a desire for pleasure and control, the same desires that lurk behind the male motivation to rape.

This is because abortion is the female manifestation of objectification. Men of sufficiently weak character see the female body as a vehicle through which they may achieve pleasure. Female objectivation sees the fetus—a body they voluntarily created—as cannon fodder in the gender wars. My friend's logic was brutal, but a rational expression of this reality. In her quest to build the life she desired, the body of another human being was disposable to guarantee her access to as many twenty-second orgasms as she desired. Bringing indiscriminate pleasure to her own body was worth the degradation of a human being she knowingly created.

Under the veil of "bodily autonomy" lies the dark proclamation "my bodily pleasure is worth the destruction of human bodies I create." The only differences between the male motivation to rape and the female justification of elective abortion on demand are the objects of degradation and social support. Rape has never been codified as a right, while abortion is the foundation of the modern woman's perception of her personhood.

CHAPTER 8
Love

IS LOVE A LIE?

I struggled to conceive of love's existence through experience or tangible evidence. Instead, these forms of reality taught me the opposite was true. Although my skepticism of love's existence was theoretical, this doubt derived from my experience with the two women who claimed to love me the most: my mother and older sister.

My mother's hate-based relational behavior was clear, my sister's more complex. Growing up without the possibility of external friendship meant sibling relationships were more costly. Without another source of human connection, these relationships became a battleground for obtaining the bare necessities of emotional support and human attachment.

The social hierarchy of my family conferred status and power based primarily on the traits of gender and age. My mother favored boys and allowed my older siblings to utilize the superior strength and mental abilities of age against weaker family members. Of the two traits, age was more important because an older sister could outfox a younger brother. However, such distinctions made no difference to me, because as the youngest female, there was no one beneath me in the familial pecking order.

My siblings, particularly those close in age, used this lowly status against me. Thus, this relational ecosystem meant that growing up required constantly trading my dignity for affection. Sometimes trade-offs were simple and relatively painless, like laughing at a silly, self-deprecating joke to build relational rapport. Other times, it necessitated internalizing cruelty in exchange for access to community.

"Leslie is ugly and stupid," represented the normal sibling cruelty most people experience, but messages about my unworthiness took a darker turn, encouraged by the verbiage commonly used by my mother, most notably the descriptor "half-aborted."

"You're worse than an animal," one brother said. "Animals can be pets that make people happy. You are just a burden. The family would be better off without you, and if you died, no one would miss you."

My reactions to these verbal attacks varied, but fighting back came at a heavy cost because my position in the family hierarchy guaranteed a negative outcome. The best result was a verbal conflict that escalated until I could no longer handle the emotional torment, at which point I would escape the room to cry. Unfortunately, sometimes my tears were overheard, causing my mother to take me aside for comfort.

"Leslie, they are just trying to get a rise out of you," she would say. "You can't take it personally."

Angered by the injustice, I responded, "Why don't you ever talk to them? I didn't start the fight. You don't care, you never tell them to stop!"

"If I told them to stop, you wouldn't have an opportunity to learn," she said. "When people try to hurt you, you can either grow resentful or become stronger. Don't you want to be strong? The more pain you feel—particularly if it is not deserved—the closer you will be to God. Jesus deserved none of the suffering he felt, yet he never lashed out, he certainly didn't cry. Don't you want to be more like Jesus?"

What began as anger moved to uncontrollable rage, "No!" I cried. "I don't want to be weak like Jesus. I want to fight back!"

This, I learned, was the wrong response. Mom's face swiftly turned to face mine. She grabbed me by the shoulders and fiercely shook my body.

"Blasphemy!" she yelled. Her eyes gripped mine, her voice was cold, and her body stiff. She shook me again.

"You do not speak of Jesus, the Son of God, as weak!"

In an instant, her eyes changed from anger to ridicule, and soon her words followed. In a voice dripping with mockery, she reminded me of my worth.

"You know who *is* weak? A little girl who cries and whines when their brothers tease her. She is weak. God gave you the gift of brothers and you reject it! I prayed for brothers and never had any. You don't deserve the life you have been given."

I wriggled my body to try to escape, but she held me tighter. "Let me go!" I screamed, but my cries were in vain.

"No," she said. Her voice had transformed once again. She no longer spoke with ridicule, now opting to express love. "Momma loves her Leslie," she said, moving my thrashing head to force eye contact. "Momma wants Leslie to grow up strong and strength doesn't come through crying and whimpering about trivial things. The boys will always tease you, and if you respond they will only tease you more. You must learn not to respond."

Desperate to escape as quickly as possible, I held back tears and feigned a smile. Despite my physical protestation, Mom had moved me into her lap. My small eight-year-old frame was no match for an adult.

"Now," she said, "let's pray."

Mom prayed. I cursed.

Over the years, I learned to avoid crying at all costs. When crying was necessary, I found private places to shed tears. Unfortunately, I had many run-ins with Mom's "comfort" before this skill was fully developed. Eventually, I became accustomed to the regularity of abuse, until only the most vicious, relentless verbal terror campaigns were able to elicit tears.

However, I soon learned that friends—not foes—should be more deeply feared. My brothers' attacks were mean, but overt and predictable. The pattern was consistent, and they used the same source material to shame me. These attacks were humiliating, demeaning, and insulting, but it came from enemy fire. Of course, I would have preferred to live with friends, but adversaries were impossible to avoid.

By contrast, my sister was ostensibly my friend. When my brothers attacked me, she gave genuine comfort, and when my mother berated me, she hugged me afterward, saying, "That isn't fair." For years, I never questioned her loyalty, until the day I learned love is limited by self-interest.

While playing, we got into a minor dispute over food preferences, landing on opposite sides of belief on whether lasagna is palatable. My sister put forth her best arguments in favor of lasagna, but I was unpersuaded. The taste of ricotta cheese, I contended, was unsavory at best, and repulsive at worst. I would sooner go hungry than chew and swallow lasagna.

After several hours of passionate arguing, I began to sense our dispute ran far deeper than mere food preferences. The fight moved from a petty squabble to all-out war, with both of us blaming the other for starting the unnecessary spat. Neither party was willing to back down. We instead chose to intentionally push each other to greater anger until my sister pulled rank.

At this point we were close to one another, passionately screaming, when she pushed me against the wall of the bedroom closet and held my wrists against the wall.

"Apologize now!" she cried.

"No," I said, "I didn't do anything wrong."

She let go of my arm, but the fight was not over.

I heard her stern, calm voice: "If you don't apologize, I will never play with you again. I will gang up on you with [our brothers]. You will be completely alone and no one will ever love you."

The illusion of love shattered.

I tried to protest. "You don't mean that," I said, and waited for her reply, but received none. After several minutes, she spoke. "I won't talk to you again until you apologize," she said before walking away.

How long she refused to speak to me is lost to time, but, to my eight-year-old mind, I refrained from apologizing for as long as I could. During this period, I mulled over my options. I checked a calendar, counting the years until college.

"*Ten*." I tried to conceptualize what it would be like to live without a friend for such a long time. "*That is longer than I have been alive*." Another voice spoke within me: "*But, Leslie, if you apologize, you won't* really *have a friend, just a fake playmate.*"

I sat in my closet, crying behind the dresses, before I came to my senses. "*Stop! You can't cry for long. Dry your tears before someone finds you.*" Outwardly, I pulled myself together, still wrestling with my decision. "*Whether I apologize or not, I won't have a friend. But, if I do what she wants, I can at least pretend to have a friend.*" The pretense of friendship, I determined, was worth the price of shame.

So, I swallowed my pride and apologized, only vaguely aware that my dignity was not the only victim. As I buried my self-respect, I laid to rest my naive, childish belief in unconditional love.

LORD OF LOVE

The phrase "God loves you" is intended to evoke positive emotion. However, to those who do not believe in God, it is perceived as condescending, naive, even offensive. To those agnostic toward belief in God *and* love, the phrase is absurd.

Prior to adopting a worldview, I was one such agnostic. My personal experiences made me suspicious of persuasion techniques rooted in emotional appeals to values based on affection, care, and love. Though this suspicion would not prove justified in all situations, it did equip me to see the hollowness in some popular but nondescript claims about love.

"LOVE IS LOVE" IS INHERENTLY MEANINGLESS

I grew up in the early 2000s, when the LGBTQ fight to legalize gay marriage was a movement rapidly advancing. I knew it was a hot-button issue in policy and culture, but remained perplexed by the movement's slogan, "Love is love." I was familiar with supporters of marriage equality using the tautology to call the public's attention to the moral superiority of those who placed love above religious conviction. To say nothing of the merits of the cause itself, the phrase "love is love" implies that "good people" believe homosexual relationships are self-evidently valid expressions of romantic and sexual affection, no argument required.

The substantively shallow phrase is nevertheless brilliant marketing. Rather than focusing on *why* the definition of love should change, it appeals to innate emotions most people feel, but never question. The phrase assumes three things. First, that the listener believes in love. Second—based on the context of the debate—that the listener believes love can be subjectively defined. Lastly, that the listener places love at the top of his values hierarchy.

I was confused by these assumptions because many of the same people who rejected a belief in God as illogical uncritically accepted a belief in love. Both are unfalsifiable claims, but the evidentiary standards applied to validate these claims are radically different. While God is questioned, love is assumed, despite centuries of human brutality undermining its existence.

I did not share the commitment to a belief in love presumed by the slogan. As an agnostic, I was unsure of my belief in God, and the same held true for my belief in all forms of relational love. The claim that human beings share love between one another is unprovable, and the external actions used as evidence of love's existence are, at best, ambiguous. What many believe to be the expression of love could just as easily be nothing more than a strategic attempt to use others' emotions to advance one's own self-interest.

At the crux of the love problem is the inherently mysterious nature of people.

Understanding human motivations is no easy task, and people routinely present a different version of themselves to the world than they do to themselves. Even without intentional acts of deceit, people cannot easily parse reality from fiction, especially in relationships. An episode of *The Twilight Zone* shows the absurdity of believing human beings can easily engage in honest relationships. Hector Poole, a bank employee, obtains the ability to read minds for one afternoon. Poole quickly learns the dissonance between people's internal and external presentation, and his own attempts at accurately interpreting others' thoughts leads to mixed results. When he reads the thoughts of a long-time employee too literally, Poole falsely accuses his colleague of plotting to rob the bank.

To understand oneself is hard enough; to believe people truly love one another despite the complexities of human relationships sound naive. This is why I was puzzled by the secular embrace of love and the use of this subjective value to change public policy. If error-ridden human relationships are all that exist, then would it not make sense to abandon the fairy tale of love in favor of realistic, transactionally rooted relationships? Would it not be more persuasive to state gay people should be able to marry simply because they want to? Why appeal to "love" at all?

WHY APPEAL TO LOVE?

Perhaps the movement appealed to love because, unlike God, love is universally revered. Christians and seculars alike claim to worship love, making it important enough to fight a culture war over its proper definition.

Understanding how to navigate this culture war through the application of the Christian definition of love is frequently discussed in Christian circles. During my youth, I watched Christians contemplate how to express their beliefs about love in a manner that could minimize offense to individuals with conflicting worldviews.

Among the most frequent moral dilemmas discussed regarding attempts to redefine love through legalizing gay marriage is how to ethically approach an invitation to a close friend or family member's gay wedding or civil ceremony. One specific conversation, spoken over coffee in the church lobby, showed the structural similarity between the Christian and secular arguments.

In most church settings, discussion participants operate from a set of shared assumptions. This generally includes a commitment to similar views on sexuality, including a heterosexual definition of marriage and the rejection of premarital sex as sinful. However, this conversation was unique because one participant was secular, the other a devout Christian.

To the secular, the answer was obvious. Christians, he argued, should place their religious beliefs regarding the morality of homosexuality aside and attend the wedding to show support, compassion, and *love* to their friend or family member. Love, he argued, should come before religious conviction. The Christian dissented, stating it was neither loving nor supportive to celebrate actions—in this case homosexual sex acts—that draw people away from God. Instead, he argued that love requires abstaining from celebration by refusing to attend the wedding.

They argued passionately for their views, but spoke past one another. Neither walked away with a better understanding of his opponent's view, and both failed to see how their fundamental difference had nothing to do with homosexuality and everything to do with their definition of love, and, by proxy, God. Both treated their definition of love as absolute, revealing a belief in love as the highest good. Functionally, the religious man said, "God is love, and God defines sexual love as between a man and a woman, therefore it is not good, or loving, to participate in gay weddings because they violate God's love," and the secular implicitly replied with "Love is God, and God is man. Man has determined all sexual unions of two persons, regardless of gender, are valid expressions of human love, therefore the good, loving man celebrates gay marriage because it is an expression of love."

To the Christian, God embodies love, and through this provides a complete and perfect definition of the word. In the secular worldview, love is both fluid and fixed. Individuals and people can define love differently, which is why a more diverse range of romantic arrangements are celebrated. However, the definition is also fixed because those who fail to recognize the validity of a relationship involving consenting adults are fiercely condemned.

Although the arguments are structurally similar, they are not equally strong. The Christian argument could be wrong, but it is coherent. If God created the world and all that it is, he has the just authority to define the boundaries of human love. Of course, if Christianity *itself* is wrong, then this conception of God—and love—crumbles. However, the secular argument rests on a weak foundation. Why does the secular reject God, but accept a belief in the unfalsifiable concept of love? And how do secular people decide where to place boundaries around their definition of love: Why, for instance, do most secular people still maintain that sexual love is only valid when it exists between two people? I wondered if the Mormons, well-known for their traditional practice of polygamy, would consider the prevailing secular definition as senselessly narrow.

Regardless, even if love does exist and is accurately defined by the secularist, why should the Christian bow before a type and character of love he rejects by affirming relationships he believes to be harmful to the participants? Indeed, why would a gay couple want guests to participate begrudgingly? Would it not be preferable for conscientious objectors to be encouraged to peacefully abstain to uphold the virtue of honesty?

INTOLERANCE AS LIBERATION

"Tolerance" is a doctrinal word in modern culture's religion. Those who embody tolerance are seen as good, while the intolerant are scorned. Damned is the man who "hates," and honored is the man who "loves."

This transcends disputes over gay marriage, and instead represents the fundamental orientation of leftwing beliefs. Those who self-identify as "progressive" see themselves as loving, tolerant, kind, and compassionate.

The faithful signal their religious zeal through typical methods. Just as a "Jesus Saves" or "Faith Lives Here" sign resides in the homes of Christian commoners, so to the followers of various secular creeds express their devotion with decor stating "Hate Has No Home Here," or "In This House We Believe…". The beliefs that follow take the reader through the scenic route of leftist thought, touching on politically charged topics ranging from Black Lives Matter and women's rights to LGBTQ advocacy, to the extent to which the layman should trust scientific experts. Spoiler alert: Skepticism of scientists is decidedly *not* welcome in these homes.

At its core, a belief in one's own "goodness" can create a similar form of self-righteousness often associated with religious conceit.

Devout followers of religion are familiar with this critique. Christians are routinely chided by the broader culture for their inability to empathize with "out groups." This was displayed in the conversation I observed as a youth. The man who demanded the Christian place affirmation above religious conviction appealed to love and empathy. Who is harmed by the Christian's attendance at a gay wedding? Ironically, the secular spoke as a pot does to a kettle. Had he taken time to empathize with the Christian, the possible harm would have been self-evident. Engaging in actions contrary to one's internal beliefs is precisely what causes people to suffer from the pain of a guilty conscience.

After enjoying decades of moral authority, leftwing conceptions are running into the same problems religious adherents have faced for centuries. The progressive worldview may claim to welcome dissidents, but it creates as many out-groups as it resolves. This is because inclusion *requires* exclusion, and the most influential leftists have always understood this truth.

Herbert Marcuse, one of the most influential left-leaning scholars of the twentieth century, advanced the idea of "liberating tolerance."[160] To liberate oppressed minorities, he argued for the strategic use of intolerance as a mechanism of advocacy. This means "intolerance against movements from the Right and toleration of movements from the Left." Putting Marcusean values into practice represses speech because intolerance against the right should be shown "before the deed, at the stage of communication in word, print, and picture."

Marcuse understood his values involved eviscerating civil rights. He argued this was necessary to avoid the worst forms of right-wing ideas by first contemplating whether the Nazi movement would have been effectively quashed by banning speech related to its campaign. After laying a foundation for what he hopes to prevent, Marcuse posits a post-fascist world is inherently dangerous, and the extremity of this danger justifies destroying constitutional rights to advance the interests of oppressed minorities.

Tolerance, Marcuse says, is perverted when it protects a repressive society by preventing men from conceiving of a better world. This perversion creates a false consciousness in people's minds by preventing them from seeing the abuse they experience. Because this perversion is created in the mind, so too is the cure. The antidote to the corruption of individual consciousness is "censorship, even precensorship," that can "break through" false consciousness to emancipate the mental captives.

---

[160] Marcuse, Herbert. "Repressive Tolerance (Full Text)." Herbert Marcuse, November 2, 2015. https://www.marcuse.org/herbert/publications/1960s/1965-repressive-tolerance-fulltext.html.

Marcuse died in 1979, but his ideas transcend the grave and provide necessary context in understanding the vitriolic nature of many self-described "tolerant" leftists. While Marcuse's name may be obscure, his beliefs had an enormous impact on academics, and millions have absorbed his ideas through cultural osmosis.

FIGHTING IMAGINED ENEMIES

The progressive tendency toward censorship is becoming a cliché, but it has dire consequences that are increasingly self-evident to the general public. Despite enjoying a favorable cultural landscape for decades, the same ideas never retain broad social favor forever. All worldviews have a shelf-life, and progressive ideas are no exception.

Like all worldview adherents, progressives are lashing out as their worldview moves from cultural dominance to one of many equally valid options. The pending death of progressive moral superiority is inseparable from the rise and strength of Trump's political career. From the moment Trump announced his presidency, the left has reviled him. However, among the wide array of insults levied against him, the narrative that he is a Nazi comparable to Adolf Hitler has been among the most consistent progressive talking points.

This created dissonance within the progressive worldview. Traditionally, progressives are known for humanizing social villains by advocating conservatives understand how the conditions of injustice, rather than character, give rise to evil. Yet, over the past decade, the most devout leftists have *created* a villain and declared themselves worthy of condemning both the object of their imagination and his supporters.

Whatever Trump is, a Nazi he most certainly is not. To even make such a comparison is to cheapen the gravity of the rise of the Third Reich and the Holocaust left in its wake. Before turning to politics, Trump was wildly famous, and popular among those who now view him as Satan in human form. He was a real estate mogul, and the host of the popular TV series, *The Apprentice*. He was known for being blunt, crass, and, in many ways, unlikeable. His tagline was "You're fired," hardly the catchphrase of a man prone to kindness, and his numerous marriages and divorces hardly indicated a commitment to traditional sexual values.

Although much ink has been spilled analyzing why Evangelical Christians remained committed to the presidency of a man lacking in Christian virtues, the reasons are remarkably simple. Evangelicals, like the other members of Trump's diverse coalition, want a seat at the table and they believe the left's hatred of them will preclude that possibility.

Whether a Christian's commitment to voting MAGA is hypocritical theologically is another matter that depends on a wide array of factors unrelated to this analysis. However, the political practicality is obvious, and indicative of how far left the nation has already moved. Trump's politics are neither traditionally Republican nor conservative. Indeed, there is no mainstream conservative political movement in the United States, at least not by traditional definitions. There are, no doubt, conservatives, and the political philosophy of the movement lives on, but it is well understood that traditionally conservative values are politically unpalatable. Thus, those who adhere to such values are naturally going to gravitate to the political movement that maximizes their ability to impact culture, law, and policy.

Conservative now simply means "non-leftist" or perhaps "anti-progressive." This is because cultural meaning is still being defined according to progressive values, and the consequence of failing a progressive purity test is being labeled "conservative," even if the individual in question has little—or no—commitment to traditionally conservative beliefs. Despite being able to put most of reality, including immutable characteristics like sex, on an imagined "spectrum," progressives are terrible at contextualizing political, philosophical, and religious beliefs in a similar manner.

Because this strips people of their complexity, it guarantees the purity tests moderate democrats and leftists decry. Rather than recognizing the people will come to different conclusions on various issues related to numerous political and cultural issues, those on the left assume that compassion has a set definition that they created. Thus, those who fail to adhere to their version of compassion become enemies. Women who do not support abortion are "internalized misogynists," lesbians or gays who reject the left's vision of transgender rights are traitors to the LGBTQ movement, and so on.

LIVING OUT LOVE IN A PLURALISTIC SOCIETY

The broken discourse surrounding the definition of love begs an answer to the following question: If love is a concept in crisis, is it worth salvaging?

Under some philosophic systems, the answer would be no. Ayn Rand, for example, would prefer to elevate selfishness from vice to virtue while tossing sacrificial love aside.[161] However, love need not involve trading honesty for political correctness, or coercing others to abide by religious ethics they do not hold.

What it *does* require is honesty, even if expressing that honesty means speaking in a way that offends, irritates, or annoys. The simplest definition of Christian love is a "desire to act in someone else's best interest." Christ did not die on the cross because He was a masochist. His prayer in Gethsemane shows a desire to avoid the excruciating pain of crucifixion. Rather, Christ sacrificed Himself for the best interest of those He *voluntarily* served.

Men and women, being mere mortals, are not capable of shouldering the sin of the entire world; no one is capable of acting in *everyone's* best interest. This is why pleas for "inclusion" miss the mark. Individuals are limited in their capacity to and receive compassion, mercy, and grace. Criticizing someone for failing to include everyone is limited because "everyone's" interests cannot be adequately considered by anyone who is not God. The mere mortals walking the Earth today are not Jesus, and attempting to force mutually exclusive cultures into coexistence is often a recipe for creating conflict, animosity, and chaos.

However, refocusing love on operating in people's best interest allows individuals to clearly align their values and actions, maximizing the compassion they have to extend and receive, while giving them clarity on how to avoid harming those it may be best to avoid.

---

[161] "The Virtue of Selfishness 1964." Ayn Rand, accessed January 30, 2025. https://aynrand.org/novels/the-virtue-of-selfishness/?nab=0.

FREEDOM OF ASSOCIATION CREATES CLARITY AND SAFETY

Operating in someone's best interest does not mean agreeing with the beliefs about God, love, sexuality, or a host of other philosophical or political stances. Instead, it means respecting one another's decisions and clearly communicating our beliefs. This will undoubtedly create boundaries within relationships, with some relationships being inherently limited by numerous barriers of belief.

This, however, is desirable, for there is no virtue in a false pretense of relational intimacy that is built on a foundation of lies and obfuscation. Such an approach is intuitive and practical because it is often the underlying purpose of group formation. Christians meet weekly to worship God, study His word, and encourage one another in the faith. Secular humanists meet to discuss their worldview and ethics. Political parties organize to carry out an agenda based on shared beliefs. Even niche communities form based on shared philosophical assumptions. LGBTQ ally groups on campuses form under the assumption that all members affirm the validity of same-sex relationships.

People should not feel obligated to "include" individuals into their groups when those individuals bring hostility to their deeply held convictions. Tearing down boundaries does not necessarily create connection; instead, it can foster fear. When people feel pressured to pretend as if they accept beliefs they do not hold, they erode their own convictions, live out a lie, and inevitably fail to fully include those whose beliefs do not align with their values.

An overlooked aspect of freedom of speech is the ability to associate without undue interference. As with all constitutional rights, the freedom to associate refers to living without undue restrictions from the government. However, *cultures* that embrace this value reap its benefits.

Applying this to the question of gay weddings, for example, creates clarity and encourages mutual respect. The issue should be approached in a manner similar to the secular interaction with religion. When an atheist is invited to church, he is not *expected* to attend a service based on ideas he believes to be untrue and, if he chooses to observe a church service, he is advised not to take communion. The same boundaries can easily govern religious observation and/or participation in homosexual weddings. Like some atheists, certain religious people may feel deeply uncomfortable attending a gay wedding. These people should be left alone. Those who do attend may observe, but carefully avoid the appearance of active participation. Once again, just as an atheist would feel put off by indignation at his refusal of the eucharist, these individuals should not be pressured to engage in behavior that violates their conscience.

EMBRACING OFFENSE AS PART OF PLURALISM

The cost of pluralism is the acceptance of routine offense. Pluralistic societies have numerous, conflicting cultures living within their borders and, when different ethnicities, religions, and philosophies share close geographic proximity, it is inevitable that individuals will offend one another. This is because, as beliefs vary, so do values, and if there are more values to consider when speaking, there are more opportunities to cause offense.

Under current progressive norms, an enormous burden is placed on speakers that tells them to avoid offending *anyone*, minus heterosexual, Christian white men, of course. Political correctness and language policing are rampant on the left. Even after the Democrats' embarrassing loss to Trump in the 2024 election, a CNN commentator shouted down a co-panelist, claiming he was "transphobic" for referring to disputes over sports eligibility as involving "boys playing in girls' sports."[162]

Culture now faces a difficult, and dangerous, predicament. The US is facing the edges of tolerance on a host of contentious issues. Pluralism can only go so far, and the absence of *any* shared values within a nation are destructive. Our nation is learning this in real time as political wars over so-called gender affirming care and abortion rage on. Is it abuse or health care for a woman to kill her offspring? Is it abuse or health care for a parent, under the guidance of a medical professional, to give her physically developmentally healthy eleven-year-old boy hormones to prevent puberty?

No amount of tolerance can solve these problems. States may differ in their approach, but legally speaking, pluralism has hard limits. However, social relationships are not legislative chambers, and most people have no direct control over state or federal statutes.

---

162 Hains, Tim. "CNN Panelist: I'm Not Going to Listen to Transphobia, Saying Boys Are Playing Girls Sports Is a 'Slur.'" Real Clear Politics, November 10, 2024. https://www.realclearpolitics.com/video/2024/11/10/cnn_panelist_im_not_going_to_listen_to_transphobia_saying_boys_are_playing_girels_sports_is_a_slur.html.

Individuals can better live with one another—even if they lose legally—by accepting deep philosophical differences of opinion as a default. Assuming a stranger may cause offense frees people to focus on engaging with ideas rather than petty squabbles over terms, like civility, that are impossible to universally define. It also allows for the opportunity to disengage before relational entanglements take hold. There are millions of people in this country, each with unique experiences and philosophic and religious convictions contrary to their own. Some with differing opinions can productively connect, others mix like oil and water.

In a pluralistic system, it is wise to allow people with divergent views or differing personalities the opportunity to easily disengage with unproductive and explosive social situations. Thus, one of the easiest ways to dial down the temperature in a heated cultural moment is to allow people to quickly observe and determine whether another individual—or group—is an appropriate fit for social engagement. This goal is frustrated by an attempt to prevent the articulation of ideas, beliefs, or viewpoints that cause offense.

FIRST, DO NO HARM

Lastly, pluralistic societies should also adopt a relational ethic akin to the Hippocratic Oath: First, do no harm. This can only be achieved in a culture that embraces freedom of association and offensive speech. In such a society, people should use their freedom responsibly by following the ethic "First, do no harm." By analyzing their speech and expression through this lens, individuals are effectively asking, "Am I intending to harm someone through my expression?" This is distinct from "Am I saying something offensive?" Suggesting white people are inherently racist, for example, is offensive to some, but it may well be communicated out of a genuine desire to spread a belief someone believes to be true. A harm-based analysis accounts for the reality that offense does not necessarily equal harm.

In the medical context from which the Hippocratic Oath emerged, this is acknowledged. Doctors do not refuse to tell their patients when they develop cancer, even though the diagnosis will undoubtedly cause grave mental distress. When someone communicates what they believe to be true, society should categorize this expression as "not harmful."

Instead, harm should be narrowly defined, and viewed (socially, not legally) as a direct attempt to provoke. A simple and practical way to implement such a principle would encourage disengaging from unproductive dialogue.

Take one of the most heated disputes in culture, the trans debate. According to some activists, failing to call an individual by preferred pronouns is a form of harassment. Others view this differently, with some contending it is a form of compelled speech to force some people to pretend as if gender is a mutable characteristic. If neither party is willing to compromise—and it appears they are not—they should be encouraged to separate. No one is served by trying to force one another to engage in forms of blasphemy against our own gods.

LIVING A LIFE OF LOVE

A personal example of these principles can help people—regardless of their philosophical definition of love—to express their values authentically to others.

In college, I routinely worked a variety of blue-collar customer service jobs to make ends meet. Most of these involved working in the food industry, including both Chipotle and Chick-fil-A. During my time working at these chains, disputes over the legalization of homosexual marriages was a major cultural flashpoint, and I worked alongside LGBTQ colleagues at both jobs.

While on a break with a coworker at Chipotle, the topic of politics came up. I knew my coworker was a lesbian and that we likely had vastly different philosophical beliefs and political predispositions. She expressed disappointment at the widespread cultural rejection of homosexuality in her hometown as well as Oklahoma generally, and I told her I understood why the social norms surrounding her would be frustrating for her to navigate.

She knew I was a Christian and asked me my views on gay relationships and marriages. I expressed hesitancy at answering her question.

Wanting to avoid either lying or unnecessarily offending her, I said, "Sarah,[163] I don't think you will like my perspective on these issues. Feel free to share your viewpoints, it won't bother me, but if this is going to upset you, I'd rather not talk about it."

She looked at me pleasantly surprised, before responding.

"No, it won't bother me, I'd really like to know what you think."

Internally hesitant, but always willing to take relational risks, I responded honestly.

"You know I am a Christian. This means I hold values in accordance with my understanding of Christian doctrines. I

[163] Name changed to protect this individual's privacy.

believe living out Christian values are best for both individuals and society as a whole.

"However, I don't expect other people to agree with me. Thus, my opinion on how people should live is not necessarily the same as what I would like to see codified into law. That being said, all laws are created based on a system of values that limits human action to some degree. The idea that people should not legislate their morality is naive, legislation does not exist in a moral vacuum."

I searched her face, waiting for signs of offense, wondering if she would report me to the manager for proselytizing. I knew sharing my opinion, even if done with no intention of conversion, was a major risk.

But she showed no signs of anger, and instead asked a follow-up question.

"Do you think gay marriage should be illegal?"

"Honestly, I'm not sure. I don't have a strong opinion regarding its legality. I understand the conservative case against legalizing gay marriage. However, there are a lot of problems that come with trying to change culture through the use of law. And culture is simply not conservative."

Sarah remained intrigued. "Don't you think it is judgmental to define marriage so narrowly? I can't imagine God would make someone gay if it wasn't good."

"I understand why you would think that way, but I don't think whether a definition is narrow is what makes it good or bad. Judgment isn't a dirty word. All morality is based on judgments, no one never judges others. Of course, people can judge inappropriately or be too harsh, that happens all the time. I'm sure you have run into Christians who are like that, which is unfortunate. As to why God would make someone gay if it isn't good? I have no idea, but I believe it is somewhat irrelevant. God allows people to face thousands of various types of struggles in life for reasons no one will ever be able to explain.

But, for what it's worth, I do think the conservative movement can be too quick to ignore experiences. Ultimately, I have no idea what I would believe if I were a lesbian. However, by the same token, those on the left don't know what they would believe if they lived the lives of conservatives. At some level, everyone ends up making value judgments and then living accordingly. No one is above judgment, or prejudice, people just approach issues from different perspectives, and that changes the flavor of their prejudice."

After this, the conversation trailed off in another direction, Sarah told me about her new girlfriend, we laughed at the annoyance of customers coming in just prior to closing, and I talked to her about how excited I was to get married the next spring. As we were getting up to go back to work, she looked at me and said, "You know, Leslie, I like you. You're too religious for me and I don't agree with you at all, but you're not like the Christians I've met. You're just a regular person."

I laughed and returned the favor. "I like you too, thanks for chatting, and just know that even though we disagree I don't look at you as anything other than a normal human being. I don't expect you to live out values you don't believe in."

We returned to work. I was never reported and our working relationship was unaffected by our lunch conversation.

When I think back to this conversation, I am struck by how much riskier this would have been today than it was in 2013, and how many more cultural flashpoints there are for people to worry about. From Trump to trans politics and everything in between, *talking* across divisions of belief are increasingly rare because they come with enormous risks.

However, this need not be the case. Politics is, and always has been, personal, and never has the political become more personal. This is particularly true in a culture where one side of the political aisle defines their politics as the only correct way to act out love and compassion. Yet, ultimately, love is not embodied in political action but in human relationships, and whether one wins or loses the culture war, we will all be faced with living with others, including those with deep political and philosophical differences.

Living together peacefully will require that we abandon the idea that love is synonymous with affirmation of someone's beliefs, choices, or viewpoints as "good." Neither I nor my coworker affirmed one another's beliefs or choices; instead, we understood our perspectives were lightyears apart. Additionally, it was self-evident that our voting patterns, and thus the policies we would like to see enacted in law, did not align. Still, neither of us attempted to convert the other. We both recognized that such an endeavor was useless and unproductive.

In short, to live in love, we must revive the connection between honesty and compassion. Dancing around our beliefs is neither compassionate nor kind, and love is, at its core, inseparable from the truth.

CHAPTER 9
Vengeance

THE RISKS OF REVENGE

"Vengeance is mine, I will repay, says the Lord."[164] This singular verse stood as an invisible demarcation line between myself and God. Regardless of the number of times I read Romans 12 or its cross reference, Deuteronomy 32,[165] my position remained the same. "*No!*" I responded, "*I will create my own vengeance.*"

By ten years old, my patience with God—who appeared to be either apathetic or impotent—had worn thin. After years of oscillating between prayer and indignation, justice was clearly not coming from above. Without a friend to fight on my behalf, I saw myself as the only person available to avenge my suffering, and,

---

[164] Romans 12:19 (ESV) *The Holy Bible: English Standard Version.* Wheaton, IL: Crossway, 2016.

[165] Deuteronomy 32:35 (ESV) *The Holy Bible: English Standard Version.* Wheaton, IL: Crossway, 2016.

like a Santa Claus of death, I had an internal checklist memorializing those I wanted to kill.

Yet, even the most righteously angry ten-year-old is nothing more than a child. Practically speaking, I had no idea how to enact vengeance.

At this age, anger at my predicament clouded my mind. Rage, not rationality, was all I could understand. This soon changed.

Although love was not the basis of familial life, sibling play and banter were not universally negative. Instead, they were infused with unspoken rules and expectations, created through thousands of iterative interactions. While communal activities were at times positive, they always had the possibility of volatility, and when things exploded, I knew I was going to be at the bottom.

One day, my sister, brother, and I were goofing around like typical children, playing with a voice recorder. This device, archaic by modern technological standards, used a cassette tape. For reasons that elude memory, my sister begged my brother to promise he would not listen to a portion of the recording, and he obliged. Unfortunately, the oral promise of teenage boys should not be trusted, and he quickly reneged, a fact I knew by listening at his bedroom door, determined to prove myself right. After all, I had warned my sister against making a deal with the devil.

Upon gathering proof of my superior reasoning, I proudly marched to the bedroom I shared with my sister to inform her how clever I was, but this soon led to a cascade of unintended consequences. Rather than responding by praising my instinct toward distrust, my sister became angry, demanding how I knew of my brother's malfeasance.

I thought explaining might chill the situation, but this assumption was soon disproven. After listening to me describe hearing the recording through my brother's bedroom door, she stormed down the hallway and into his room, screaming. This, predictably, started an argument. As the dispute crescendoed, my sister approached my brother and hit him on the top of the head. Now, the fight had moved from verbal to physical. Until this moment, my sister had expressed fury while my brother's tone indicated playful banter. She was angry, and he was happy to have provoked her.

After being struck, his demeanor turned. He lunged forward from a seated position, grabbed my sister by the throat, pushed her out of his bedroom and into the hallway, and pressed her back against a closet door.

His eyes were red, his nose puffed with rage, and he maintained an iron grip. She struggled to free herself, but he only asserted more dominance by grabbing her left hand and pinning it to the wall. He spoke, but I could only make out some of them, the last of which was a short, simple command, "Never hit me again." After this final sentence, he released her and returned to his bedroom while my sister collapsed to the ground.

I walked toward her and saw her face was filled with fear. With wide eyes, she walked back to our bedroom. She rebuffed my attempts to fully discuss the incident, only speaking of it in passing and quickly changing the subject each time I tried to engage her.

While the event was short in duration and resulted in no physical injuries, it replayed in my mind often, as I tried to understand its meaning. The interaction itself was disproportionate on both ends. Neither the offense of listening to the recording or the smack on the head warranted its response. After months of rumination, my best interpretation told me my siblings' immediate overreaction was connected to the deeper suffering nurtured in the home.

I was at the bottom of the familial totem pole, but I was wise enough to know that, in relation to most children in society, my siblings existed in one of the lowest social classes: isolated homeschoolers. While other children socialized with friends, we were, to use a familial term of art, "ratholed," meaning we weren't allowed to associate with other children outside the family. The damaging effects of this isolation was universally acknowledged among myself and my siblings.

Still, my brother's violent reaction, even if born from the pain of forced social rejection, was simultaneously confusing and illuminating. Although unlucky among society's children, he was treated with favor in my family. Of the seven children, he was my father's favorite, and this favoritism came with perks. He was the only child allowed to work, date, and establish semi-consistent friendships prior to college. This incident occurred before those milestones, but my parents' propensity to bend the rules for him was already well established. I knew this because they were swift to praise him and slow to punish.

I knew my brother was aware of this status, making his violent reaction to my sister low risk. Taking anger out on her was unlikely to cause him any trouble, especially if he left no visual evidence of his assault.

"*He made his own vengeance,*" I mused, "*but he targeted the wrong person. She didn't lock him in the prison of childhood. Mom and Dad did.*"

After this moment of clarity, I began to question my hit list. Power, it seemed, was easy to abuse and the desire to avenge pain was not easily channeled to target the person, or people, directly responsible for a person's suffering.

VENGEANCE AS PSYCHOLOGICAL WARFARE

My mother was an expert at emotional manipulation, and pitting her children against one another was a critical aspect of maintaining her power. When we fought among ourselves, we weren't fighting against her. Yet this strategy is not limited to broken, dysfunctional families. It is among the most powerful forms of psychological abuse represented in politics and culture. Despite its dangers, misdirected vengeance is useful, both as a mechanism to enrich power, and as a tool victims wield in a feeble attempt to secure long-denied justice.

Political movements, composed of thousands of individuals, are driven by human passion. Justice and peace are the ideals they claim to strive for, but vengeance, envy, and other darker desires often reside at the heart of them, past and present. The Democratic Party, for instance, roots itself in identity politics, which leverages vengeance to further a distorted form of justice, one that seeks to right wrongs based on the status of the marginalized rather than principles of equality under the law.

VICTIMHOOD AS VIRTUE

The hero's journey is the most compelling narrative arc in literature because it gives humanity an ideal to which each person can strive. Diversity in experience between characters does not negate the principles of goodness that they uphold. Tolkien's *The Lord of the Rings* is a superb example of numerous heroes' stories told concurrently, and the diverse array of characters fighting to uphold goodness, truth, and beauty add depth to his work. While seeking to destroy the One Ring is the practical element uniting the characters' journeys, their philosophical unity is found in a commitment to principles and conviction in spite of pain. Each character is dealt a heavy hand, none are blessed with an easy road. Of these, the hobbits stand out as unique. They abandon the heavenly Shire to set out on a journey with unknown pitfalls and no expectation of glory, riches, or rewards.

The beauty in this story comes from a once-common understanding of virtue and merit. There was a time when merit was associated with virtue: To possess virtue, an individual needed to display the ability to pursue goodness without an expectation of glory. Humanity's best attained their position by remaining steadfastly committed to the principles of justice even when under immense pressure. When the threat of sanctions is held over the head of a just man, he does not shrink. Instead, he continues in his pursuits because fear does not dissuade him. Goodness, in his eyes, is worth suffering.

Progressives redefined virtue, and in so doing transformed those who seek vengeance from sinners to saints.

In influential subsets of progressive culture, merit and virtue are connected to a person's *circumstances*, not their conduct.

Enduring pain and speaking of this endurance makes one worthy of praise, for it shows their ability to acknowledge the destructive forces of "bigotry" and "hatred." Thus, modern leftist heroes have one thing in common: the experience of pain—often specific to one's group identity—and a desire to seek retribution either for their own pain or for the suffering of their respective social class.

Because of the power reputation holds in the digital age, retribution can be sought through nothing more than raising one's voice. This is why Jussie Smollett could create a racist hoax out of thin air and receive almost no serious scrutiny from the mainstream press.[166] It is why, in the wake of merely accusing Brett Kavanaugh of sexual assault, Christine Blasey Ford was showered with prestigious accolades and awards. The truth of her story, which was dubious, paled in comparison to her symbolic power. Ford was placed on a short list for *Time* magazine's 2018 Person of the Year award,[167] invited to present *Sports Illustrated*'s Inspiration of the Year award,[168] nominated for the University of

---

[166] Williams, Ashley R., Megan Thomas, Sandra Gonzalez, and Lauren Mascarenhas. "Jussie Smollett's Conviction Overturned in Alleged Hate-Crime Hoax: How We Got Here and What's Next." CNN, November 23, 2024. https://www.cnn.com/2024/11/22/entertainment/jussie-smollett-conviction-overturned-whats-next/index.html.

[167] Halleman, Caroline. "Meghan Markle Is on the Shortlist for *Time*'s Person of the Year." *Town & Country*, December 10, 2018. https://www.townandcountrymag.com/society/tradition/a25456642/meghan-markle-shortlist-time-person-of-the-year-2018/.

[168] Boren, Cindy. "Christine Blasey Ford Presents SI 'Inspiration of the Year' Award to Rachael Denhollander." *The Washington Post*, December 12, 2018. https://www.washingtonpost.com/sports/2018/12/12/brett-kavanaughs-accuser-presents-sis-inspiration-year-award-larry-nassar-victim/.

North Carolina at Chapel Hill's Distinguished Alumna Award,[169] and received a Courage Award from the ACLU.[170] Their stories were assumed to be true, because virtue was imputed to them as a consequence of the immutable characteristics of their race and gender and because they claimed to have been wronged in ways sympathetic to progressive prejudices.

In 2019, Ford also received a feature story in *Time*'s annual list of one hundred most influential people in the world. She was nominated to *Time* 100 by none other than her home state senator, Kamala Harris.[171] Describing Ford in her review, Harris states Ford "risked everything to send a warning in a moment of grave consequence." I beg to differ. By 2019, the social incentive structure, particularly in elite spaces, richly rewarded victims speaking out when their stories called traditional values into question. While it was true that Ford's testimony would undoubtedly bring her criticism, the idea that a woman who lived in one of the most liberal areas of the country "risked everything" by accusing a white man of sexual crimes is a gross exaggeration. Indeed, it was far more courageous for Kavanaugh to vote his conscience in *Dobbs*. In the wake of this decision, he was relentlessly attacked

---

[169] Kelly, Caroline. "Christine Blasey Ford Nominated for UNC Distinguished Alumna." CNN Politics, October 10, 2018. https://www.cnn.com/2018/10/09/politics/ford-unc-distinguished-alumna-award/index.html.

[170] Johnson, Alex. "Kavanaugh Accuser Christine Blasey Ford Makes Rare Appearance to Accept Award." NBC News, November 18, 2019. https://www.nbcnews.com/news/us-news/kavanaugh-accuser-christine-blasey-ford-makes-rare-appearance-accept-award-n1084696.

[171] Harris, Kamala. "Christine Blasey Ford." *TIME*, accessed January 30, 2025. https://time.com/collection/100-most-influential-people-2019/5567675/christine-blasey-ford/.

by activists outside his home and nearly assassinated.[172] He awaits not his glowing feature stories and Courage Awards, for they will never materialize.

PAIN AS MERIT

The veneration of victims speaking and acting out of pain creates numerous perverse incentives in society because it elevates people based on a false premise. More pain does not necessarily equate to greater virtue, and accusations alone—even those that are controversial—do not reflect an individual's propensity to uphold truth or goodness. Additionally, it both glorifies and demonizes suffering. By granting glory based on the amount of pain a person has sustained, progressive culture encourages people to exaggerate or invent suffering to access social capital. On the other hand, suffering sustained by the historically marginalized is used as a mechanism to evade accountability. Since pain is difficult to bear, the vices of victims should be overlooked.

It is important to understand the conflation of pain and merit because the left is often criticized for abandoning merit in favor of diversity, equity, and inclusion. Pain is not, in fact, connected to an individual's qualifications for any given position of prestige or authority. However, part of the reason progressives are comfortable with identity politics is because they equate membership in marginalized groups with greater experiences of pain, and they

---

[172] Lybrand, Holmes, and Tierney Sneed. "FBI Says Man Accused of Attempting to Kill Brett Kavanaugh Said He Was 'Shooting for 3' Justices." CNN Politics, July 27, 2022. https://www.cnn.com/2022/07/27/politics/kavanaugh-roske-arrest-warrant/index.html.

believe these experiences of suffering infuse the sufferer with a greater capacity for truth and goodness.

Conflating pain with a higher base capacity for sound character, wisdom in discernment, and capability in governance has been a central theme in progressive advocacy for decades.

However, in recent years, the pretense of operating under prior definitions of virtue and merit has collapsed. Harris was selected as vice president, at least in part, *because* of her gender, so too was Supreme Court Justice Ketanji Jackson.[173] Criticism of this politicized pandering was met with accusations of bigotry.

When constitutional scholar Ilya Shapiro, for example, made the obvious observation that President Biden's commitment to nominating a black female undermined his ability to choose the most qualified candidate and guaranteed the tarnishing of his nominee's legacy, he was met with hostility by Georgetown Law. The law school stated Shapiro's commentary is "at odds with everything" the institution stands for and damages its culture of diversity, equity, and inclusion.[174] Shapiro was then placed on administrative leave before he eventually abandoned the university altogether.[175]

---

[173] Choi, Matthew. "Biden Vows to Select a Woman as His Running Mate." Politico, March 15, 2020. https://www.politico.com/news/2020/03/15/biden-woman-vice-president-131309.

[174] Cho, Aimee, and NBC Washington Staff. "New Georgetown Law Administrator on Leave after Supreme Court Tweet." NBC4 Washington, January 31, 2022. https://www.nbcwashington.com/news/local/new-georgetown-law-administrator-on-leave-after-supreme-court-tweet/2955413/.

[175] Hartocollis, Anemona. "A Conservative Quits Georgetown's Law School Amid Free Speech Fight." *The New York Times*, June 6, 2022. https://www.nytimes.com/2022/06/06/us/georgetown-ilya-shapiro.html.

In the progressive view, the pain victims feel not only entitles them to opportunities, but also exculpates them from accountability. After Harris lost in a landslide to President Trump in November 2024, commentators were quick to remind the public that racism and misogyny were material elements in Harris's defeat.[176] Her inability to answer questions profoundly important to the public was sidelined. The fact that she had no track record of broad public support was ignored, as was her inability to communicate on the issues more important to swing voters, such as the economy and immigration. Harris's defects as a candidate are invisible to progressives because holding historically marginalized victims accountable for their shortcomings is one of their cardinal sins.

One of the most obvious problems with the progressive view of pain is that it grossly stereotypes people and groups. While there are always intergenerational effects of marginalization, it is transparently false to equate race, gender, or ethnicity with systemic disadvantages. Ford's background is from an elite prep school. Justice Jackson is the daughter of an attorney and school principal. Her uncle was the police chief of the Miami Police Department. Harris was the daughter of university researchers. On a systemic level, the hardship these women faced pales in comparison to the difficulties shouldered by someone like J. D. Vance. But in the progressive system, individual hardships are

---

[176] Land, Olivia. "Fuming Joe Scarborough Blames Racism, Misogyny from Black and Hispanic Voters for Harris' Loss." *New York Post*, November 6, 2024. https://nypost.com/2024/11/06/us-news/fuming-joe-scarborough-blames-racism-misogyny-among-black-and-hispanic-voters-for-harris-loss/.

irrelevant because public figures hold symbolic power. The overt, yet unstated, assumption is that their existence in the broader groups of women, and black women, make them avatars for others' pain—or in the case of a white, Christian, man, others' privilege. However, as discussed soon, pain—and privilege-by-proxy—always loses out to real suffering and advantage.

GLORIFICATION AND DEMONIZATION OF SUFFERING

Progressives hold a schizophrenic view of suffering because they are equally comfortable with condemning and creating pain, depending on the circumstance. Their views on abortion, race, and sexual assault elucidate this reality.

For those who read prior chapters, the ways in which abortion causes suffering are readily apparent, although it is invisible to progressives who can only acknowledge suffering that aligns with a particular hierarchy of victimhood.

In racial matters, the left is attuned to the suffering of those whose ancestors faced slavery and discrimination, but it uses this historic suffering as a justification for enacting vengeance against the descendants of those who committed egregious, racially motivated, crimes, like slavery and Jim Crow. The problem is that the targets of this vengeance had no part in committing the offenses for which they are punished. Instead, the price of ancestral sins is borne by those who lacked any control over their commission.

Schoolchildren in modern America have no embodied connection to the oppression of the past, yet they are chided for their race, gender, religion, and sexuality, and are constantly reminded that "historically marginalized" groups, like racial minorities, women, and members of the LGBTQ community, have less "privilege" than their white, cis, heterosexual, male counterparts.

This can be seen in how regulatory bodies instruct schools to address privilege as a concept. The National Association of School Psychologists (NASP) instructs schools to teach students about privilege by having students ruminate on the ways in which they either have or lack privilege.[177] When defining privilege, NASP encourages leaders to have students define the terms subjectively or to use the Merriam-Webster dictionary, which defines privilege as a right or favor granted or an exemption from burdens or evil based on group membership.

After defining privilege, students are encouraged to make a line and move forwards or backwards in response to prompts from the leader. Upon hearing a prompt, students are encouraged to physically move themselves in accordance to their new standing in society's hierarchy of pain. Sample questions asked range from the inane, "If you ever tried to change your appearance, mannerisms, or behavior to fit in more, take one step back," to the overtly sensational, "If there was ever substance abuse in your household, take one step back." Positive life experiences, such as attending schools with people like oneself, or enjoying media representations (even if not perceived as typical) of one's identity, correspond to taking steps forward.

---

[177] "Talking about Race and Privilege: Lesson Plan for Middle and High School Students." NASP, 2016. https://www.nasponline.org/resources-and-publications/resources-and-podcasts/diversity-and-social-justice/social-justice/social-justice-lesson-plans/talking-about-race-and-privilege-lesson-plan-for-middle-and-high-school-students.

These methods represent emotionalized vengeance in action. Rather than encouraging children to focus on circumstances they can control, these exercises force students into comparative thinking, with the exercises ending when students assess where they stand in relation to one another.[178] Not only is the accuracy of such a test impossible to assess (for example, some students will understandably refuse to move positions based on an unwillingness to disclose private details), but it also encourages shallow thinking and stereotyping. Students cannot understand the complexity of their own—or others'—lives based on answers to preconceived, ideologically driven questionnaires.

Accurately assessing where an individual lands relative to others in society requires a degree of knowledge no one person possesses, hence why traditional wisdom rendered the judgment of a person's heart to God. A student with all the markers of privilege may live with judgmental parents unwilling to nurture her heart, or her privilege could evaporate in a year when her parents file for divorce. An African American student could feel well-represented in media based on the media he consumes, until his parents relocate and his attempts to fit into a new set of social conditions cause him to change his patterns of media consumption. A child in poverty could view herself as immeasurably blessed due to the nurturing home in which she lives, until she attends a privilege walk in school and learns she stands at the bottom of a totem pole she never knew existed. Now, she notices as her classmates

---

[178] "Privilege Walk Lesson Plan." Peace Learner, March 14, 2016. https://peacelearner.org/2016/03/14/privilege-walk-lesson-plan/.

look upon her differently after learning they have a reason to view her differently than themselves.

Comparison has always been the thief of joy, and emotionally well-adjusted adults do not encourage children to compete with one another over privilege points earned or denied based on ancestral decisions. Research is beginning to expose the obvious flaws in culture's newest attempt to create community by breeding enmity between people with disparate life experiences. Researchers at the Network Contagion Research Institute (NCRI) and Rutgers University's Social Perception Lab found that "anti-oppressive" exercises cause participants to become combative.[179] "The evidence," they conclude, shows that despite attempting to mitigate bias, anti-oppression narratives "engender a hostile attribution bias and heighten racial suspicion, prejudicial attitudes, authoritarian policing, and support for punitive behaviors."[180] Support for punishment was widespread even without evidence of a transgression worthy of discipline.

VENGEANCE AS POLITICAL WARFARE

Modern culture is in confusion because it lacks a principled commitment to beliefs transcending tribal alliances. The problem of individuals living in safe internet silos that reinforce their preexisting perceptions of the world is often discussed, but this

---

179 "Instructing Animosity: How DEI Pedagogy Produces the Hostile Attribution Bias." NCRI, November 24, 2024. https://networkcontagion.us/reports/instructing-animosity-how-dei-pedagogy-produces-the-hostile-attribution-bias/.

180 "Instructing Animosity: How DEI Pedagogy Produces the Hostile Attribution Bias," NCRI.

issue cannot be divorced from the culture in which the internet arose. People crave tribal safety when cross-cultural trust is lost, and the privilege narrative of the left places an enormous cost on cross-cultural communication.

As previously discussed, these costs are not necessarily connected to individual harms. Instead, diversity is celebrated while people are simultaneously punished for behavior typical of cross-cultural dialogue. Take, for example, the rise of microaggressions. A creation of the academic left, the word "microaggression" has made its way into the dictionary and is defined as a comment or action that subtly, unconsciously, or unintentionally expresses prejudice against members of a marginalized group.[181]

According to left-leaning institutions, microaggressions are a major problem. Speaking with the American Psychological Association, Derald Wing Sue, Columbia professor of psychology and education, stated microaggressions are an issue because they are "reflections of worldviews, of inclusion, exclusion, superiority, inferiority, and normality, abnormality."[182] He goes on to explain all marginalized groups are subject to microaggressions, noting their applicability to race, gender, and sexual orientation.

Notably absent was a discussion of how microaggressions can be used against groups progressives perceive as privileged. This is because the concept is designed by progressives as a punitive measure to change and mold culture according to their

181 "Microaggression." Merriam-Webster, accessed January 30, 2025. https://www.merriam-webster.com/dictionary/microaggression.

182 Wing Sue, Derald. "How to Combat Microaggressions." American Psychological Association, August 2023. https://www.apa.org/news/podcasts/speaking-of-psychology/microaggressions.

presuppositions, and one of those presuppositions is that cultural power hierarchies in America have remained relatively unaltered since the nation's founding.[183] White, Christian, heterosexual men are presumed to live outside of the realm of possible marginalization because, historically, these identity characteristics have been socially beneficial. But when people are told they possess innate and unalterable unconscious biases[184] that could unintentionally harm those in historically marginalized groups, the incentive to engage with people across lines of vast difference obviously diminishes.

The problem progressives must face is that their model of reality is broken. Society is now a generation into the twenty-first century, and from Hollywood to academia, the benefit of being born a white male extinguished years ago. What progressives call "white privilege" is actually a function of the slow changes in culture. Because being a white male was once socially advantageous, there are remnants of this benefit, primarily connected to generationally high-status families. This is why almost half of Harvard's white population comes from legacy admissions, athletes, or

---

[183] Indeed, the misguided—and historically inaccurate—view that America was founded on slavery is promoted by *The New York Times* 1619 Project. "The 1619 Project." *The New York Times*, August 14, 2019. https://www.nytimes.com/interactive/2019/08/14/magazine/1619-america-slavery.html.

[184] For example, "white privilege." See definition, "White Privilege." Merriam-Webster, accessed January 30, 2025. https://www.merriam-webster.com/dictionary/white%20privilege.

students related to donors and staff.[185] However, younger generations disconnected from elite wealth face an entirely separate set of circumstances. Children participating in privilege walks implicitly know they will be targeted as holding power if they were unlucky enough to be born a white, Christian male because cultural messaging now demonizes what its practitioners perceive as historically "privileged" groups.

Functionally, progressives treat historical conditions of marginalization as static and unchanging while simultaneously arguing for a fundamental change in social relationships. This inconsistency is progressivism's Achilles heel. Through control of culture's academic centers, progressives have even been able to control the definitions of words integral to the practice of their philosophy, but this linguistic control is eroding as society's social hierarchies shift.

THE CYCLE OF POWER

Those on the left *assume* it is clear which groups are marginalized. With this definition firmly fixed, the objects of punishment are identified in relation to the victims whose interests should be avenged. This is why the negative social effects of cultural practices analyzed by Ivory Tower professors focus disproportionately on criticizing religious, conservative, and traditional worldviews.

---

[185] Silva, Daniella. "Study on Harvard Finds 43 Percent of White Students Are Legacy, Athletes, Related to Donors or Staff." NBC News, September 30, 2019. https://www.nbcnews.com/news/us-news/study-harvard-finds-43-percent-white-students-are-legacy-athletes-n1060361.

While progressives focus heavily on countering historical privilege by punishing individuals connected to groups with historical privilege, they ignore the real-world effects of their actions. As they tear down ideas, statutes, and traditions, they erect new ones in their stead, thus redistributing, not abolishing, the hierarchical power dynamics they critique. By treating the world as a zero-sum power game, the left fights for those historically oppressed by creating new victim groups, thus guaranteeing vengeance will become a brutal cycle of competing power.

However, progressive cultural power has always relied on the use—and abuse—of language. Without the ability to control important cultural concepts, like marginalization, oppression, power, and privilege, the left is losing its control over language, causing a linguistic collapse and a reordering of tribal affiliations. In recent years, the left has lost practical control of the narrative, while their opposition on the right shows signs of using elements of the leftist playbook against progressive interests.

Human emotions, and therefore language, culture, and society, are cyclical. The evolving nature of culture has often been used by the left to argue for reform because, as the meaning of language evolves, so too should social practices. The left's problems come into sharp focus when they fail to treat power and privilege as evolving. While the meaning of marriage, family, freedom, happiness, equality, and other concepts deeply connected to the cultural identity of people and the nation are treated as fluid, power and victim hierarchies are viewed as fixed. Regardless of social upheaval, the white, Christian, heterosexual man is assumed to *always* reside at the top of the social hierarchy in all cultural contexts.

This, of course, is not true. Victims and victors constantly trade places, both individually and collectively. The oppressed becomes the oppressor, and the man who was punished yesterday may deserve today's protection. However, despite radical changes in social conditions, all of which favor progressive interests, those on the left struggle to understand their own propensity to unfairly punish others in cultural, relational, political, and legal contexts.

The progressive problem is, to some degree, internal. Because they view themselves as champions of the oppressed, leftists struggle to see their own prejudice, thus making it difficult for them to acknowledge their propensity to mete out unfair punishment. Luke Conway, a professor who teaches about prejudice, researched left-wing authoritarianism and his results align with what one would expect from a culture committed to Marcusean values.

Conway surveyed over five thousand Americans by giving people a standard questionnaire on authoritarianism. After completing the survey, participants were asked whether they viewed themselves as dogmatic and authoritarian. Conservative Americans who scored high on authoritarianism answered in the affirmative, but their liberal counterparts did not. In fact, the higher liberals scored on the authoritarian scale, the less likely they were to see themselves as dogmatic or authoritarian.[186]

Among the questions that measured authoritarianism—regardless of political orientation—included whether participants agreed with statements such as:

---

[186] Conway, Luke. "The Left Has an Authoritarian Problem (but Doesn't Know It)." Presser, accessed January 30, 2025. https://www.pressermag.com/september-2024/the-left-has-an-authoritarian-problem.

- Society should punish those they disagree with, and
- The nation would be better off if certain groups would just shut up and accept their group's proper place in society

Participants' answers to these questions show progressive prejudice in action. Those who identify as tolerant are often quite comfortable with utilizing intolerance to advance their mission of building a good society.

This lack of self-awareness is creating practical problems for Democrats because the language of power, oppression, and privilege is changing, and the public is becoming more aware of the leftist propensity to use authoritarian measures to abuse power.

PRACTICAL LINGUISTIC PROBLEMS

Progressives ran into a major roadblock in 2022, when Elon Musk acquired Twitter. This one acquisition broke the left's suppression of voices dissatisfied and disillusioned with leftist monopolization of culture's understanding of power and privilege. The timing of this acquisition is important because it came in the wake of an enormous effort to stifle online expression that was brought on by the 2020 presidential election and the COVID-19 pandemic. This is because Musk's decision to co-invest $44 billion into the social media site was motivated by a belief in the necessity of securing freedom of speech, and the necessity of preventing a philosophical "mind virus," from having an information weapon with which to propagate a corrosive civilizational ideology.[187]

Musk's decision broke the stranglehold leftwing ideas have on the media in modern America and was a focal point in a fundamental realignment of tribal interests in American politics. The privilege narrative the left used, and bolstered through cultural gatekeeping of academia, entertainment, and news, is now untenable because it relies on convincing the public to treat past cultural prejudices as a fixed, rather than fluid, reality, and fails to acknowledge the harms perpetrated by those who are ideologically committed to progressive presuppositions.

Simply put, an increasingly large swath of the American public's daily life is largely removed from historical prejudices. While the residue of biases based in racial, gender, or sexual stereotypes exists, there are new prejudices far more relevant to the immediate experience of millions of Americans—most notably, prejudices rooted in viewpoint discrimination and the condescension of experts who seek to impose their will onto the public.

Musk's acquisition of Twitter was powerful because it allowed a freer flow of online information unregulated by far-left interests. This stymied attempts to censor viewpoints unapproved by adherents to progressive, or left-leaning worldviews, and provided legitimacy to Americans who dissented from left-wing orthodoxy.

---

[187] PowerfulJRE. "Elon Musk on Buying Twitter and Turning It Into X." YouTube, October 31, 2023. https://www.youtube.com/watch?v=N-8Nf56srwcA&t=185s. Fox News. "Elon Musk Reveals the Goal of the New Twitter." YouTube, April 18, 2023. https://www.youtube.com/watch?v=qbxStDmHFAE&t=1s.

It also gave widespread public representation to someone sympathetic to Trump's campaign.

Most importantly, in combination with censorship of election and COVID-19 information, the belief that an elite segment of American society was marginalizing and victimizing regular Americans began to grow. This is among the many reasons the numerous lawsuits against Trump did not sway the public against his candidacy. For years, his messaging tied his interests to that of the lay public. It was easy for him to frame the numerous lawsuits against him as politically motivated because this is, at the very least in part, undeniably accurate. The infamous Steele dossier that alleged Trump was colluding with Russia created a multi-year scandal presented to the public as evidence of Trump's corruption. Over five years later, the dossier has been debunked, and with it the credibility of the news media, an industry that continues to report record-low levels of public trust.[188]

The events that unfolded during the COVID-19 pandemic also opened the public's eyes to the abuses that come from government overreach, particularly to fundamental freedoms such as speech, and, ironically, bodily autonomy. Additionally, the ease with which social media companies—the source of most

---

[188] Cohen, Marshall. "The Steele Dossier: A Reckoning." CNN Politics, November 18, 2021. https://www.cnn.com/2021/11/18/politics/steele-dossier-reckoning/index.html.
"Trump-Russia Steele Dossier Analyst Charged with Lying to FBI." BBC, November 5, 2021. https://www.bbc.com/news/world-us-canada-59168626.
Brenan, Megan. "Americans' Trust in Media Remains at Trend Low." Gallup, October 14, 2024. https://news.gallup.com/poll/651977/americans-trust-media-remains-trend-low.aspx.

Americans' news—can be functionally wielded as arms of the state with no legal recourse, became one of the most important 2024 presidential election issues, with nearly two-thirds of Americans identifying this issue as a determinative factor in their vote.[189]

Given the benefits afforded to leftwing ideas in culturally powerful institutions, including government agencies, it should come as no surprise that there are major partisan divides regarding the integrity of elections or voting rights.[190] Between Republican concerns with the integrity of vote counts, and Democratic concerns regarding voter suppression, only 20 percent of the public has faith in the overall integrity of US elections.[191]

During the Biden-Harris administration, the public observed numerous attempts by the government to collaborate with powerful technology companies to silence speech. This ranged from the revelations of the Twitter Files, released after Musk acquired the company, to Biden's now-defunct Disinformation Governance Board, which was briefly headed by Nina Jankowicz, a leftwing ideologue who, ironically, promoted the disinformation that the Hunter Biden laptop story was fake news.[192]

---

[189] Bannister, Craig. "Free Speech Issue Weighed Heavily in 2024 Elections." mrcTV, November 6, 2024. https://www.mrctv.org/blog/craig-bannister/free-speech-issue-weighed-heavily-2024-elections.

[190] Agiesta, Jennifer. "CNN Poll: A Growing Number of People Lack Confidence in American Elections." CNN Politics, February 11, 2022. https://www.cnn.com/2022/02/10/politics/cnn-poll-democracy/index.html.

[191] Shepherd, Brittany. "Americans' Faith in Election Integrity Drops: POLL." ABC News, January 6, 2022. https://abcnews.go.com/Politics/americans-faith-election-integrity-drops-poll/story?id=82069876.

[192] Schorr, Isaac. "Meet Nina Jankowicz, Biden's New Disinformation Czar." *National Review*, April 29, 2022. https://www.nationalreview.com/news/meet-nina-jankowicz-bidens-new-disinformation-czar/.

As the 2024 election approached, the choice Americans faced was increasingly driven by a sense of fear surrounding fundamental freedoms. The progressive problem is that they have possessed asymmetrical cultural and institutional power for over two generations, making it more practically difficult to sell the idea that their opposition is a grave threat to democracy. It is hard to preach against privilege while controlling institutional power.

APPROPRIATION OF THE LEFT'S LINGUISTIC STRUCTURE

The practical problems of progressives leave them vulnerable to opponents using their own theories against them. Just as Christians struggled to explain the congruence of their definition of love paired with seemingly unloving actions, so to the left is floundering to explain how they fight privilege while enjoying its benefits.

Trump, a notoriously brilliant marketer, has exploited this weakness by appropriating leftist linguistics against itself. The left, Trump alleged, were liars, performative actors who signaled virtue while upholding a system that *oppressed* the will of regular Americans whom they detest. Included in his fold are Americans of all races, creeds, and beliefs.

No criticism has stuck to Trump. He has faced relentless, often highly exaggerated and hyperbolized media coverage for almost a decade, including numerous debunked stories, ranging from the claim that he called neo-Nazis "very fine people," to the accusation that he instructed the American public to consume bleach as a way to treat COVID-19.[193]

Although employed differently, Trump strategically uses the language of oppression, privilege, power, and vengeance. After nearly a decade in politics, his 2024 bid for the White House built on the foundation of his 2016 campaign. In a Conservative Political Action Conference (CPAC) speech, Trump signaled his commitment to justice for the oppressed public, stating, "In 2016 I declared, I am your voice. Today I add, I am your warrior, I am your justice, and for those who have been wronged and betrayed, I am your retribution."[194]

Trump's sustained popularity can be attributed to his direct and consistent messaging designed to reach Americans who felt silenced, shamed, and ignored by coastal progressive elites. Cultural commentators often marvel at the loyalty of Trump's base, but he has no secret sauce aside from speaking clearly and passionately to a population facing decades of invisibility. This theme can be seen throughout his political career and began with his speech announcing his 2016 presidential campaign, where he focused on how America's commitment to the consent of the

---

[193] Hardinges, Nick. "Trump Didn't Say People Should 'Inject Bleach' to Tackle COVID-19. Here's What He Said." Snopes, August 23, 2024. https://www.snopes.com/fact-check/trump-bleach-covid-19/.
PerryCook, Taija. "No, Trump Did Not Call Neo-Nazis and White Supremacists 'Very Fine People.'" Snopes, June 20, 2024. https://www.snopes.com/fact-check/trump-very-fine-people/.

[194] Schwartz, Ian. "Trump: I Am Your Warrior, I Am Your Justice, and I Am Your Retribution." Real Clear Politics, March 4, 2023. https://www.realclearpolitics.com/video/2023/03/04/trump_i_am_your_warrior_i_am_your_justice_and_i_am_your_retribution.html.

governed is undermined by Washington, DC elites who work for special interests rather than the people they purportedly represent. Although those on the left often criticize the public for believing a billionaire like Trump operates in their best interest, he turned his wealth into a selling point, stating he can reform the government because he is not a politician, can't be bought, owes politicians nothing, and is beholden to no one aside from the American public.[195]

Whether progressives agree with his assertions is irrelevant because, although they interpret his actions through a cynical lens, his behavior over the past decade has been remarkably consistent. Americans who agree with Trump's premise that an elite class seeks to oppress the public by denying regular Americans the opportunity to fully participate in the uniquely American experiment of self-governance view the attacks against Trump as attacks directly against them.

The left fails to understand that Trump's appeal comes from direct messaging that ties his candidacy to the interests of the public. In 2016, his campaign slogan, Make America Great Again, was accompanied by a theme of giving a voice to those who languish in silent suffering under the oppression of those with power. This is highlighted by Trump's focus on illegal immigration, the drug problems that come with it, and the incorporation of Make America Healthy Again (MAHA) as an ally of the MAGA movement.

---

[195] Roll Call Factbase Videos. "Speech: Donald Trump Announces His Candidacy in New York, NY - June 16, 2015." YouTube, October 29, 2017. https://www.youtube.com/watch?v=aV-nyOM4_gc.

By positioning himself in this manner, the attacks against him fell flat. Left-wing reactions to his presidency were severe and easily parodied. In 2016, he was depicted as Julius Caesar and stabbed in a New York performance of *Shakespeare in the Park.*[196] In 2017, the Russian collusion narrative was circulated almost immediately after Trump took office, and popular leftist criticisms of the president continued to take a shockingly violent approach as symbolized by Kathy Griffin's tweet featuring her holding Trump's bloody, severed head.[197] While news outlets routinely portrayed Trump's words in the worst light possible, a CBS news report discussing Griffin's tweet painted her as the victim, "Death threats, cancellations, investigations: Kathy Griffin says she would do it all again," the headline reads.[198]

This need to break the left's monopoly on power was a motivating factor in the change of political alliances that occurred toward the end of the presidential campaign. Trump selected a vice-presidential candidate who once called himself a "Never

---

[196] Dobnik, Verena. "Shakespeare in the Park Show Features Stabbing of Trump Look-Alike." NBC4 New York, June 9, 2017. https://www.nbcnewyork.com/news/local/trump-mock-assassination-shakespeare-in-the-park-new-york-city-controversy-kathy-griffin/164591/.

[197] "Death Threats, Cancellations, Investigations: Kathy Griffin Says She Would Do It All Again." CBS News, March 24, 2019. https://www.cbsnews.com/news/kathy-griffin-on-death-threats-cancellations-investigations-over-trump-severed-head-photo/.

[198] "Death Threats, Cancellations, Investigations: Kathy Griffin Says She Would Do It All Again," CBS News.

Trumper," before later issuing an apology saying he once bought the lies of the mainstream media.[199]

Similarly, Robert F. Kennedy Jr., a man who once issued fierce criticisms of Trump,[200] endorsed Trump's bid for the presidency because he viewed the Democratic Party as an existential threat to freedom. His reasons centered around similar concerns that led Musk to acquire Twitter, including his belief that the Democratic Party and leftwing political interests were in alignment with government actors. In his speech suspending his campaign and endorsing Trump, Kennedy stated he is concerned because his former party turns "to censorship and media control and the weaponization of the federal agencies" to achieve their goals.[201]

Kennedy's commitment to free speech and a peace deal in Ukraine were factors in his decision to back Trump, but it is his passion for addressing the often-ignored chronic health epidemic in the US that ultimately led him to back the controversial former president. It is his concern that elites are "poisoning the poor" by advancing the interests of pharmaceutical interests over the health

---

[199] Diss, Kathryn, and Lucy Sweeney. "How JD Vance Transformed Himself from a Never Trumper to the Republican Pick for Vice-President." ABC News, July 16, 2024. https://www.abc.net.au/news/2024-07-17/how-jd-vance-transformed-himself-from-never-trumper-to-vp-pick/104106988.

[200] Kaczynski, Andrew. "RFK Jr.'s Long History of Attacking Trump Melted Away After He Endorsed Him for President." CNN Politics, August 26, 2024. https://www.cnn.com/2024/08/26/politics/kfile-rfk-jr-trump-endorsement/index.html.

[201] The Editors. "RFK Jr. Address to the Nation: Full Transcript." Real Clear Policy, August 24, 2024. https://www.realclearpolicy.com/2024/08/24/rfk_jr_address_to_the_nation_full_transcript_1053865.html.

and well-being of America's citizens.[202] Trump's commitment to giving Kennedy a seat at the table—and thereby the opportunity to address chronic health—created an unexpected alliance. Make America Great Again now merged with the newly created Make America Healthy Again.

However, despite the general support for Trump, a substantial portion of the electorate continues to view him as an existential threat to democracy, and they are likely to view his attempts at enacting the justice he promised his supporters as vengeance.

WARRING SYSTEMS OF VENGEANCE?

Moving forward, American politics is increasingly characterized by attempts to avenge the grievance of populations oppressed by the inappropriate use of power. Thus, after winning the 2024 election, Trump's vow to be the people's "retribution" will be subject to mutually exclusive interpretations based largely on political affiliation, and an individual's prior assumptions about not only Trump, but also the Democratic Party and its progressive base.

In an indirect way, the progressive definition of who was oppressed was on the ballot, and it suffered a devastating setback. To declare it dead would be an overstatement; the left still controls major sources of cultural power and young adherents to their ideologies will rise to positions of authority, thus guaranteeing their perspectives will retain significant power for the foreseeable future. However, the public, at least for the moment, had grown weary of the fixation on progressive virtue signaling, and a new

---

202 The Editors, "RFK Jr. Address to the Nation: Full Transcript."

slate of prominent voices has begun to push against the progressive narrative of oppression, power, and justice.

Trump's initial selections for important cabinet positions are indicative of the retribution he seeks to enact and all have a common denominator: The individuals selected are those viewed with scorn by the agencies they would lead. Those on the left will continue to portray Trump, and those aligned with him, as threats to democracy. However, unless the conditions of tyranny emerge, they are likely to only burn through more political capital.

CHAPTER 10
The Devouring Mother

MOTHER KNOWS BEST

As described in later chapters, I eventually resolved my indecision in favor of Christianity, and life moved on in its scheduled direction. Not long after solidifying my religious and philosophic identity, I enrolled in freshman courses at the University of Oklahoma and, during my second semester, I met my husband, Tim. After meeting, we quickly became best friends, meeting up regularly to hang out on campus and talking on the phone for hours after returning to our respective homes.

By the end of the semester, we were dating, and our conversations took an uncomfortable turn. When Tim would ask about my family, I struggled to find appropriate verbiage to describe its relational dynamics. Without extensive personal knowledge of my family home, he struggled to appropriately contextualize the relationships, particularly the combative relationship between my mother and I. For hours, I would recount conversations we had growing up, but these left him with more questions than answers.

This turned into a vicious cycle of questions and answers that reached no mutual understanding. Finally, to explain my family's interpersonal dynamics, I told Tim my birth story, how my mother called me half-aborted.

He looked at me in disbelief, "Your mother called you half-aborted. What does that even mean?"

I said the adjective had no specific, known definition before reverting to social training that minimized her behavior.

"She said I was born from Satan. I don't really know what that means either, but she always blamed her doctor. She said the doctors and nurses destroyed our mother-child bond by cutting my umbilical cord too early, and letting me cry for too long in the nursery."

Tim adamantly refused to accept these attempts at minimization.

"That's insane and makes zero sense," he said angrily. "There is something seriously wrong with her. What kind of mother says that to her own child? There's no excuse for that behavior."

This conversation opened a can of worms that carried on for weeks. Tim was curious about my circumstance, and wanted to understand my family to help me navigate the situation with minimal emotional damage. The more I talked about my family, the more disturbed Tim became. After hearing how I was barred from having friends before college, he became exasperated by the absurdity of the home and sighed, "Sounds like your parents run a cult," he said.

I was neither ready to fully accept this observation, nor did it quite fit the circumstances.

"No," I said, "it wasn't really a cult, it was...I don't know, it's hard to explain." I paused for several minutes before continuing,

"It wasn't a cult because it was just my family, they weren't interested in bringing in converts. My mom just didn't want her kids to grow up, especially the younger ones. She was obsessed with babies and always wanted to have infants around, so it felt like being constantly infantilized and stunted from developing."

"Oh!" he said, finally able to relate. "So your mom is like the old witch from *Tangled*."

I had heard of the movie, but never watched it. Disney movies were not generally in the family film repertoire and *Tangled* had been released approximately my senior year of high school.

"Maybe?" I said, still hesitant to accept such an unsavory reality. "That just sounds really dramatic. I don't think it was *that* bad."

To test Tim's analogy, we watched the movie together. The story line, which follows the life of Rapunzel, the princess who spends her life in a tower under the coercion and control of her mother, was instantaneously relatable. Although the entirety of the movie was deeply uncomfortable due to an uneasy feeling of familiarity, one scene and its corresponding song was especially jarring and revelatory.

"Mother Knows Best" painted a vivid and accurate picture of female predation by showing how the mother uses emotional manipulation to justify her tyrannical control. The witch attacked her child's competency, saying the world was scary and highlighting Rapunzel's youth, inexperience, and perceived flaws, in an attempt to convince her daughter that entering the world would lead to disaster. If these reasons were not enough, the witch resorts to emotional manipulation, reminding Rapunzel of who cared for her during her childhood. The extensive demands of motherhood were strategically used to keep Rapunzel in her place. No one knows better than a mother,

After the movie concluded and the credits rolled, it was difficult to argue with Tim's logic. "Was that what it was like growing up?" he asked.

"Yes," I replied, "it was pretty accurate, scarily accurate actually."

CONTROL AS "CARE"

The abuse and infantilization perpetrated against Rapunzel by her devouring mother are fictitious, but the underlying relational dynamic is real and represents an under-discussed aspect of cultural development. The fairy tale and subsequent Disney adaptation shows the extremes of female predation, bringing the worst image of the devouring mother to life.

However, in practice, all predatory behavior falls on a spectrum. Just as a man yelling at his wife is not necessarily indicative of abuse, instances of overprotective mothering are not always problematic. Still, at some point that defies absolute definition, both masculine and feminine behaviors move from the realm of human error into the category of abuse.

As previously discussed, society is comfortable naming and discussing male-driven forms of abuse while female forms of predation are generally minimized. Discussion of female-perpetrated abuse is often mischaracterized as "misogyny," making it difficult for victims to gain social sympathy and support.

Assessing the extremes of female predation can assist in understanding how perverted femininity operates throughout society, including in ideologically and politically charged contexts. The worst form of female predation is female-perpetrated sexual abuse of children, a social taboo that has frustrated research efforts for decades.[203] Obtaining accurate statistics on the number of female perpetrators of sexual abuse is difficult because, although all forms of sexual abuse are underreported, this underreporting is even more exaggerated in cases involving a female perpetrator.[204] Some researchers estimate the number of female child sexual abusers represents between 5 percent to 20 percent of overall cases. This enormous range of possible error shows how difficult it is to access the scope of this form of female predation.[205]

Despite the dearth of reliable information on the topic, some information about female perpetrated abusers is known. Most abusers are the victim's caregiver, either a mother, close relative, or nanny. Additionally, social attitudes allow female abusers to remain undetected because attitudes toward male abuse generates far more social outrage. News reports, professors, law enforcement, and mental health providers have all been found more likely to react to female-perpetrated abuse with dismissal toward

---

[203] Tozdan, Safiye, Peer Briken, and Arne Dekker. "Uncovering Female Child Sexual Offenders—Needs and Challenges for Practice and Research." *Journal of Clinical Medicine* 8, no. 3 (2019): 401. https://doi.org/10.3390/jcm8030401.

[204] Rymanowicz, Kylie. "Keeping Kids Safe: Characteristics of Child Sexual Offenders." Michigan State University, August 17, 2017. https://www.canr.msu.edu/resources/keeping-kids-safe-characteristics-of-child-sexual-offenders.

[205] Augarde, Sophie, and Michelle Rydon-Grange. "Female Perpetrators of Child Sexual Abuse: A Review of the Clinical and Empirical Literature—A 20-Year Update." *Aggression and Violent Behavior* 62 (January–February 2022). https://doi.org/10.1016/j.avb.2021.101687.

victims.[206] Predatory male behavior is simply more recognizable and subject to greater levels of social scorn.

SPECTRUM OF PREDATION

As previously mentioned, predatory behavior exists on a spectrum. A man who beats his wife once is abusive, the man who beats his wife daily is far more abusive. The same is true of female predation, a phenomenon that hides behind presumed moral innocence and the trust of caretaking.

Ironically, while feminists often complain that women are socially expected to perform more emotional labor, they are the last to discuss the power and control caretaking often provides.[207] Indeed, as mentioned in prior chapters, feminists have been historically reluctant to discuss female forms of predatory sexual behavior, a phenomenon inherently wrapped up in perverse forms of "caretaking," because they are fearful this will generate misogynistic backlash.

Yet, less overt and extreme forms of female predation are obvious in culture; all one needs to do is open their eyes to the ways in which femininity can be perverted to see this truth. Because female predation relies on weaponizing empathy and infantilizing children to ensure their perpetual dependence, it stands to reason

---

[206] Tozdan, Briken, and Dekker. "Uncovering Female Child Sexual Offenders—Needs and Challenges for Practice and Research."

[207] Morgan, Kate. "'The Extra Shift': The Unpaid Emotional Labour Expected of Women at Work." BBC, March 14, 2024. https://www.bbc.com/worklife/article/20240313-invisible-emotional-labour-women-in-workplace.

that as society embraces female predation, empathy and caretaking will become similarly perverted.

This is already occurring throughout the western world, including the United States. There is a growing body of discourse discussing problems related to caretaking and empathy. Journalist and author Abigail Shrier's past two books address the topic, one covering the troubling rise of gender dysphoria in young girls, and the other shedding light on how therapeutic interventions for children often undermine their mental growth, making it difficult for younger generations to assertively move through the world as competent adults.[208] Furthermore, debates over identity politics are innately bound up in this problem with critics referring to those on the left as embodying "suicidal empathy,"[209] and failing to understand the destruction of their own actions due to a "mind virus."[210] It is this mind virus that Musk sought to combat through the acquisition of Twitter and subsequent alliance with Trump.

Other examples of this growing awareness come from the transgender movement, which is heavily criticized for the ease with which abusive parents can groom their children into believing they were born in the wrong body. Jordan Peterson, whose license has been threatened by Canadian Psychologist regulators

---

[208] "Abigail Shrier: Independent Journalist." Substack, accessed January 31, 2025. https://www.abigailshrier.com/.

[209] The Ayaan Hirsi Ali Podcast. "Suicidal Empathy and the Decline of the West | Gad Saad EP02." YouTube, November 8, 2024. https://youtube.com/watch?v=NknDCkgdENQ.

[210] "Books." Dr. Gad Saad, accessed January 31, 2025. https://www.gadsaad.com/.

due to his controversial political and social commentary,[211] is among the few discussing the political implications of the devouring mother,[212] including the exponential growth of the transgender youth. In an interview with Joe Rogan, Peterson criticized a Disney executive who claimed to have two children, one trans and one pansexual, stating the probability that this woman is a devouring mother who pathologically sacrificed her children to compassion are so astronomical as to almost be certain.[213]

Although uncomfortable, Peterson's observation that female predation will inevitably be expressed politically is correct. A failure to address this reality will result in continued social disintegration because it will allow predatory behavior to run unchecked and there is only so long the public can be preyed upon before they fight back.

While left-leaning commentators reflect on the sexist implications of Trump's electoral victory, a more honest analysis would include the public's legitimate fear that female forms of predation threaten to devour the public's independence, making people perpetual infants, dependent upon Mother Government for permission to even think, speak, and act contrary to her will.

---

211 Tunney, Catharine. "Jordan Peterson Agrees to Social Media Coaching After Supreme Court Declines Free Speech Case." CBC News, August 8, 2024. https://www.cbc.ca/news/politics/supreme-court-jordan-peterson-1.7288497.

212 *Joe Rogan Experience #1933 – Jordan Peterson*. *YouTube*, 2024. https://www.youtube.com/watch?v=oU-AQ2Rfmn4.

213 General Video. "Jordan Peterson Speaks to Mother of Trans and Pan Children." YouTube, May 16, 2024. https://www.youtube.com/watch?v=aaHHGACtEac.

FEMINISM AND INFANTILIZATION

The difficulty faced by victims of female-perpetrated abuse is magnified in fields where left wing and feminist thought predominates. I experienced this first-hand while seeking care in the aftermath of realizing my mother was a sexual predator. Because my abuse sits at the intersection of the most sympathetic social groups, women and mothers, navigating mental health services was indistinguishable from self-masochism.

Therapists and counselors are like pastors or mentors. Good ones are worth their weight in gold, while bad apples make a career out of emotional destruction. Professional ethical guidelines may bar therapists from projecting their beliefs onto patients in therapy sessions, but there is no practical way to enforce these guidelines. Aside from overt, egregious, and extremely well-documented cases of obvious abuse, counselors, therapists, and psychiatrists can impose their worldviews on their clients in clinical settings with almost no recourse.

Despite my decision to become a Christian, and therefore abandon my desire to die, I continued to struggle with persistent suicidal ideation during my college years. This yearning carried a quality of forbidden lust, for it was impossible to squelch and left me with a deeply felt sense of longing that expressed itself as an invisible hole of unfulfilled heartache. I did not merely think of committing suicide; I craved death and coveted the blessing of an early earthly exit.

However, this desire was in tension with my philosophical beliefs. Christians, after all, recognize the sanctity of all human life, including their own. Despite being sexually abused by my mother for over a decade, I was incapable of accurately naming her behavior until after I was married. Like all of society, I viewed women—my mother included—as misguided caregivers. Mothers could be controlling, but not sexually predatory. I still recall the moment I understood the weight of my mother's actions.

I was in Washington, DC, completing a summer academic and internship program, an eight-week endeavor I embarked on just two weeks after Tim and I were married, on the summer before our senior year of college. Unlike others raised in religious environments, I have never had a single shame-based sexual thought during my relationship with Tim, either during dating, engagement, or marriage. Thus, I was taken aback when, despite my excitement and enthusiasm for sexual activity, my desires and bodily functions warred with one another.

Well-aware of the anti-religious biases of sex therapists, I was unwilling to seek assistance from people who would blame my problems on my religious faith. I simply had no interest in paying money to argue with someone who incorrectly believed I was a victim of my own choices. Instead, I pondered the problem, searching for an answer. One night as I was completing a run through the National Mall, I stopped abruptly near the Lincoln Memorial, taken aback by an awareness of reality I had never contextualized before.

A wave of memories flooded my mind. None were new, but all had previously been categorized as mom being controlling, not necessarily abusive, certainly not in a sexual manner. To get my bearings, I began asking myself how I would interpret these memories if I stated the same events but replaced my mother with my father. Instantaneously, the truth was self-evident. What my mother called "child care" was sexual exploitation.

This realization shattered my entire world. I was terrified of the consequences, both to myself and Tim. After doing everything in my power to disclose the difficulty of my life circumstances to him, I saw myself as a failure because I had not done enough due diligence to make him aware of this life-altering problem prior to marriage.

Terrified to tell anyone for fear of disbelief, I instead fell into suicidal ideation. Soon, I was actively encouraging the suicidal thoughts I had trained myself to ignore. This quickly spiraled out of control, and within six months, I unsuccessfully attempted suicide through medication overdose. In the wake of this, Tim asked me for an honest answer as to why I tried to end my life. With nothing to lose, I responded honestly:

"My mom is a pedophile. She raped me for years when I was a child, but I didn't understand that her actions were sexually abusive until…." I broke eye contact, looked down, and allowed my voice to trail off, unable to voice the obvious.

Tim understood and rushed to embrace me. He told me we would move through the process of unpacking the abuse together. I felt numb, destroyed, and incapable of receiving his compassion. I wanted to run, convinced he deserved someone "better," untainted by the horror of pedophilia, but knew I could not refuse to seek help. For his sake alone, I sought professional mental health care, putting nagging concerns aside to fight for the preservation of our marriage.

Within weeks, I entered the mental healthcare system. A field dominated by women, my first appointment was with a female psychologist. I was hopeful, but pragmatic, cautious, and deeply resistant to trust. Unwilling to spend money I did not have for the services of someone who may pity my existence, I broached the topic of my half-aborted label early, curious to observe her response to my mother's abusive behavior. This, I reasoned, would test how this provider addressed female-perpetrated abuse without bringing the sensitive topic of sexual abuse into the conversation.

Within two sessions, it became clear to me that progressive, feminist biases clouded her judgment to a degree that would make a cult devotee blush. At every turn, she justified my mother's decision, informing me children are "difficult to care for," men compound this problem by being "unwilling to bear emotional labor," and postpartum depression "causes mothers to engage in poor behavior that isn't their fault." Everyone—except my mother—it seemed, was responsible for her maternal abuse.

I wondered if her response would have been less forceful if I had chosen to give myself a fake, but equally emotionally abusive childhood nickname. I exited her office and tried another therapist. This time I steered the conversation toward other demeaning names my mother had called me, like "half-human," and "born from Satan."

This woman's defense of my mother was clear, but less strident…until I brought up "half-aborted." After hearing this, her attitude toward me turned to skepticism. Postpartum depression was once again brought to the forefront of our conversations. "You have no idea how hard motherhood is," she said.

Moving forward, she began to undermine my own memories, routinely asking me if my mother's behaviors were, in fact, the actions of my father.

"Are you sure you are not misremembering? You grew up in a deeply patriarchal home. Perhaps your father engaged in some of this conduct that you now believe should be attributed to your mother."

I was shocked, but not surprised. To avoid creating tension, I paid for another two sessions before refusing to schedule more. I tried more therapists, psychiatrists, the exact number of which is lost to memory, perhaps even intentionally blocked. These were, after all, universally terrible, even retraumatizing experiences. With no exceptions, every female therapist displayed a tenacious determination to minimize my mother's actions by either placing blame on me for misinterpreting her "care," or offering numerous excuses to exculpate her abuse.

While her name is no longer in my immediate consciousness, I will never forget the last conversation I had with a secular female mental health provider. This time, I avoided the abortion issue entirely, instead trying to focus directly on the problem of suicide. In an unfortunately vulnerable state, I detailed stories of my mother's sexual abuse, and tied this to my suicidal desires. "It touches every aspect of life and seemingly always will. I don't know how to deal with the fact my mother raped me. It feels so defeating, like a mountain I cannot climb. I just want to die."

She raised her eyebrow, puckered her lips, and remained silent. Tension filled the room until she began to speak. "Your mother is not a rapist. While you may have felt hurt she was trying her best to take care of you, she acted in your best interest. Motherhood is hard. You don't understand the sacrifice it entails. Mothers do not rape their daughters."

At this point, I had been attempting to seek care for years, paying precious money I did not have for "services" that were making me sicker. I decided I no longer had to speak to counselors so ideologically possessed they were incapable of seeing my pain. I left that appointment, took the prescription drugs the psychiatrist had given me, flushed them down the toilet and vowed to manage my mental health through strict adherence to diet and exercise. Never again would I seek the care of those who sought to profit from my emotional anguish.

THE NEED TO INOCULATE AGAINST IDEOLOGY

There are many lessons to be gleaned from the inadequacy of mental healthcare, but among the most valuable is the connection between doubt and ideology. Society is familiar with the problems associated with absolute certainty. Religions are routinely criticized and mocked for preventing humanity from freely living out the desire of the heart. These criticisms have some merit. When taken to an extreme, rule-based religions can easily replace God's just authority with a cheap counterfeit. Since no man, or woman, can fully understand truth, doubt can serve as a productive mechanism to prevent the abuse of humanity through unnecessarily constrict rules.

However, although absolute certainty comes with its own set of problems, doubt can just as easily be leveraged to cause harm.

DOUBT, IDENTITY, AND IDEOLOGICAL CONVERSION

Doubt has always been a powerful motivator, but it is never neutral. Before a cheater commits adultery, she first doubts the integrity of the relationship...or herself. Of course, doubt can also be positive. No woman would leave an abusive relationship before first doubting whether it was good. Doubt also lies at the heart of moral, philosophical—and increasingly—political narratives. The atheist doubts God. The believer doubts the plausibility of life without a creator.

Because doubt is both revelatory and uncertain, it is a state of vulnerability, thus leaving the doubter subject to emotional exploitation. This is why it makes sense to view emotional, rock-bottom religious conversions with skepticism. While rock bottom can rationally lead someone to the truth, it can just as easily guide them to its deceitful counterfeit.

America is currently a nation in doubt. Most Americans lack a concrete worldview, instead absorbing a hodgepodge of beliefs based on cultural practices and convenience.[214] In bygone years, this haphazard approach was more manageable. "Do as thou will" is easy when community trust is high. However, the trust and shared cultural assumptions that once held society together have unraveled. Institutions that once held broad public trust, like newspapers, churches, and law enforcement, are increasingly viewed with suspicion. Social media has made it easy to isolate

---

214 Barna, George. "American Worldview Inventory 2021: America's Dominant Worldview Syncretism." Arizona Christian University, April 13, 2021. https://arizonachristian.dspacedirect.org/items/75db4da7-64be-4d30-90e0-1d7c02c1d0b0.

into ideological silos and even geographic trends show citizens are self-selecting into comfortable communities full of like-minded people. Thus, our politics is reflective of our people. We are confused, divided, and unsure of what, if anything, to trust.

In short, the nation is facing an identity crisis. Without a clear understanding of truth, reality, or core values, America is locked in a cold psychological war. This is why elections are now spoken of in apocalyptic terms. Because the premises of both sides of the aisle cannot be represented in law, policy, and culture, each is concerned they will lose power permanently. Ultimately, the culture wars will have a victor, and, until quite recently, progressives were justified in assuming they would take all the spoils. Their worldview was destined to destroy the archaic, backward viewpoints of the "deplorables" who bitterly "cling to guns or religion or antipathy to people who aren't like them or anti-immigrant sentiment or anti-trade sentiment as a way to explain their frustrations."[215]

The progressives, led by an army of experts marching in ideological lockstep, were going to save America from its racist founding and the backwards conservative hicks residing in the nation's heartland.

THE PUBLIC NOW BROADLY DOUBTS THE CREDIBILITY OF EXPERTS

However, over the past decade the excesses of the left have been revealed by the rise of Trump, COVID-19, and their embrace of

---

[215] Spross, Jeff. "How Obama Diagnosed Trumpism Way Back in 2008." The Week, March 8, 2016. https://theweek.com/articles/610945/how-obama-diagnosed-trumpism-way-back-2008.

transgender ideology. It is the embrace of transgender identity, particularly in relation to minors, that highlights the public's increasing wariness of leftist values. This has opened the public's mind and eyes to the emotional manipulation tactics commonly deployed by progressives who, hellbent on possessing absolute social, cultural, and political control, are determined to colonize the confused American mind by ideologically possessing the public consciousness and therefore indirectly controlling people's perception of justice, goodness, and truth, guaranteeing individuals will internally utilize a leftwing perspective when determining how to assess their own motivations, behaviors, and actions.

By making the public dependent on their worldview to understand reality, progressives seek to dominate from the inside out. They want to devour the public to save it from itself. The Democratic machine, full of faux compassion and love, are the devouring mother. Increasingly, the public is skeptical of their compassion and unwilling to accept their political care.

Unfortunately for the progressive cause, people are increasingly distrustful of professions dedicated to caretaking. This is expressed through the now pervasive distrust of medical professionals. In a post-COVID world this should be unsurprising, but trust in the medical system enjoys a small two-point advantage over religious institutions,[216] and the gap is narrowing. In 2021, 44 percent of Americans trusted the medical system, while only

[216] Saad, Lydia. "Historically Low Faith in US Institutions Continues." Gallup, July 6, 2023. https://news.gallup.com/poll/508169/historically-low-faith-institutions-continues.aspx.

37 percent trusted religion. Gallup now shows those percentages at 34 percent and 32 percent, respectively.[217]

Plummeting trust in religious institutions is understandable, an expected outcome in a secular age where most culturally powerful elites are deeply biased against religious belief. However, medical professionals enjoy broad elite support, thus begging the question: What caused this precipitous decline in public trust?

EXPERTS AS EMOTIONAL MANIPULATORS

As discussed in the prologue, the devouring mother embodies a tyranny perpetrated for the good of its citizenry. Culture experienced this during COVID-19 and has yet to fully comprehend its implications. The possibility of ideological capture is now seared into the American consciousness, and the public is now cynical to expert claims rooted in a purported concern for compassion and care. It is not that people distrust all experts, but appeals to expert organizations, whether medical, news, or educational are no longer broadly persuasive. Instead, individuals trust *specific* experts, while others are viewed as professional manipulators. Mixed messages surrounding the efficacy of masks, social distancing, and the COVID-19 vaccine have exposed the ease with which the scientific process can be abused by powerful actors.

Dr. Anthony Fauci is now the poster child of an abusive medical system. After proclaiming himself synonymous with "the science," he later admitted the social distancing guidelines

---

[217] Augarde and Rydon-Grange. "Female Perpetrators of Child Sexual Abuse: A Review of the Clinical and Empirical Literature—A 20-Year Update."

he preached were not evidence based and instead "sort of just appeared."[218] Despite maintaining the respect of those on the left, Fauci stands accused of various types of wrongdoing and illegal behavior by a select committee of the US House of Representatives. His alleged malfeasance includes engaging in a conspiracy to hinder US government operations by using personal emails to evade Freedom of Information Act (FOIA) requests and deleting records related to COVID-19.[219]

Initial claims regarding the efficacy of the COVID-19 vaccine were also grossly exaggerated, with Fauci and media allies repeating the false claim that vaccinated individuals could neither contract nor pass on the virus to others. Biden's White House used this falsehood to attempt to shame and manipulate individuals refusing the vaccine into taking the jab. In now-infamous remarks, Biden drew a clear, and implicitly moral, distinction between the vaccinated and unvaccinated:

> For unvaccinated, we are looking at a winter of severe illness and death—for unvaccinated, for themselves, their families, and the hospitals they'll soon overwhelm.

---

[218] Etzel, Gabrielle M. "Fauci Unmasked: Clearing the Record on Masks, Social Distancing, and Vaccines." *Washington Examiner*, June 18, 2024. https://www.washingtonexaminer.com/policy/healthcare/3045129/fauci-unmasked-clearing-record-masks-social-distancing-vaccines/.

[219] "New COVID Select Memo Details Allegations of Wrongdoing and Illegal Activity by Dr. Fauci's Senior Scientific Advisor." Committee on Oversight and Government Reform, May 22, 2024. https://oversight.house.gov/release/new-covid-select-memo-details-allegations-of-wrongdoing-and-illegal-activity-by-dr-faucis-senior-scientific-advisor/.

> But there's good news: If you're vaccinated and you had your booster shot, you're protected from severe illness and death—period.[220]

In the early years of the pandemic, discrimination against the unvaccinated was so widespread it resulted in the Supreme Court halting the Biden administration from enforcing a broad requirement that employers require employees to either show proof of vaccination or submit to routine COVID-19 testing.[221] Additionally, Americans watched as Canadian officials took increasingly draconian measures, including debanking individuals involved in supporting truckers who took to the roads to protest mandatory vaccination.[222]

The COVID-19 pandemic was undoubtedly a major factor driving public distrust, but a runner up[223] is the medical commu-

---

220 Malloy, Allie, and Maegan Vazquez. "Biden Warns of Winter of 'Severe Illness and Death' for Unvaccinated Due to Omicron." CNN Politics, December 16, 2021. https://www.cnn.com/2021/12/16/politics/joe-biden-warning-winter/index.html.

221 Howe, Amy. "Fractured Court Blocks Vaccine-or-Test Requirement for Large Workplaces but Green-Lights Vaccine Mandate for Health Care Workers." SCOTUS Blog, January 13, 2022. https://www.scotusblog.com/2022/01/fractured-court-blocks-vaccine-or-test-requirement-for-large-workplaces-but-green-lights-vaccine-mandate-for-health-care-workers/.

222 Fung, Katherine. "Banks Have Begun Freezing Accounts Linked to Trucker Protest." *Newsweek*, February 18, 2022. https://www.newsweek.com/banks-have-begun-freezing-accounts-linked-trucker-protest-1680649.

223 "Medical Association Statements in Support of Health Care for Transgender People and Youth." GLAAD, June 26, 2024. https://glaad.org/medical-association-statements-supporting-trans-youth-health-care-and-against-discriminatory/.

nity's embrace of transgender treatment for minors. The public views this issue through a lens of common sense, innately rejecting the ideological belief that some children are "born in the wrong body." Thus, when regular, non-ideological parents with children who suffer from gender dysphoria are advised to alter their child's natural development using medication, or mutilate their child's healthy body through gender reassignment surgery, they are naturally not only hesitant to accept such "medical care," but prepared to fight any system that seeks to impose obvious harm onto their children.

This represents yet another manifestation of progressive culture that embodies the devouring mother. The increasingly common, cliché response parents receive when they seek psychological or psychiatric care for their gender-dysphoric children is overtly manipulative, "Would you prefer a dead daughter or a trans son?" The medical community's embrace of gender ideology is clear, alarming, and rapidly degrading public confidence in mainstream psychological care.

In the American Psychological Association's preamble of ethical principles, the association states the goal of its ethics is to provide for the welfare and protection of those who seek psychological care.[224] In 2024, the association adopted a policy supporting access to gender-affirming care to minors.[225] The APA then

---

[224] "Ethical Principles of Psychologists and Code of Conduct." American Psychological Association, 2017. https://www.apa.org/ethics/code.

[225] "Position Statement on Access to Care for Transgender and Gender Diverse Individuals." American Psychiatric Association, 2018. https://www.psychiatry.org/about-apa/Policy-Finder/Position-Statement-on-Access-to-Care-for-Transgend.

jumped directly into the political fray by advocating for federal protections for gender-affirming care. These protections, they argue, are necessary to prevent states from passing laws limiting a child's access to medical interventions, such as puberty blockers. Such state laws, they claim, are passed without any evidence to support the concerns legislators cite in support of the law, instead putting transgender youth at risk for poor mental health outcomes.[226]

The APA is not alone. As Gay and Lesbian Alliance Against Defamation (GLAAD) notes, major medical associations are in support of gender-affirming care for minors, including the American Academy of Pediatrics, the American Academy of Child and Adolescent Psychiatry, and the American Medical Association. However, no amount of expert consensus can negate reality, and the positions these associations have taken are nakedly ideological.

Every day, Americans can understand several obvious realities. First, the drugs given to children during hormone therapy to block the effects of puberty are experimental and come with irreversible effects. Second, surgical interventions to create neo-vaginas or neo-penises are extreme interventions that children neither appreciate nor fully understand. Lastly, children are not mentally, emotionally, or psychologically capable of providing informed consent to such life-altering medical decisions.

---

[226] "Urging Congress to Protect Access to Gender-Affirming Care for Transgender Youth." American Psychological Association Services, August 9, 2023. https://www.apaservices.org/advocacy/news/gender-affirming-care-transgender-youth.

VOTERS DON'T SUPPORT GENDER-AFFIRMING CARE FOR MINORS

The 2024 election occurred within a context of increasing skepticism, as the difference between the average American's perceptions of reality and expert opinion widened from a gap to a chasm. From the impact on athletic opportunities for young girls, to the obvious problems associated with allowing young people to chemically or surgically castrate themselves, the progressive view on this issue is deeply out of touch with the viewpoints of average Americans.

Because the leftist position on transgender care for minors flies in the face of common sense, voters understandably react with a skepticism that is difficult to override. Recent polls show 68 percent of Americans oppose allowing ten- to fourteen-year-olds access to puberty blockers.[227] The same poll also shows broad support for banning male to female transgenders from competing in sports with biological women, and the viewpoint that sex is determined at birth.[228]

With the Supreme Court considering a constitutional challenge to Tennessee's law banning access to puberty blockers and hormonal treatment for allegedly transgender minors, the left is in unfamiliar territory. They found themselves on the opposite side

---

[227] Gans, Jared. "Majority of Americans Oppose Gender-Affirming Care for Minors, Trans Women Participating in Sports: Poll." *The Hill*, May 6, 2023. https://thehill.com/blogs/blog-briefing-room/3991685-majority-of-americans-oppose-gender-affirming-care-for-minors-trans-women-participating-in-sports-poll/.

[228] Gans, "Majority of Americans Oppose Gender-Affirming Care for Minors, Trans Women Participating in Sports: Poll."

of the public's attitudes on a major culture war issue, and, instead of being able to persuade the public to convert to their viewpoint, the opposite has occurred. Rather, most of the voters support passing a version of Tennessee's law at the federal level, by codifying a ban on the use of puberty blockers or the performance of gender reassignment surgeries on minors.[229]

Progressive privilege that allowed leftists to self-righteously judge their political opponents as backward bigots reached a tipping point in the Trump years. It is now progressives who are at odds with public opinion.

Keeping in mind that voters, especially swing voters, are not doing a systematic review of issues before casting their vote, it is worth reviewing how the Democratic messaging undermined its own credibility while failing to address the public's concerns.

THE ROLE OF SCOTUS

The role of the Supreme Court is heightened in public consciousness due to the Kavanaugh debacle and the *Dobbs* decision. Given Harris's aggressive abortion messaging, it is clear she believed there was an opportunity to capitalize on this issue by stoking fears that miscarriage care is now illegal in pro-life states and routinely rallying her base by declaring women's rights had been taken away.

---

[229] Martinell, TJ. "Poll: Majority of Voters Favor a Federal Ban on Transgender Procedures for Minors." The Center Square, October 13, 2024. https://www.thecentersquare.com/national/article_513f3242-8818-11ef-aba3-2b7497f57024.html.

However, it is no longer 1970. In 2024, women have dozens of birth control options, and many states with no gestational limits on the procedure. While a small portion of the electorate may struggle to drive across state lines, there are only two states, Louisiana and Mississippi, that do not border a pro-abortion state. Despite hysteria, the procedure is practically easy to obtain for most women.

Furthermore, many women are understandably shocked at the thought of conflating abortion and miscarriage. While the left-wing narrative is that abortion bans impact miscarriage, these cases are more complex, generally involving intervening causes such as medical mismanagement both from abortion providers and hospital staff. Those without strong views on abortion are likely to view the Democratic effort to demonize Republicans as callous people who don't care about women having miscarriages as extreme, which is why Harris's $2.4 million investment in ads targeting voters on reproductive issues in the swing state of Georgia failed.[230] This highlights an uncomfortable reality; while progressive culture views pro-life people with scorn, most Americans do not hold extreme views on abortion in either direction. Harris's inability to articulate any gestational limits and a callous attempt to conflate natural miscarriage with induced abortion was viewed unfavorably by people in the middle.

[230] Mukherjee, Neha, Ocheze Amuzie, Eryn Davis, and Phoebe Quinton. "Harris Spent $2.4m on Reproductive Health Ads in Georgia after State's Abortion Ruling." *The Atlanta Journal-Constitution*, November 4, 2024. https://www.ajc.com/politics/harris-spent-24m-on-reproductive-health-ads-targeting-georgia-voters-in-campaigns-closing-months/XWT3A34MKNHZXGWKW6CUMSZDE4/.

Additionally, highlighting the Supreme Court cuts against the public's viewpoints on the transgender issue, a problem that is far more salient than abortion. The public opposes the *Dobbs* decision, but because the issue is now handled at the state level, the impact of the president is of limited value. However, the Court's decisions regarding transgender issues are yet to be litigated. Although it is unlikely the Court will rule against states passing laws in opposition to gender-affirming care for minors, the public implicitly knows Trump's choice of justices is the primary reason half the states in the union are able to craft their own laws on this issue rather than being forced to comply with judicial fiat.

Furthermore, the issue of men in women's sports—a problem highlighted at the summer Olympics immediately prior to the election—was another problem for Democrats. The vast majority of the electorate favors barring biological men from competing in women's sports, even after they have transitioned.[231] Given the power the executive has to steer policy through Title IX and the ideological leanings of federal judges and Supreme Court Justices, those against the progressive view on transgender issues had no reason to vote for Harris.

And, in relation to SCOTUS, there is reason to believe the transgender issue and the makeup of the Supreme Court was a major factor in the election that swung in Trump's favor. Abortion has already been decided by the Supreme Court, but the trans issue is just reaching major appellate litigation. Moderate pro-choice voters can make their voice heard at the state level on

[231] Gans, "Majority of Americans Oppose Gender-Affirming Care for Minors, Trans Women Participating in Sports: Poll."

abortion, but having a left-wing Supreme Court could cement deeply unpopular precedent related to transgender issues. Over half of voters who became aware of Harris's position on allowing children access to sex change surgeries were likely to vote for Trump.[232] Similarly, half of those who knew Harris supported taxpayer-funded transition surgeries for prison inmates also broke for Trump.[233] A slightly smaller, but similar percentage of voters broke for Trump after learning Harris supported allowing biological men to compete in women's sports.[234]

In light of the broad public backlash against transgender ideology, highlighting the importance of voting to ensure judicial outcomes aligned with a voter's preference likely backfired because the Democratic view on both abortion and transgender care is that there should be uniform federal policies preventing states from crafting their own laws.

MISINFORMATION, MEDIA, AND REALIGNMENT OF PUBLIC TRUST

The hyper-politicization of everything in society comes with a cost, and one of the costs political commentators struggle to understand is the interrelation of subjective and objective "truth."

---

[232] "New Poll: Transgender Issue Ads Moved Voters to Trump, Republicans." American Principles Project, November 26, 2024. https://americanprinciplesproject.org/elections/new-poll-transgender-issue-ads-moved-voters-trump-republicans/.

[233] Ibid.

[234] Ibid.

Many on the left place the blame for this on social media[235] and Trump, claiming Trump ushered in a "post-truth" society.[236]

However, this starting point inverts reality. The American public has been steeped in postmodernism and relativism—both beliefs that negate the existence of truth—for decades, well before the existence of social media or Trump's political career. Instead, social media and the Trump effect, characterized by both his hyperbole *and* an often hysterical and deeply irrational response to his candidacy and presidency, amplified existing problems in American society and culture.

Additionally, words and discourse itself have become cheapened to the point of absurdity. A Supreme Court Justice stated, unironically, in a Senate hearing that she needed to refer to a trained biologist to determine what constitutes a man and a woman. Mis-, dis-, or malinformation is obviously used as a cudgel with which to bludgeon political opponents, and the ease with which fallible human actors can destroy institutions by perverting a facially good purpose is clear.

---

[235] Littau, Jeremy. "Social Media Has Collapsed Good Debate." *The Atlantic*, June 24, 2023. https://www.theatlantic.com/technology/archive/2023/06/joe-rogan-rfk-jr-interview-debate/674515/.

[236] Pazzanese, Christina. "Politics in a 'Post-Truth' Age." *The Harvard Gazette*, July 14, 2016. https://news.harvard.edu/gazette/story/2016/07/politics-in-a-post-truth-age/.

Norman, Andy. "The Cause of America's Post-Truth Predicament." *Scientific American*, May 18, 2021. https://www.scientificamerican.com/article/the-cause-of-americas-post-truth-predicament/.

Sachs, Jeffrey D. "Opinion: Amy Coney Barrett Showed She's Ready to Be Part of Trump's Post-Truth Strategy." CNN, October 18, 2020. https://www.cnn.com/2020/10/18/opinions/amy-coney-barrett-trump-post-truth-sachs/index.html.

Increasingly, the public is aware of the profound truth of human fallibility, both in themselves and others. Doubtful of legacy outlets and tech platforms that are quick to censor ideas challenging the premises of mainstream wisdom, people have begun to seek information through longform, interview-based podcasts.

Through this medium, individuals are exposed to highly credentialed experts who dissent from the prevailing viewpoints of their respective professions. From psychologists like Jordan Peterson, to medical experts, such as Jay Bhattacharya and Peter McCullough, millions of Americans are becoming more likely to trust *individuals* rather than institutions.

This is because expertise and related concepts—such as "myths" and "misinformation"—have been cheapened by a commitment to ideology over all else. From public health officials and the police, to the FBI, the Department of Justice, and newscasters, impersonal entities of legal, social, or cultural power no longer garner automatic trust.

Trump understands this dynamic, and it is one of the reasons he has withstood every attack against him. He is committed to no overarching ideological cause, and instead sold his ideas, candidacy, beliefs, and brands as an individual. His ability to connect with audiences is unmatched in current politics, and, for all his flaws, including his crass commentary, crude behavior, and egotistical personality, he stands as the polar opposite of a manipulator. Voters may dislike him, but Trump lacks the finesse and political tact of someone interested in emotionally manipulating the public.

The diametrically opposed ways that Trump and Harris engaged with the public spoke to their respective levels of confidence and doubt. Trump was everywhere all the time, he routinely gave long-form discussions of policy issues, and willingly went on any and all forms of media platforms, from broadcast to podcast formats. On the contrary, Harris was clearly uncomfortable with speaking off-script, and unwilling to engage in free-flowing, authentic dialogue.

This realignment of public trust has thrown progressives off-kilter because, for the first time in decades, they are being forced to contend with the troubling problems of conversion. Religious and traditional Americans are familiar with this issue, the perception that Christians proselytize for self-motivated, or misguided ideological reasons are widespread.

The left must now contend with similar concerns from those not already aligned with their ideology. Most Americans don't appreciate being forced to act as if they believe in a worldview they neither understand nor affirm, and, because the devouring Democratic machine is losing its assumption of "compassion," gone are the days when progressive prejudice receives unscrutinized, unearned privilege. Increasingly, voters who swing elections are deeply skeptical of progressive beliefs, see many of their ideological positions as creating, rather than alleviating harm, and view many of its sacred cows with suspicion, or even scorn.

In short, the public is beginning to doubt the integrity of the devouring mother's claim to compassion and love.

CHAPTER 11
The Price of Life

CONSENT AND ACCOUNTABILITY

The coerced baptism and concurrent vow of church membership further solidified my need to determine my belief system prior to college. It was clear to me that there is no such thing as a free ride and, contrary to common messaging, agnosticism is neither neutral nor cost-free. Instead, it comes at a steep price, because refusing to decide renders one susceptible to the influence of those whose wills are firm and whose minds are at peace with their beliefs.

I began to conceive of choosing a worldview as the price of living in the world, as what gives people skin in the game of life. Without making that choice, I was concerned natural, yet subtle, and destructive emotions would take over. The desire to be liked, to please, and to enter a community are unavoidable and strong. Without convictions, people are prone to being led down paths they never intended to follow, floating downstream on the river of life, fearful of rocking the boat lest they capsize and drown.

A 2009 Tim McGraw album, *Southern Voice*, captured my interest in its exploration of these themes. Captivated by the sound of his voice and the stories he told, I found in the album a perfect escape from the walls of my housc. It was dark and dense, providing the oasis I needed in an otherwise barren land.

I analyzed the album as I did any other. First, I listened through the album twice to understand the music's narrative arc, and identify common themes before moving into the meaning of specific songs. The album's first song reminded me of the human capacity to experience past memories in the present. Its last song, "Love You Goodbye," tackled the theme of redemption, describing a teenage boy's difficult decision to leave home in the wake of his parents' troubled relationship and subsequent divorce. Wedged in the middle was a song titled "If I Died Today."

It was this song that caught my attention, and the fourth verse most clearly related to my own reasons for considering suicide by asking whether the afterlife would bring shame and regret.

I rewrote the lyrics in my mind as a description more closely aligned with my circumstances, removing questions of shame and regret and inserting words that showed my sense of worthlessness. For I knew that if I died, no one would care, because few knew I existed, and the people aware of my life saw it as useless.

Without meaningful choices, shame and regret lose their meaning. With choices, on the other hand, comes accountability: Those who choose must face the consequences of their actions. At the time, I had few consequences to face because my life was so controlled across all dimensions.

Thus, the prospect of an adulthood in which my choices mattered brought a unique sense of dread.

In five or ten years, will I feel shame and regret for the choices I make? Will those choices be worth the price of living or will they only create more destruction? I have had years to contemplate what I want to believe, whatever actions I take. It will be impossible to say I was unaware they could come with negative effects. Is it better to close the book of life now, before there are strong reasons for regret? Is God more willing to forgive suicide than the millions of mistakes I could make over a lifetime?

I knew no amount of thinking could prepare me for the reality of living in the world, of being confronted with thousands of daily choices, all of which would have a cumulative impact I could neither predict nor control. Worst of all, these choices had to be made in the presence and community of people, thus impacting the lives of untold numbers of individuals. Would this impact be positive or negative?

How would I know?

DECEPTION WEAPONIZES DOUBT

The previous chapter of this book discussed the cost of doubt by addressing the ease with which individuals can be emotionally manipulated when in a state of vulnerability. To doubt is to open oneself up to personal change that can cause either positive or negative effects.

America's identity crisis began as all do. The nation began to question whether the values, beliefs, and worldview of its founding was good, true, and beautiful. These questions are, of course, rational. No person or nation is perfect. If pursued, each person, nation, or culture could spend an eternity critiquing oneself and still find no bottom to the depths of their own unique iniquity.

The left-wing perspective in America has traditionally been an insurgent one. It thrives when America suffers, because this cultural pain provides the public with compelling reasons to change. This role is neither always played by the left nor universally bad. The right, at least in the sense of the Republican Party, rightfully waged war against slavery, and 1960s left-wing revolutionaries rightfully fought against Jim Crow laws. Their communist sympathies do not negate the truth that slavery and Jim Crow laws brought immense suffering to millions of African Americans who were brutalized by Southern aristocratic elites.

However, while identity crises can result in positive change, they almost always come with negative side effects, particularly when undertaken collectively.

Yet, America's past is almost exclusively analyzed through a lens critical of its tradition with no corresponding critique of how the past several generations—all dominated by leftism—have created intergenerational problems and pain. Instead, the damaging impact of leftism's rise and consolidation of power has evaded public discourse for decades because the continued national identity crisis itself is welcomed by those who stood to benefit from cultural chaos, including those in positions of power at universities and public schools and in the entertainment, journalism, and technology companies that propel the knowledge economy.

Our collective failure to critique progressivism's negative impact on public life has caused incalculable harm because perpetual self-doubt comes at a steep cost. It is healthy to question and assess the wisdom of our own actions, but chronic, unrelenting self-doubt is psychologically damaging. Because people's worldviews and beliefs are formed—and updated—based on the sum total of their human experience, perpetual self-doubt can cause a person to develop a perversely negative view of oneself.

In modern America, self-doubt is invoked by encouraging people to perpetually question their own moral self-worth by requiring individuals to upend their lives by learning to accommodate the beliefs of a small fraction of the population.

Failure to comply is costly socially and legally.

THE PRICE OF LIFE IN MODERN SOCIETY IS LIVING OUT A LIE

The left won the culture war by taking advantage of the nation's collective doubt. Like a devouring mother observing her prey, progressives in power leverage emotions for political benefit and seek to micromanage relational activity.

Deception is a critical element in the progressive playbook because it breeds further confusion. Understanding the use of deceit through the devouring mother metaphor is useful because the left's perversion reflects a form of toxic femininity. While feminists still complain of the patriarchy, the modern world is not governed by masculinity. This is true regardless of whether men retain more numerical positions of power.

Unlike historical eras, our current world is increasingly digital, not physical. Gaining power no longer necessarily involves physical feats. From warfare to work, reality is increasingly governed using language, expressed either through mathematical code or traditional language. Men may dominate science, technology, engineering, and mathematics (STEM), but most of society's social relations are governed by a feminine understanding of ideal social relationships and using feminist approaches to categorizing and punishing unwanted social behaviors.

Masculine and feminine ways of governing have always existed across the globe and are embodied in patriarchies and matriarchies, respectively. Both are prone to human error, but only one is compatible with the individual rights Americans have long cherished. Heide Goettner-Abendroth, an anthropologist who specializes in studying matriarchal societies, states such societies are non-hierarchical, governed by consensus, and rooted in nurturing. Their economies are based on need, private property is nonexistent, and political decisions are reached through consensus. The metaphysical and spiritual narrative of these societies is based on female superiority, evidenced by the acceptance of the concept that the universe is a Great Goddess who birthed the world. Thus, every member of society's worth derives from "being a child of the Great Mother Nature."[237]

In such a culture, to be rejected by Mother is to be rejected by society because Mother is society. Interestingly enough, Goettner-Abendroth describes these cultures as "societies of balanced economic reciprocity, based on the circulation of gifts," and "egalitarian societies of consensus."[238]

Whether stated or not, the left seeks to transform Western culture into a matriarchy, at least according to Goettner-Abendroth's

---

[237] Goettner-Abendroth, Dr. Heide. "Matriarchies Are Not Just a Reversal of Patriarchies: A Structural Analysis by Heide Goettner-Abendroth." Feminism and Religion, February 16, 2020. https://feminismandreligion.com/2020/02/16/matriarchies-are-not-just-a-reversal-of-patriarchies-a-structural-analysis-by-heide-goettner-abendroth/.

[238] Goettner-Abendroth, "Matriarchies Are Not Just a Reversal of Patriarchies: A Structural Analysis by Heide Goettner-Abendroth."

description. The same words may not be used, but the results would be identical. The price of adopting the left's perspective is the abolition of individual rights as traditionally understood by Americans. In many ways, the United States already embodies a matriarchy, ruled by an unseen devouring mother that operates in a borg-like conglomerate of power created by the alliance of ideological interests across society's culture-making institutions.

This can be seen in how the left understands human rights, the purpose of politics, and the role of the individual in relation to the collective. As discussed in prior chapters, the left views human rights, specifically the right to exist, as derivative of the will of women alone. Women can, and should, control who participates in life. Thus, the rights of children are subservient to the needs of mothers, and people should be grateful to exist because, if the Almighty Mother determined abortion was in society's best interest, she is *always* right. Mothers must not be questioned.

The insistence on abortion as a human right makes sense under a matriarchal framework because, in such a system, there is no authority beyond the maternal. Mother is akin to the Supreme Court, there is no one to appeal to, thus those whose lives she deems unworthy are tossed into the trash bin where they justifiably belong.

All societies regulate human relationships, both legally and culturally. Because men and women represent approximately half of any given society's population, the tendency to favor either masculine or feminine relational practices is understandable. The problems with patriarchies are well-known; however, the downsides of feminine cultures are equally troubling. Chief among the concerns of those who live under oppressive female societies is the pressure to lie to preserve social standing.

LEGISLATING RELATIONAL MORALITY

Fans and foes of Jordan Peterson are familiar with one of his rules for life. It reads as follows: "Tell the truth, or at least don't lie." This is sound advice, but the cost of living rules out in modern society are harsh, especially for young people, primarily because living requires money, and to obtain money individuals generally need a job. Unfortunately, in an attempt to create a culture rooted in compassion, human resource departments micromanage the relational activities of employees to ensure individuals are sufficiently inclusive and not inappropriately discriminatory.

Anti-discrimination law is created at both the federal and state level and can be derived from statutes passed by Congress (or state legislative chambers) and rulings from the judiciary, with Supreme Court rulings impacting the entire nation. These laws are designed to prevent discrimination against protected classes by barring employers, businesses, schools, or government entities from basing hiring, firing, housing, educational, or access to government benefits on characteristics such as race, sex, religion, national origin, and sexual orientation.

One of the fundamental ideas behind these laws is that, by barring discrimination, an individual's equal protection under the Fourteenth Amendment is guaranteed. Unfortunately, the efficacy of these laws is questionable and the practical trade-offs they require are underdiscussed. Although a minority view in progressive dominated academia, the threat anti-discrimination laws pose to fundamental civil liberties, such as speech and association rights, is well-known, and is the subject of sound academic critique and numerous Supreme Court cases.[239]

This tension between anti-discrimination and associational rights is clearly shown in the first Supreme Court case addressing the issue. In *Roberts v. United States Jaycees*, the United States Jaycees, a national organization for young business leaders that historically only accepted men as members, began to change their practices by admitting women as associate members with no voting privileges. Leadership of the national chapter threatened to revoke two Minnesota chapters after they sought to admit women as full members. This rift resulted in a lawsuit when the Minnesota chapters sued, arguing the state's public accommodation laws barred discrimination against women.[240]

The national chapter of the Jaycees argued they possessed a First Amendment associational right to limit membership to the purpose of their organization, which was the promotion of "interests of young men." Admitting women, the Jaycees argued, risked altering the organization's political positions because of the "gender gap" in political viewpoints.[241] This argument won in federal court, but lost at the Supreme Court. Writing for the Court, Justice Stephen Brennan narrowly interpreted the First Amendment right to expressive association.

According to Brennan, the Jaycees presented no valid evidence that accepting women would impact the organization's

---

[239] *Roberts v. US Jaycees*, 468 US 609 (1984). Justia US Supreme Court, accessed January 31, 2025. https://supreme.justia.com/cases/federal/us/468/609/.

[240] Ibid.

[241] Ibid.

content or speech, stating such beliefs rested on gender stereotypes. Furthermore, even if Minnesota's law did infringe on associational rights, this infringement was justified because the state has a compelling interest in eliminating sex discrimination important enough to justify intruding on First Amendment rights.[242]

The crux of the problem with anti-discrimination laws is that they seek to regulate relationships, placing the government—and possible legal sanctions—between individuals engaging in economic and educational activity. There are undoubtedly social ills that anti-discrimination laws seek to cure, and this writing is not intended as a complete analysis arguing against the utility of these laws writ large. However, the combined forces of law and cultural changes are increasingly large, and a complex web of anti-discrimination laws has created a culture of silence that erodes individualism across the nation.

Anti-discrimination laws present another barrier to entry for individuals seeking to engage in economic activity. Barriers to entry are fixed costs placed on new entrants into a marketplace divorced from performance metrics, such as sales or other productive activity. Because these costs are fixed and disconnected from merit, they are an impediment to newcomers in a market or economic industry, thus stifling competition and creative destruction, a phrase used by economists to describe the ever-evolving process of innovation.

Individuals drive innovation, and when there are costs placed on social relationships, creativity is inherently limited, thus stifling innovation. This occurs for two reasons. First, behavior the law

---

[242] Ibid.

prohibits is behavior it will punish. To avoid the risk of legal sanctions, companies seek to mitigate their risk exposure by regulating corporate relationships to protect the company. Hence, the rise of human resources departments. HR manages hiring, firing, and employee relations with the purpose of cultivating a productive workplace that maximizes the employer's profit while minimizing its exposure to liabilities, including anti-discrimination lawsuits.

The Supreme Court's analysis in Jaycees is indicative of a broader problem with anti-discrimination law. In this case, the court determined stereotypes alone drove the Jaycees' decision to limit its membership to men only. However, a significant portion of speech inherently rests on stereotypes that are simply standardized mental conceptions of individuals within group settings. It is therefore impossible to place a legal cost on *all* forms of stereotyping because, just like discrimination, stereotyping operates on a spectrum.

Some forms of stereotyping and discrimination are not only valid, but possibly life-saving. This is now routinely, passionately, and justifiably argued by women who seek to discriminate against men seeking entrance into spaces designed exclusively for women. The dispute over biological men entering women's locker rooms, bathrooms, and sports categories is predicated on whether it is appropriate to allow groups to discriminate based on a person's genitalia.

MENTAL COLONIZATION

The left may wish to eliminate the government from the bedroom, but they want Uncle Sam to intervene in nearly every other human relationship, under the guise of protection. To accurately reflect what the left wants requires renaming the government, for progressives want a *mother*, not an uncle. An uncle is prone to tough love, but a mother is known for coddling, and it is coddling the modern left desires.

As previously mentioned, discrimination, stereotyping, and all other forms of prejudice are inherent to the human condition. They also operate on a spectrum related to a person's core values and beliefs. Thus, the regulation of discrimination is necessarily the regulation of morality and speech. These laws regulate interracial, intersexual, and interreligious relationships, barring people from living out worldviews that the law defines as inappropriately "discriminatory."

Because compliance, either as an employer, employee, student, or government worker is required, the ability to act in accordance to one's values is hampered. This leads to a form of mental colonization because actions and beliefs are deeply interconnected. Cognitive dissonance occurs when there is tension between someone's beliefs and their actions. This is expressed biblically when the Apostle Paul addresses the impact of sin, stating, "I do not understand my own actions. For I do not do what I want, but I do the very thing I hate."[243]

Speech is one of the most difficult human behaviors to control because speaking is so easy. Entering the marketplace of ideas is as simple as opening one's mouth. Thus, laws that regulate speech actually target the mind. What someone dwells on tends to come

---

[243] Romans 7:15 (ESV).

through in patterns of speech, and, as Peterson observed, the man forced to think one thing while speaking another becomes a liar.[244]

It is no secret that people internalize the norms created by law and culture; this is precisely why the culture wars will always rage on. Powerful ideologies, beliefs, and religious viewpoints will trade places, but ultimately ideas war for cultural and legal power because people respond to social and legal sanctions. As physical prowess becomes less relevant to gaining and maintaining power, linguistic competence has never been more valuable, or more regulated.

Whatever the merits of anti-discrimination laws, current culture is now generations deep in both legal and cultural anti-discrimination practices. Culturally, discrimination is seen as sinful, to discriminate against a group perceived as historically marginalized is to cause grave harm.

Discrimination is a dirty word, even though it is synonymous with discernment. The real problem with discrimination is not that it occurs, but rather that individuals use the wrong moral map when exercising judgment by conflating race or gender with human value. The degree to which Americans self-censor is directly connected to the cultural propensity to champion "diversity" and "inclusion" above all other virtues. Whatever the original intention of anti-discrimination, it is now undoubtedly a force at odds with a commitment to individual rights and expression.

However, disincentivizing individuals from cultivating their own worldviews and then living them out, even when this is at

---

[244] Peterson, Jordan. "Truth in No-Man's Land." In *12 Rules for Life*, 203–206. Random House Canada, 2018.

odds with what others believe is good and true, has a cost. This regulation of morality comes at the cost of individuality, it seeks to control an individual's conception of what is good and forces people to constantly weigh the cost of speaking against possible social consequences judged according to subjective, ever evolving moral criteria.

CHAPTER 12
The Cost of Discipleship

DOUBT AND DESPAIR

After the baptism at age sixteen, my desire to determine what I believed rapidly accelerated. I read incessantly, focusing on apologetics to get my bearings regarding the historical accuracy of scripture, Christ's resurrection, and questions surrounding rationality and faith. However, reading brought more questions than answers. While it was readily apparent that common atheistic beliefs about the Bible were often untrue and rooted in anti-religious bias, no field of study—particularly in the humanities—breeds absolute certainty.

From biblical history to scientific theories about the origins of life, the more I read, the more aware I was of the inherent subjectivity of the questions I sought to answer. Yet, despite this subjectivity, logic dictated that mutually exclusive answers could not be true. There was a truth, but my ability to discern this truth was clearly limited. The problem was my limitation was not unique to me, even the most intelligent experts in any given field had a finite mind. Trusting them to give me the truth was a cop out to doing the hard work of pursuing truth on my own.

This was an unsolvable technical dilemma. I knew that in a hypothetical conversation with any given subject matter expert, I would lack the expertise to competently debate the material at hand. On my own merit alone, I could neither confirm nor refute any given perspective in history or human origins. Additionally, if I wanted to be able to competently debate without merely citing to more authoritative sources, I would need PhD-level knowledge across numerous domains. Given the finite nature of time, it was not reasonable to predicate my worldview on such an extensive level of knowledge. The earliest I could obtain *one* PhD would place me in my late twenties.

Thus, the more extensive knowledge I required to justify any given worldview would trade against the valuable currency of time. This was not only irrational, but naive. No twenty-five-year-old operates without a worldview, such a person is a fiction. Instead, mired in indecision, the perpetual agnostic seeks what she can never find: absolute certainty.

This jarring awareness of my own limitations brought a sense of anxiety and relief. Anxiety because no matter which worldview I chose, lingering doubt would always exist within my mind, and relief because this doubt was an inescapable aspect of being human.

Satisfied that my acceptance of a worldview had to be based on my own viewpoints, not the opinion of experts, I moved away from seeking to justify these opinions to hypothetical third parties and into the practical realm. To avoid the perpetual hamster wheel of doubt, I focused on what could be known with as much certainty as the order of the seasons and the rise and fall of the sun. This brought me to an irrefutable constant: time.

I now had two constants—truth and time. If truth could be known, then it must occur over some period of time. If someone accepts the truth and lives accordingly, then this individual would gradually become more attuned to truth. The pursuit of truth would lead to a positive feedback loop where its disciple becomes more impervious to the seduction of lies. Of course, the opposite would be true of the man who follows lies. Those deceived by lies would, over time, become attuned to falsehood. The more a man lied, the higher the cost of turning away from lies and toward the truth.

Since youth is characterized by an inability to consent, naming one's understanding of truth at an early age brings clarity. Even if initially wrong, the believer is aware of what they follow, thus reducing the price of repentance should their understanding of truth prove to be incorrect.

Because it was clear no man, or woman, lived in a vacuum, it was inevitable that seeking the truth would require submission. Unless I was willing to claim to *be* the truth, a statement of divinity, then to pursue truth, could not be disentangled from the act of following. In the Christian tradition, this diligent pursuit of truth is discipleship, and those who embark on the journey are sanctified, that is, drawn closer into truth through an unfolding, ever deepening, relationship with the divine.

Through this analysis I reoriented my thinking from processes that focused on answering the materialistic skepticism of modern atheists by asking a different set of questions.

"*What would discipleship in secular atheism versus Christianity look like?*"

As I continued to ponder the best path forward, I struggled to understand discipleship in practice. I continued to read as broadly as I could, but I found no author directly addressing this topic from a place of both theory and practice. Books about living out Christian values were a dime a dozen, but they generally focused on following rules, only some of which were easily traceable in historic Christianity.

Since truth is absolute while one's knowledge of it is unfolding, I was highly skeptical of Christian works that prescribed detailed life advice. The Bible was too complex for such analysis. From textual analysis determining the validity of various scriptural translations to the nuanced nature of understanding the Bible in the context of the time and place in which it was written, it was easy to see how people could be tempted to insert, or remove, sections of the Bible based on personal preference or prejudice.

However, truth is neither a rule book nor an *a la carte* menu. Determined to pursue truth with enough rigidity to provide stability while having enough intellectual humility to change over time, I focused my analysis only on necessary personal implications of secularism and Christianity.

During this time, boredom was ever-present. With my sister in college, my days were a blur of school and navigating the tense relationship with my mother. A cloud of despair was ever-present and thoughts of suicide spiked. Even reading as a mental escape began to lose its appeal and I found myself in an unbearable depression. For days I stared at the walls of my childhood room, wondering if there was any escape from destruction. Suicide presented itself as a peaceful solution, one that could remove me from the torment of life at home and the terror of integrating into a world where my own existence was deemed a horrific mistake.

In an attempt to avoid spiraling thoughts of death, I went to one of my parents' bookshelves and combed through titles in search of new content. I had already read most titles, but I continued to look until my eyes landed on a green paperback book I had never seen before.

I pulled the book from the shelf and read the title, *The Cost of Discipleship*. This, it seemed, was at least related to the questions plaguing my mind.

"Dietrich Bonhoeffer," I said. "He's German. I wonder when it was written." I looked inside the book and saw it was published in 1937, during the rise of the Third Reich. The book was not thick and appeared to be a rather quick read, so I brought it to my bedroom and turned to the first page and read.

"When Christ calls a man, he bids him come and die."

"Finally!" I sighed. "A book about Christianity worth reading."

CONFRONTING CHRIST

Over the next two years, I read *The Cost of Discipleship* and Eric Metaxas's biography of Bonhoeffer no fewer than four times. Reading this book was easily the most transformational experience of my life, and it permanently reordered my perception of Christ.

Prior to reading *The Cost of Discipleship*, I was deeply ambivalent about Christ's work on the cross. Lingering within me was a concern that his death was a form of masochism and weakness. Why would a God allow himself to die? How could this death be a form of strength? And, although I had heard the resurrection story a million times, it was not until encountering Bonhoeffer that I reframed my understanding of the Christian conception of life and death.

The book initially derailed my worldview analysis because I became so mentally consumed with understanding it that I could not focus on determining what I believed. It was as if all prior life endeavors—including my intense suicidal ideation—were placed on an indefinite pause as I tried to gain mental clarity regarding the meaning of the Christian faith.

After multiple reads, I was struck by several truths.

CHRIST AS MEDIATOR OF TRUTH

Growing up in a religious setting, I was aware Christ was "the Truth," but Bonhoeffer fleshed out what this meant, without concern for social convention, political affiliation, or other concerns that pervasively polluted American Christianity.

Instead, Bonhoeffer spoke to a universal duality within the human spirit by bifurcating humanity's sense of identity into two distinct concepts that ran through the entirety of his work. First, there was the experience and identity of fallen men and women. Second, there was the experience of the Christian, that is, the man or woman who is given a new identity through the work of Christ.

To be a Christian was to die to the fallen state of humanity and instead voluntarily live in the truth of Christ's resurrection. This means the Christian is both profane and holy. Unlike Christ, they cannot strip themselves of the stain of sin; however, their belief in Christ defines their outlook, conduct, and orientation toward all of reality. By aligning with Christ's truth, the Christian performs for an audience of one, God. But, because the standard of this God is nothing short of perfection, the Christian's diligent pursuit of Christ over time requires them to adopt a favorable disposition toward the world.

This involved rejecting bitterness and resentment, repaying evil for good, and living a life committed to the pursuit of holiness, even if this resulted in physical death, for death was merely temporal, not eternal.

LIFE AND DEATH

This reframed my understanding of life and death. According to a secular worldview, life is all there is, death is final. Thus, under this theory, actions on earth have either no value (nihilism) or absolute value.

However, for the Christian, actions on earth are not disconnected from the afterlife. The phrase "You only live once," could be reworded to "You only *die* once." This is what Bonhoeffer meant when he spoke his final words, "This is the end, for me the beginning of life." The end of earthly life meant an end to the duality and struggle men and women face in the world. In heaven, life is no longer characterized by a struggle between the flesh and spirit; instead, by living in spite of death, as Christ the Redeemer did, the Christian's wrestling with pain is complete upon death. Life goes on, but without suffering.

This deeply complicated my analysis, for Bonhoeffer posited that belief and action were deeply intertwined, "to believe is to be obedient, and to be obedient is to believe." This logic appeared to be irrefutable. The man who says he believes in marriage, but cheats on his wife, is clearly a liar. Indeed, the man who struggles to understand the need for loyalty within marriage, but who remains faithful to his wife from marriage until death do them part *shows* belief. Showing, not telling, gives literary characters value, and ultimately, actions speak far louder than words. This begs the question: Is the doubter who lives as if Christianity is true better than a hypocritical Christian? Or is the hypocrite really a Christian at all?

However, more importantly for me, was suicide the ultimate act of apostacy? For, if we are made in the image of God, then taking human life is a direct assault on His will and His creation. Furthermore, if Christ is truth and He commands His followers to uphold the dignity of all human life, would this not render suicide the ultimate act of irredeemable rebellion? For example, how could one restore relational peace with God after severing the relationship through intentional self-destruction? I knew blasphemy against the Holy Spirit was, according to Jesus, an unforgivable sin. In Matthew, He spoke clearly, stating, "Whoever speaks against the Holy Spirit will not be forgiven, either in this age or in the age to come."[245]

Was speaking limited to speech or did it encompass other forms of expression? I had no obvious answer; this, it seemed, would require more astute knowledge of the passage in context than I presently had. Perhaps, I reasoned, I would need to speak blasphemy while in the act of suicide, but it remained unclear. Indeed, even if suicide was not a form of blasphemy against the Holy Spirit, it most certainly is incongruent with the fruit of

---

[245] Matthew 12:32 (ESV) *The Holy Bible: English Standard Version*. Wheaton, IL: Crossway, 2016.

the spirit by which Christ claimed Christians could be known. And, since belief and obedience were intertwined in a manner so infinitely complex as to deny humanity's fallible access to knowledge, what assurance would I have that suicide would accomplish my stated goal, that is, the absence of life?

If suicide increased my pain, I wanted nothing to do with it. This placed me in an impossible predicament because the only way to determine whether suicide would increase, or cease, pain involved taking a final action (death) from which there was no return. I had already experienced the horror of consciousness, the searing pain of my earliest days, learning my life came with an asterisk, and understanding millions of people would wish I had never existed at all. The thought of killing myself only to relive the misery of gaining consciousness to face a reality of perpetual pain, from which there was no escape, brought a sense of terror and panic.

COUNTING THE COST

However, I did not want to make such an important decision in a state of such intense anxiety. Thus, after spending well over a year ruminating on Bonhoeffer's work, and reading the Bible considering this newfound perspective on life and death, I asked myself the following question:

"*Assume each set (atheism versus Christianity) of truth claims are valid, what is the cost of following each set of beliefs? What is the cross you would must bear to live out these beliefs? Act like this is a geometry proof. Do not skip steps.*"

Placing a concrete price tag at the intersection of my personal life simplified the process, cut out the noise of anxiety, and focused my analysis on the most important question: Did I want to *live* or *die*? First, I analyzed the cost of atheism, then Christianity.

Under atheism, the question was a simple cost/benefit analysis. Was the pain of life sufficient to justify continued living? If it was now, was it subject to change? If so, how could I protect myself against excessive pain by reevaluating the pros and cons of suicide at a later date?

ATHEISM, SUICIDE, AND SOCIOPATHOLOGY

I already knew my transition from high school to college was going to involve an enormous amount of psychological and emotional suffering. From navigating a culture in which developing close relationships was remarkably risky, to finding ways to process my childhood in a healthy manner, the future was inescapably bleak.

The reality of time only made matters worse. Since the past informed the present moment and the present then created the future, it was self-evident that the first eighteen years of my life, almost one-quarter assuming an eighty-year life span, was going to negatively impact my future until death terminated my natural life.

Unfortunately, since I had been afforded no opportunities to make friends, work, or gain practical skills that could lead to gainful employment, I had no option but to attend college. There was simply no other path outside my childhood home. Furthermore, this relational poverty guaranteed that creating solid relationships, either in friendship or romantic settings, was going to involve clearing numerous barriers to entry. My position in the marketplace of relationships of any kind, both personal and professional, was unbearably weak.

It is tempting to think I had conceived of the worst of this scenario, but such an assumption is incorrect. More reflection revealed greater difficulty. Since college prepares young adults for jobs with success that depends on navigating complex social networks, it was apparent that I would have to pay a heavy price to enter and succeed in the modern workforce. Thus, to sustain life outside my parents' house would mean accepting a steep learning curve involving rejection, the implementation of overwhelming volumes of negative feedback, and ignoring the inevitable landslide of criticism and judgment that comes from a progressive culture hellbent on converting homeschooled "victims" into progressive saints.

I assessed my willingness to undertake this endeavor under the philosophical assumptions of atheism and determined I had no desire to even begin this journey. I knew I did not like, nor trust, people. While I was interested in learning about the world and curious to gain experiences, I knew I was not interested in forming trust-based relationships with other individuals. Placing my trust in people was laughable. Thus, accepting atheism as true meant embracing a form of sociopathology. I could embrace learning human relational systems to leverage them to my advantage, but I had no intention of becoming emotionally entangled with people who could do me harm.

While psychologists pathologized manipulation, deceit, and aggression while venerating compassion, empathy, and love, under the rules of atheism, all forms of human interactions are fair game. If people had no inherent value, I had no intention of pretending they did, except to the extent it was externally necessary to fulfill my own objectives. Under a secular framework, I could not understand the pathologizing of antisocial behavior and, when donning an internal atheistic disposition, I mocked fellow seculars as unwilling to accept the implications of their beliefs.

Therefore, the cost of atheism was becoming a sociopath.

CHRISTIANITY AND SELF-SACRIFICE

Running the same analysis through a Christian worldview produced an entirely different outcome. Premises relevant to my suicide dilemma stated:

1. My life did not belong to me.
2. Life was eternal, death temporal.
3. Suffering was not only an inherent aspect of life, but essential to the development of goodness. To become like Christ, individuals must wage war on the malevolence within their own heart, regardless of how rational the propensity for evil.

If Christianity were true, it did not alleviate the conditions described above related to the difficult transition from homeschooling to college. Instead, those conditions represented the cross I was required to bear, not because it was fair, but because it was reality. It became obvious that, contrary to popular opinion, Christianity is not a religion designed for those who seek comfort from pain, nor is it a belief system for the faint of heart.

Instead, I was guaranteed to face significant suffering as a precondition of ever finding joy, or comfort. Indeed, there was no guarantee of earthly joy or comfort. This felt brutally harsh and unbelievably unfair. Still, it was consistent with the world as described by the Bible because, if Satan was real, then his reality must be contended with. If Satan was the master of lies who successfully duped some people into rejecting the truth, then pain on earth is, unfortunately, unavoidable. A world void of pain and suffering is heaven, not earth. Additionally, if the infinite types of human pain could be quantified, it would be irrational to assume suffering would be equally dispersed. This is because such a reality would require God to destroy all aspects of human will, and I knew the debate over predestination and free will raged on in secular and religious communities alike, practically speaking each person's actions impacted generations to come.

My own encounter with Bonhoeffer was evidence of this. It was rather remarkable to realize a man's written work from 1930s Germany was deeply influencing the philosophical, religious, and ethical beliefs of a teenage girl in America over seventy years after it was written. Words and actions reverberate through history. Since this must be equally true of good and evil actions, people and places whose beliefs and actions are more aligned with goodness create more joy and less pain. Similarly, evil compounds, creating pain across generations.

The Christian approach to pain is inspirational but mercilessly hard. It is to accept suffering, no matter how senseless, with a resolve to fight evil by becoming good, a process which, in itself, requires shouldering an unknown amount of future pain.

Applying this to my own life meant contextualizing my own unholy desires in the broader context of history. Each person's inclinations, both for good and evil, are, to some degree, a product of their nature and nurture. When a person acts out evil, he harms himself by becoming more evil, and by passing pain on to other people who now have another reason to view resentment as rational. Thus, the greater the evil perpetrated against an individual, the more rational the desire to embrace revenge and resentment. This desire, however, should be abandoned because reason alone does not lead man to that which is good.

In my life, this meant the evil perpetrated against me made my flirtation with sociopathology make sense, but, if Christianity was true, these desires had to be overcome, not embraced. From history, I was familiar with the work of Aleksandr Solzhenitsyn, the Russian dissident who won the 1970 Nobel Prize of Literature for his book, *The Gulag Archipelago*, which raised awareness of the oppression occurring in Soviet Union prison camps. Among the most famous lines in his book was the observation that the line between good and evil cuts through every human heart.[246]

Bonhoeffer's work highlighted similar truths. He observed how defeating injustice involved driving a spoke into the wheel of evil. This could not be done without confronting one's own duality,[247] refusing to bestow goodness upon ourselves, but instead embracing a lifelong journey of discipleship towards goodness.[248]

This embrace of the high cost of seeking Christ, for example, goodness, also meant fighting this internal battle among a sea

---

[246] "The Gulag Archipelago 1918–56: An Experiment in Literary Investigation." The Aleksandr Solzhenitsyn Center, accessed January 31, 2025. https://www.solzhenitsyncenter.org/his-writings/large-work-and-novels/the-gulag-archipelago.

[247] Metaxas, Eric. "Bonhoeffer's Innermost Thoughts." In *Bonhoeffer: Pastor, Martyr, Prophet, Spy*, 461–465. Thomas Nelson, 2010.

[248] Bonhoeffer, Dietrich. "Costly Grace." In *The Cost of Discipleship*, 45–60. MacMillan Publishing Company, 1963.

of enemies. When discussing Christ's life and work, Bonhoeffer made this clear, stating:

> Jesus Christ lived in the midst of his enemies. At the end all his disciples deserted him. On the Cross he was utterly alone, surrounded by evildoers and mockers. For this cause he had come, to bring peace to the enemies of God. So the Christian, too, belongs not in the seclusion of a cloistered life but in the thick of foes.[249]

Therefore, the Christian life required me to accept the realities of my position as normative. The life I was about to enter, one full of criticism, judgment, and desire to turn my attention from the divine to the progressively profane, was simply the specific cross I was called to bear:

> The kingdom is to be in the midst of your enemies. And he who will not suffer this does not want to be of the Kingdom of Christ; he wants to be among friends, to sit among roses and lilies, not with the bad people but the devout people. O you blasphemers and betrayers of Christ! If Christ had done what you are doing, who would ever have been spared (Luther).[250]

---

249 Bonhoeffer, Dietrich. *Life Together*. (New York, New York: Harper & Brothers, 1954), 17.
250 Ibid.

This meant the acceptance of Christianity was bittersweet. If true, it is inspiring, full of courage and hope. Yet, it forces its adherents to confront the world as it is, full of evil, destruction, and malevolence. Entering a den of lions, surrounding myself with "evildoers and mockers" was hardly a comforting message. But the question was not, "Is this comfortable," but rather, "Is this true?" And, if so, "Is this a sufficient reason to reject suicide in favor of life?"

The answer was, if Christianity is true, then suicide was the ultimate act of rebellion against God. Whether it prevented me from entering heaven was beside the point, because my life—and death—were not primarily about myself. Instead, suicide was removing goodness from the world because God created human beings in His image with the intention that create a better future for those on earth, even in circumstances where limited human perspectives tell them evil is the most powerful force.

Thus, the cost of Christianity was my life. It required me to abandon my desires for retribution, revenge, and suicide.

THE COST OF REPENTANCE

After analyzing the cost of atheism and Christianity, I was ready to move to the final step of the worldview formation process. This involved comparing the costs of each worldview over time, assuming I could not remove doubt because my ability to reason was limited due to the finite nature of the human mind and the inherently limited nature of knowledge.

Repentance in the Christian religion is turning away from lies and towards the truth (Christ). The greater the sin, the more costly the repentance. Bonhoeffer used the terms "cheap" and "costly" grace to describe the difference between the hypocrite and the man who lives according to his convictions. Cheap grace is the type we give ourselves; it is the disposition of a man who views God's grace as a get-out-of-jail-free card. No matter the crime, no matter how much harm one causes, God's grace covers every sin. On the contrary, costly grace is the intentional abandonment of any thought or desire out of alignment with God's truth.

The confused human mind and spirit, an infinitely complex interplay of the holy and the profane, must intentionally wage war against sin, and the Christian understands such a war is futile without Christ's grace because to perfectly embody the law is to be a God, and this station is already occupied.

Interestingly, however, the concepts of cheap and costly grace can apply to any worldview, because all humans tend to bestow grace upon themselves while meting out judgment to their enemies. Progressives, for example, are quick to tell Christians not to judge those who violate Christian ethical norms, but they rarely reserve grace for those who commit crimes blasphemous to their worldview. Cancel culture, rampant on university campuses, is the expression of progressive "costly grace," for there is nothing but judgment awaiting the man or woman who fails, intentionally or by accident, to use updated, "inclusive" language when describing the world. The idea that blasphemy laws only exist in explicitly religious settings can be disproved by the vigor with which seculars enforce hate crimes against "historically marginalized" communities.

This reality was not lost on me. However, what was most relevant was my understanding of the cost of repentance.

First, I assumed atheism was false, but it was the worldview I chose. What would be the cost of this decision? The cost would depend on how long I had practiced an atheistic way of life. The longer I practiced atheism, the harder it would be to turn from lies to truth. It also depended on how well I acted out my self-proclaimed sociopathic ethic. The more I sinned, the harder it would be to remold my identity according to the values of Christ. It would not be impossible because, unlike a get-out-of-jail-free card, Christ's atonement on the cross is a reminder that even the most evil of men, *if they truly repent*, can transform from evil to good. However, it is undoubtedly true that the man who commits mass rape and slaughter, or the woman who kills her children in utero for easy access to orgasms, has a much higher price to pay because atoning for such grievous sins requires an enormous amount of time and effort.

Therefore, if I practiced sociopathology and used people for my own ends, even if I did not physically harm others, turning away from this lifestyle was high cost, because it would force me to reassess my life, observe a tsunami of evil actions, and voluntarily turn away from evil to good, admitting that I had chosen evil and become that which is detestable. Such a process is neither pleasant nor avoidable because grace is not cheap, and repentance is anything but easy.

Now, I ran the analysis in reverse. If Christianity was false, but I chose to live it out, what was the cost of turning away from Christ? The answer was as easy as it was obvious, *there was no cost*. The only conceivable cost was if I wanted to kill myself. Either I needed a rock-solid plan not subject to failure, or I could save enough money to go to the Netherlands, where assisted suicide was legal.[251] However, if I decided to turn to sociopathology, following my own will was simple. Repenting of the sin of living a Christian ethic involved nothing more than internally refusing to obey the remarkably difficult commands of the Christian faith. This is why Christians are always derided as hypocrites. Its adherents have chosen an objectively impossible path, while seculars, unshackled from any truth claims, live out a different type of hypocrisy, for it is hard to be a hypocrite when you have no ethical rules you are required to follow.

This crystalized an observation I had not yet pondered. It was atheism, not Christianity, that closed an individual's mind. Attempting to be a good Christian would require me to seek answers to impossible questions, to question my actions with religious diligence to ensure my heart and mind are aligned with one another. It required me to set my pride aside, empathize with others, and love my neighbors and enemies alike. In short, Christianity would force me to productively engage with doubt.

By contrast, atheism provided ample room for self-assurance because, if there is no God, then man is the measure of good and evil. Thus, individuals have no incentive to bow before the authority of another person unless a negative consequence, such as jail, demands their obedience. Atheism gives its adherents no incentive to engage with doubt. Why ponder whether an action is good or not if morality is relative? Why question your actions if no higher authority can judge them as moral or immoral? This is why so much of secular logic is committed to convincing people

251 "Dutch 'Mercy Killing Law' Passed." BBC News, April 11, 2001. http://news.bbc.co.uk/1/hi/world/europe/1269682.stm.

that the negative effects of certain actions, like abortion, are fictitious. The sheer volume and weight of shame that would rain down on secular progressive Americans if they understood the gravity of the evil they either directly perpetuate or complicitly support would shock their consciences and souls. Perhaps such shock would be socially beneficial; however, it is individually terrifying.

Having counted the costs, I became a Christian and began the journey from death to life.

CHAPTER 13
Combating the Devouring Mother

THE SISTERHOOD'S STRENGTH

As expected, accepting the cost of Christianity did nothing to ease the suffering I was destined to face. I learned through numerous painful experiences the absurdity of the cultural belief in the empathetic nature of women. Access to compassion is culturally gate-kept by women, and, as with all gatekeepers, the sisterhood protects its own by downplaying, dismissing, and trivializing female-perpetrated abuse.

When confronted with forms of abuse they have never experienced or encountered, women react the same as men, by turning a blind eye to harms they neither recognize nor understand. To combat the inevitable cries of "misogyny" that accompany even the most tactful criticism of women, the victims of female-perpetrated abuse in the unenviable position of having to curry favor with those most likely to dismiss their pain.

Despite constant feminist complaints about emotional labor and the difficulty of caretaking, women wield enormous power by serving as society's judges of what constitutes harm, and therefore who is worthy of compassion and grace.

UNDERSTANDING VICTIMIZATION WHILE REJECTING VICTIMHOOD

Recognizing I was the victim of maternal rape was only the beginning of a longer journey.

While I was in law school, I learned that resisting the devouring mother begins in the mind.

The call to reject victimhood identity is common among those on the center right. Although a victimhood mentality has its downsides, understanding victimization is essential to reasserting agency after abuse. Unfortunately, emotional and psychological abuse—when perpetrated without physical harm—are remarkably difficult to identify. This is why progressive forms of prejudice remain hidden from the public mind. Covert abuse is always harder to pinpoint, and those viewed as helpless victims, like women, are rarely seen as capable of causing significant harm.

Before an individual can separate from the devouring mother, they must first recognize the danger of being devoured, and they cannot do this if they are incapable of categorizing female-perpetrated abuse as real.

I learned the hard way how difficult it is to categorize myself as the victim of an intentionally malicious woman. Even after disclosing to my husband that my mother had raped me, assigning intent to her actions remained taboo. Excuses, all from various women in my life, abounded:

> "Are you sure you are remembering events correctly?"
>
> "She was *trying* to love you, she just didn't know how."
>
> "Postpartum depression and anxiety are difficult. Women, especially moms, don't have enough help. If she had more support, this wouldn't have happened."
>
> "She was a victim, too."
>
> "She's your *mother*, don't be too hard on her. You have no idea how difficult motherhood is."
>
> "If your father had not been controlling this would not have happened."
>
> "You grew up in a fundamentalist, Christian home. Your mother was a victim of your father and fearful of him. She was doing the best she could."
>
> "Don't abandon your mother, she loves you."

For years, I fought silently against the thousands of lies spread by a culture allergic to holding a female perpetrator accountable for her actions, even when she caused enormous harm to my body, mind, and spirit. Internally, I always had a primal, visceral repulsion to this stream of lies, and the propensity to blame my father for actions he never took was deeply offensive. Still, it was not until I was in law school that I began to truly understand how my mother abused not only her children, but also her husband.

Despite being the victim of female-perpetrated abuse, I was prone to overlooking how men can be controlled and abused by women. However, understanding how the family law court system works opened my eyes to the ease with which malevolent people—of both genders—can manipulate laws to destroy their spouses.

False allegations of child abuse, and/or domestic abuse, known as the "Silver Bullet," are used as tools in contested divorces, particularly in divisive divorces where one, or both, spouses seek revenge.

In the cast of my family, and thousands of others, the wife was responsible for childcare, making her the familiar parent. And, one of the most well-known psychological principles is that people tend to choose the hell with which they are familiar. Caretaking, in the family law context, is power. Children are susceptible to authority and mothers are a child's first relational bond *and* first authority figure. When children are primarily raised by their mothers, they know her, are disciplined by her, attuned to her needs, and primed to view threats to her as threats to themselves. Thus, when marital relationships break down, it is easy to see how a mother can have disproportionate power when seeking to induce a child to testify on their behalf. Additionally, the cultural propensity to view men as naturally predatory only further tips the scales in favor of women.

I will never forget the deep feeling of shame that overcame me when, at the age of twenty-five, I realized I had never considered the dangers my father would have faced in the family law courts had he attempted to divorce my mother. This feeling turned from shame to anger when I participated in an interdisciplinary child abuse and neglect class. This course brought together law students, psychologists, and social workers to study child abuse and neglect. One day, the instructors had the class engage in an exercise to elucidate the practical problems of escaping domestic violence. Per the usual, the victim was assumed to be a battered woman. Access to agency was demonstrated by having students move to different parts of the room based on the removal of resources. Bank accounts, housing, and so on, presumed to be controlled by the man, were, one by one, removed, backing the abuse victim into a corner.

While this dynamic is undoubtedly real and problematic, I ran a similar analysis in my mind, but from my father's perspective. If he had attempted to protect me from my mother's abuse, *how* would he have done so? In a divorce, he was unlikely to gain sole custody. She could easily accuse him of abuse, and her ability to manipulate her children into testifying against him could remove his access to his children entirely. Furthermore, she was a stay-at-home mother in a religious home. As the breadwinner and male, he was going to be assumed to have more control over her than she had over him. And, since access to resources, such as income, is presumed to come with an emotionally coercive impact, a battered man's provision for his family is, in some ways, a legal liability.

In a litigated divorce, a judge and jury are unlikely to view a stay-at-home mother of seven children, living in a religious, conservative, Christian home as abusive. The scales on my eyes began to lift. My mother *knew* she had power. She *knew* how to play the role of submissive wife while controlling the home with an iron fist. In short, she knew emotions, when weaponized without physical evidence, were far more powerful than brute force or a bank account, especially when held over the head of a harmless, cowardly man.

She knew this, and she won. When I was in high school, I would spar with her over feminism, questioning why she was willing to play what she claimed as a submissive role rather than pursuing power or a career. Her response was consistent, but puzzling. "Leslie," she said, "when the man is the head of the household, it means he is responsible for every action within his jurisdiction. He may receive glory for victory, but he is also accountable for *every evil* that occurs within his home."

The cultural strength of feminism is so strong that women often view the appeal of perverted forms of submission practiced by fundamental religious sects as a manifestation of "internalized misogyny," however my mother articulated a different motivation, one that will never be spoken by those ideologically predisposed to advocate only in the interests of women.

An evil heart, not internalized misogyny, was my mother's problem, and she understood the power of presumed moral purity. If she was externally submissive, she could control the home indirectly because any malfeasance that occurred within the four corners of the house was, by definition, my father's fault. His headship, not physical actions, or even presence, was what determined culpability. She could rape me while he was at work, and he was still responsible for her sexual perversions. Thus, she could play the part of submissive wife and tyrannical monster, with no fear of accountability. Indeed, this bastardization of complementary gender roles incentivized my father to turn a blind eye to her abuse because, the greater her abuse, the more severe his sin.

Allowing her to abuse his children ultimately fell at his feet, yet exiting the union was a risky move, one that could easily increase her power. Emasculation and emotional manipulation were the primary problems in my parents' relationship. I simply couldn't understand this reality until I could contextualize the circumstances without assuming the moral superiority of women. Until I could see my mother as malevolent, not only toward me, but also in relation to my father, the truth was obvious yet invisible.

This was a shocking, unsettling realization because, due to the abortion issue, I had never considered myself a feminist, at least not according to current cultural definitions. Still, the social messaging was so strong that it obliterated my ability to accurately assess what was right before my eyes. My mother gloated at the awe-inspiring power she could wield simply by donning the cultural identity of a repressed housewife and mother. My mother played the gender wars, and she emerged the victor. The likelihood she will be brought to justice for her acts of sexual abuse are almost zero.

EQUAL RIGHTS, UNEQUAL BURDENS

The devouring mother is embodied in culture today through identity politics and a desire to simplify complex human relations by assuming individuals from historically marginalized are victims, rather than perpetrators, of harm.

This is a dangerous form of prejudice because it ignores the truth of a statement at the core of our national identity, "All men are created equal." Campaigns for equal rights were won, the fight for equality in the twenty-first century must move toward expanding this statement to include understanding all people as possessing an equal capacity for evil. Criticism of those marginalized, according to a leftwing ideological framework, must be disconnected from the perception of malice, hatred, bigotry, and so on.

This is already under way as the progressive grip on moral superiority is collapsing. However, moral vacuums are dangerous and our nation is at a critical juncture. If the progressive definition of compassion is eradicated, what will replace it? If the prevailing cultural understanding of tolerance collapses, will tribalism reign supreme? More importantly, will those on the center right fall into the natural temptation to bully, cancel, and legally harass their opposition to repay evil for evil?

Prejudice is a fact of life. It will shapeshift and morph with the changing culture, but it only evolves, never evaporates. America is a relativistic nation, allergic to absolute truth claims. The election of Donald Trump is evidence of this. For the Democratic Party's power came from subverting traditionally religious conservative norms. However, once those norms were culturally defeated, the public became fearful of the left's attempt to consolidate political power to impose their version of morality and truth onto the nation.

The nature of prejudice in a relativistic culture is that individuals will live under the boot of numerous forms of oppression. Each subculture—and the US has many—will marginalize different types of people. Thus, prejudices will span the ideological, political, and religious spectrums. Political rights can be equally guaranteed under the letter of the law, but the application of justice is, in practice, never blind. Judges, juries, government agencies, and other civic leaders are people, and all people carry their own set of prejudices.

Americans of all religious and ideological viewpoints should expect to face discrimination. In a world of rapid information sharing, near-constant social connection, and increasingly low public trust, discrimination is incentivized. Individuals will face unfair burdens and it will be easy to become cynical and view equality as a lie. Men will face discrimination from women accustomed to viewing males as predators. Women will face discrimination from men who experience or sense some of the problems discussed in this book. The same is true of ethnic, religious, and political groups. No one will be immune from discrimination, workplace or otherwise, because policing human nature is a political impossibility.

CREATING CULTURE

What can be done to create a better future?

An honest answer to this is not satisfying because it does not come with the dopamine rush of an immediate reward. Addressing prejudice, including the types routinely ignored and discussed throughout this book, requires actively building culture through committed, sustained communal engagement that aligns with your philosophic values.

In culture building, capitalism, an economic system rooted in voluntary exchange, is your friend. Indeed, most dissatisfaction with capitalism is rage that should be directed at culture. An economic system that operates under capitalism reflects the values input into that system. Capitalism holds a mirror before culture, revealing its virtues and vices. A morally bankrupt system will appear ugly, but this is not the fault of capitalism because capitalism has no agenda. It simply reflects the sum total of a market's economic decisions.

Aside from unenforceable transactions, for example, human slavery, people can change the culture through their freedom to associate. This is true both culturally and economically.

The first step in culture building is understanding the cultural forces surrounding you. When assessing this, look at culture as a set of rings surrounding you. The people, institutions, and other entities closest to you form your immediate cultural context. By way of example, my "culture" as a child was my family, the church my parents attended, and the local softball park. Had I landed in court, the culture of the city, Norman, Oklahoma, would have become relevant. However, for most people, their immediate cultural context is narrow and consists of people and institutions with which they regularly interface, such as school, church, and work.

Ask yourself, in this specific context what viewpoints are rewarded? Similarly, which ones are discouraged? You should be able to notice the distinctions between your workplace, church, and school. Even the subtle distinctions between the culture created within a classroom should become apparent.

Understanding these cultural dynamics is critical to productively engaging with those around you and leads to a second step—defining your worldview. It is impossible to know how to interact with others to create a better society if you have no defined values. If you are unclear what your values are, begin to explore them.

Ask yourself questions about the culture around you. What are some of the positive and negative aspects of your culture? What makes these elements good or bad? What would you change in culture if you could? Why would you make these changes? Who benefits from these changes and who loses?

If you already have a defined worldview, consider asking the following questions: Does the culture incentivize goodness and justice? Does it punish behavior that should be stigmatized or does it place social sanctions on righteousness? If you believe you live in a corrupt culture, are you willing to pay the price of living on this culture's margins or would it be better—for yourself and others—if you found a cultural space that more closely aligns with your worldview?

While there is no set formula that can be used to answer these questions, some relevant factors can be identified. I fundamentally reoriented my approach to friendship after taking inventory of the first ten years of my adult life because I noticed I was stuck in a pattern of trying to force myself to cultivate trust in conditions where trust was virtually impossible. If the culture in which you live believes your life is a mistake, cultivating trust with individuals who adhere to this culture's philosophy is unlikely to end in a productive, mutually beneficial relationship.

In my case, I noticed myself becoming internally resentful and routinely came home from social outings with "friends" emotionally exhausted from feeling the need to hide my true feelings through whatever means were most appropriate or readily available. Thus, I was gaining no benefit from my "friends" and they were interacting with a carefully crafted façade, rather than a manifestation of my true self. In other words, everyone was losing, and precious time was being wasted.

CULTIVATING CURIOSITY

After solidifying your purpose within culture, you should avoid the tendency to live within an echo chamber by finding ways to cultivate curiosity about others who think differently than you. Unfortunately, this type of curiosity has been co-opted by the left. When people think of walking a mile in the shoes of the marginalized, they *assume* this means adopting the perspective of the marginalized communities championed by progressives.

Resist this urge. Broaden your perspective; there are an unknown number of unnamed marginalized groups. These people exist in disparate settings and share one thing in common: They live under the boot of progressive prejudice. This does not mean the interests of the groups championed by the left have no merit. However, society is derelict in its duty if it pretends prejudice is a pie with a finite number of known interest groups. Human relationships are far too complex for such a reductionist approach to reality.

Cultivate curiosity for those harmed by progressive prejudice. These are the true silent sufferers of our age. They are the reason Trump won. For those who are not progressive and despise the president, it would be wise to turn your attention to the concerns of those who placed Trump into office. Show them the grace you claim their leader lacks.

The world we live in is harsh and increasingly cruel. It is easy to turn to lazy critiques based on past prejudices. Leftists routinely do this, laying the blame for society's turn toward harshness at the feet of the patriarchy, racism, xenophobia, homophobia, transphobia, and whatever new pejorative Ivy League professors concoct in faculty lounge conversation. This, however, is absurd. These types of prejudice undoubtedly exist, but the twentieth century saw the rise and dominance of secularism, feminism, and progressive values. Pretending the prejudice of the left does not play a critical role in the polarization we all feel is, simply put, delusional.

Given the disproportionate ideological asymmetrical representation favoring left-wing ideas in education, journalism, media, and entertainment, it is crucial to identify and discuss the prejudices associated with the political left.

This book addressed these prejudices from the lens of women's issues, particularly in relation to how modern feminist philosophy wages war against the dignity of children. Yet this is only one of myriad forms of progressive prejudice. Look at the "deplorables" despised by America's elite with compassion rather than scorn. Seek to understand their concerns with an eye toward the reality that these demographics may be formally uneducated, but they are no less human. Their concerns are human concerns, and their ability to articulate their pain may be frustrated by a lifetime of marginalization they cannot capture with words.

Cultivate the kind of curiosity that prevents you from wielding knowledge against your fellow man, and reject the impulse to argue from a place of authority. A true expert is humble; they don't flaunt degrees, credentials, or specialized knowledge to coerce people into agreement or action. Instead, the best experts present their well-formed opinion, wish you the best, and—importantly—*allow you to fail.*

Additionally, curiosity is a powerful antidote against coercion and control. Petty tyrants are generally outraged when their authority is questioned. Guard your mind, and by extension your heart, with your life by refusing to trust in what you do not understand. In the words of Ronald Regan, "Trust, but verify." Resist becoming dependent on bureaucratic systems. Remember that the more heavily regulated an industry is, the more its actors within are bound by policies and procedures that protect those in power.

Finally, be wary of those who seek to gain your compliance under the guise of compassion and care. The devouring mother lures the gullible into her web by promising comfort and safety; ride the dangerous tides of liberty instead. In an increasingly socially connected world, assert your independence and agency early and often. Cut the umbilical cord and separate from the devouring mother before she devours you.

ACKNOWLEDGMENTS

Although the jury is out on its commercial success, I consider this book to be the current pinnacle of my career. Politics is about people. This means speaking of unnamed social and cultural ills to assist others in understanding truth is necessary for the preservation of truth liberty, justice, and equality. The burden of evil is heavy because it obscures the light of truth. And where darkness reigns, tyranny takes hold. Thus, transforming a life lived under the weight of the worst social taboos into autobiographical and cultural analysis is a powerful form of emancipation.

Even more freeing was the feeling of completing this book while caring for my first child. Reliving these experiences while pregnant and postpartum was a reminder that the best revenge is a life well-lived. Despite the doom-filled stereotypes of the terror that allegedly accompanies motherhood, I have never been more happy, fulfilled, or further from despair.

Caring for the needs of my son, however minor, is among the most rebellious and meaningful of acts. Breaking the cycle of abuse and establishing a nurturing, love-based home, centered around the best interests of the child, may be culturally and economically undervalued, but it is the foundation of true success.

However, I could not achieve this milestone alone. First and foremost, my husband, Tim, has been by my side since I was nineteen years old. From dating to marriage, law school, and childbearing, he has provided me unwavering love, devotion, and support. Above all, he is a superb husband and father. I could not ask for a better spouse, and remain eternally grateful that I ignored conventional "wisdom" by choosing to marry at age twenty-one, just three years after leaving the extreme isolation of my childhood home.

Keith Adams has been my counselor and mentor since my early twenties. He remains the sole reason I have any positive connotation with therapy. His intellectual and spiritual guidance provided me with the wisdom and clarity necessary to navigate the journey from abuse to health.

Talia Barnes provided invaluable feedback throughout the writing process, reading numerous drafts of chapters and discussing the ideas and their organization as the manuscript moved from an idea to a final product. I also want to thank my agent, AJ Rice, and publisher Post Hill Press for their work to ensure this book could be completed and brought to press.

Lastly, thank you to my friends, all of whom I am sure prefer to remain anonymous. Your support and encouragement are a blessing for which I am eternally grateful.

ABOUT THE AUTHOR

Photo Credit: Jonathan Newton
Social (Instagram):
@jonathon.filmart

Leslie Corbly is an author, poet, and attorney. She holds a BA degree in Journalism and a JD degree from the University of Oklahoma College of Law. She writes broadly on culture, politics, and human dignity by examining the norms and corresponding taboos of the modern left.

Her prior work includes a poetry collection, *Silent Suffering*, critiquing the predicates of progressive and postmodern beliefs by exploring the suffering of those who fall on the margins of progressive philosophies.

Leslie lives in Utah with her husband, Tim, and their son, Keith. In her free time, she enjoys CrossFit, hiking, playing the piano, and reading or discussing classical literature, history, philosophy, and theology.